THE TROUBLE

WITH

LAWYERS

THE TROUBLE

WITH

LAWYERS

❦

DEBORAH L. RHODE

OXFORD
UNIVERSITY PRESS

OXFORD

UNIVERSITY PRESS

Oxford University Press is a department of the University of Oxford.
It furthers the University's objective of excellence in research, scholarship,
and education by publishing worldwide.

Oxford   New York

Auckland   Cape Town   Dar es Salaam   Hong Kong   Karachi
Kuala Lumpur   Madrid   Melbourne   Mexico City   Nairobi
New Delhi   Shanghai   Taipei   Toronto

With offices in

Argentina   Austria   Brazil   Chile   Czech Republic   France   Greece
Guatemala   Hungary   Italy   Japan   Poland   Portugal   Singapore
South Korea   Switzerland   Thailand   Turkey   Ukraine   Vietnam

Oxford is a registered trade mark of Oxford University Press
in the UK and certain other countries.

Published in the United States of America by
Oxford University Press
198 Madison Avenue, New York, NY 10016

Library of Congress Cataloging-in-Publication Data
Rhode, Deborah L., author.
The trouble with lawyers / Deborah L. Rhode.
p.   cm.
ISBN 978–0–19–021722–8 (hardback : alk. paper)
1. Practice of law—United States. 2. Legal ethics—United States.
3. Lawyers—United States. 4. Attorney and client—United States. I. Title.
KF297.R485 2015
347.73'504—dc23
2014037607

1   3   5   7   9   8   6   4   2

Printed in the United States of America on acid-free paper

For David McBride

CONTENTS

———⚬⚬⚬———

ACKNOWLEDGMENTS

THIS BOOK OWES MANY debts. I am deeply grateful to David McBride at Oxford University Press, who supported this project from the outset and shepherded it through publication. I am also indebted to Bruce Ackerman, Benjamin Barton, and Robert Gordon for their insightful comments, and to Aaron Henson for his excellent research. The staff of the Stanford Law library provided invaluable reference assistance: Paul Lomio, Sonia Moss, Rich Porter, Rachael Samberg, Sergio Stone, George Vizvary, Erika Wayne, and George Wilson. My greatest debt is to my husband, Ralph Cavanagh, whose support and guidance made this book possible.

I

Introduction

THESE ARE NOT THE best of times for American lawyers. The titles of books on the profession speak volumes: *The Lawyer Bubble, Declining Prospects, The American Legal Profession in Crisis, Failing Law Schools, The End of Lawyers, The Vanishing American Lawyer, The Destruction of Young Lawyers, The Betrayed Profession, The Lost Lawyer.*[1] Less than a fifth of Americans rate the honesty and ethical standards of lawyers as very high or high, ranking them just above insurance sales agents.[2] In a 2010 Pew survey that asked which occupations contribute most to society's well-being, law ranked the lowest of ten occupations.[3] Paradoxically, the nation suffers from an oversupply of lawyers and an undersupply of legal services for people with low or moderate incomes.

This is a timely moment for a comprehensive account of challenges facing the American bar, all of which have a human face:

- Ashley Newhall has a law degree and is licensed to practice in Pennsylvania and New Jersey. She is working for some extremely demanding clients—but most of them are under three years old. Her primary income for the last three years has come from working as a nanny. It takes three part-time jobs to keep her afloat, given her six-figure law school debt.[4]
- Billy Jerome Presley spent 17 months in a jail for falling behind in child support. He had no prior criminal record but also no lawyer. If he had been able to afford legal assistance, his lawyer could have gotten him out of jail on bail and worked out a repayment schedule.[5]

- A law firm associate at Clifford Chance chronicles a day that begins at 4:45 a.m. with a crying baby and ends at 1:30 the following morning in a vain effort to keep pace with billable hour demands.[6]

These individuals are among the thousands paying the price for failures described in the chapters to follow. These chapters explore trends in the legal market that have posed increasing problems for the profession and the public that relies on their services. The book's central premise is that the bar is failing to deal with fundamental problems in the conditions of legal practice, access to justice, diversity in the profession, regulation of lawyers, and legal education. Some problems are market-driven; others are of the profession's own making. This chapter offers an overview of these challenges.

Chapter 2 explores the conditions of practice, with a particular focus on law firms. The discussion examines how increases in the size, scale, and competitiveness of contemporary practice, together with changes in technology, have intensified economic pressures. The recession compounded these pressures as clients demanded more for less. Difficulties persisted even after the economy rebounded, and most lawyers believe that the result is permanent changes in the legal marketplace.

These pressures are amplified by the relentless preoccupation with short-term profits that drives law firm decision making. The priority of profit is responsible for the escalation in billable hours over the last several decades, and the price is paid in quality of life. Most lawyers report that they do not have sufficient time for themselves and their families, and most are unable to devote even an hour a week to pro bono service. These trends have taken a toll in lawyers' workplace satisfaction. Law does not rank among the top twelve professions for satisfaction, and a majority of lawyers would choose a different career if they had to make the decision again. Lawyers also have disproportionately high rates of depression, substance abuse, and related disorders. Responses to these problems are possible only if lawyers become more informed about the sources of professional fulfillment, and more proactive in shaping workplaces to meet their needs.

Chapter 3 addresses access to justice. It is a shameful irony that more than a third of law school graduates cannot find full-time legal employment while more than four-fifths of the legal needs of the poor and a majority of the needs of middle-income Americans remain unmet. The situation in indigent criminal defense is particularly problematic. Politicians win votes by promising to get tough on crime, not subsidize criminal defense. As a result, the system is chronically underfunded. Public defenders often have crushing caseloads. Some lawyers cope with more than 1000 misdemeanors or 500 felonies annually, almost three times the national average. Private lawyers who defend indigent clients are reimbursed at ludicrous levels. Plumbers make more per hour in some jurisdictions. The result is that lawyers take too many cases to spend time on an adequate defense. Ninety percent of criminal cases are resolved without trial, and typically without any factual investigation. In the cases that do go to trial, standards for what constitutes effective representation of counsel are notoriously lax. Convictions have been upheld where lawyers have failed to do any investigation, present any evidence, or even remain awake and sober at the trial.

Similar underfunding plagues the civil justice system. Americans do not believe that justice should be for sale, but neither do they want to pay for the alternative. Recent budgetary cutbacks for legal aid have made a bad situation even worse. The federal government spends less than a dollar per day per person per year on such assistance. Millions of Americans priced out of the market for legal services are struggling to represent themselves in systems designed by and for lawyers. Their problems have been compounded by sweeping prohibitions against assistance by qualified nonlawyer providers. Although the bar has long prided itself on filling the gaps in the justice system through pro bono service, participation rates are shamefully low. Only about a quarter of lawyers meet the aspirational standard of 50 hours of service annually that is codified in the American Bar Association's *Model Rules of Professional Conduct.*

Chapter 4 explores challenges concerning diversity. In principle, the bar is deeply committed to racial and gender equality. In practice, it lags behind other occupations in leveling the playing field. Only two professions have less diversity than law, and many do considerably better. Part of the problem lies in the lack of consensus about what exactly the problem is and what can be done to address it. There is no question that women and minorities are grossly underrepresented at leadership levels such as law firm partners and general counsel. Yet leaders of the bar tend to attribute these differences in achievement to differences in capabilities and commitment.

Such explanations underestimate the impact of unconscious bias. A wide array of evidence suggests that women and minorities lack the presumption of competence accorded to white men. Many women and minorities also remain outside the networks of mentoring, sponsorship, and business development that are often crucial for professional advancement. The problems are compounded by escalating billable hour requirements and inflexible workplace structures. The costs are disproportionately borne by women because they assume a disproportionate share of family responsibilities.

Contemporary antidiscrimination law, which provides remedies against overt intentional bias, has proven inadequate to combat the unconscious stereotyping, old-boy networks, and workplace structures that prevent equal opportunities. The high costs of bringing, and the substantial difficulties of proving, a case of discrimination keep many victims from coming forward.

Yet employers as well as individuals suffer from the unequal playing field in legal settings. Considerable research supports the business case for diversity. Diverse viewpoints encourage critical thinking and creative problem solving; they expand the range of alternatives considered and counteract "groupthink." Many practices that would improve conditions for women and lawyers of color serve broader organizational interests. Better mentoring programs, more equitable compensation and work assignments, and greater accountability of supervising attorneys are all likely to have long-term payoffs. In a world in which the majority of the talent pool is composed of women and lawyers of color, it is reasonable to assume that firms will suffer some competitive disadvantage if they cannot effectively retain and advance these groups.

Chapter 5 focuses on bar regulatory processes. The legal profession is in some sense a victim of its own success. In no country has the bar been more influential and more effective in protecting its right to regulatory independence. Yet that success and the structural forces that ensure it have shielded the profession from the accountability and innovation that would best serve societal interests. Lawyer regulation suffers from two structural problems: the profession's unchecked control over its own governance and its state-based system of oversight. Both stem from state courts' assertion of inherent and exclusive authority to regulate legal practice, and their tendency to defer to the organized bar in exercising that authority.

The problems are apparent in the bar's approach toward multi-jurisdictional and multidisciplinary practice, and in its prohibitions of nonlawyer investment in law firms. A state-based admission structure ill suits contemporary practice. Many legal matters and attorney communications do not remain within the jurisdictions where the attorneys are licensed to practice law. Nor do client needs respect disciplinary boundaries. The bar's ban on fee sharing with nonlawyers has impeded efforts to establish collaborative practices that many clients would find cost-effective. The ban has also prevented the infusion of nonlawyer capital and innovative marketing strategies that could improve the delivery of legal services. In opposing multidisciplinary practice and nonlawyer investment, the bar has claimed that lawyers will become accountable to supervisors from a different tradition with less rigorous standards governing confidentiality, conflicts of interest, and pro bono service. Yet these problems have not materialized in other countries that permit such nonlawyer involvement. Regulation, not prohibition, is the obvious solution to the problems that the opponents raise.

The bar's regulatory efforts have proven similarly flawed on matters of continuing legal education (CLE). All but five states require lawyers to complete a certain amount of CLE, typically between 10 and 12 hours annually. Although ongoing education makes sense in principle, the system leaves much to be desired in practice. There has been no showing that passive attendance at courses improves performance, or addresses the causes of most clients' complaints about lawyers. Moreover, the absence of quality control or monitoring leads to many abuses of the system. Lawyers can get credit for stress reduction through relaxation techniques and for "self-study," which does not ensure that participants are engaged or even awake while CLE tapes are running.

Discipline is another area in which regulatory processes fall short. The current system does both too little and too much. It does too little to protect clients and third parties from ethical abuses, and too much to sanction lawyers for misconduct not involving clients. Many disciplinary authorities do not even handle "minor" misconduct, such as negligence and overcharging, on the theory that other civil liability remedies are available. Here again, a basic problem is structural. State supreme courts have claimed authority to regulate lawyers but have insufficient time, interest, or capacity to exercise that authority effectively. They have delegated regulatory authority to agencies that are part of, or closely aligned with, the organized bar. These agencies also lack the resources to respond adequately to misconduct. The system is almost entirely reactive to client complaints, and fails to respond when clients benefit from misconduct, as in abusive litigation practices, or when clients lack information or incentives to file complaints. Many doubt that complaining will do much good, and they are largely correct. Only about 3 percent of complaints result in public discipline.

A final set of challenges for the legal profession involves legal education. Chapter 6 explores problems in law schools' finances, structure, curriculum, and values. Changes in the market for legal services have lent new urgency to longstanding problems. Declines in the demand for recent graduates, together with rising tuitions and greater debt burdens, have left many new lawyers in difficult financial straits. Only about two-thirds have secured full-time legal jobs, and their median salary has often been inadequate to cover average debt levels.

Part of the reason for the high tuitions is the rigid accreditation standards imposed by the Council of the American Bar Association Section of Legal Education and Admissions to the Bar. It prescribes a vast range of expensive requirements. The result is a one-size-fits-all framework for legal education, which stifles innovation. It also fails to acknowledge the vast diversity among legal practice specialties, and the need for corresponding diversity in law school preparation.

Another reason for the high cost of legal education is the role of *U.S. News and World Report* rankings, which encourage an arms race in expenditures rewarded by the rankings formula. One example is expenditures per student, which have risen dramatically since the rankings went into effect. Another example is spending that is designed to enhance reputation, including subsidies for faculty scholarship and glitzy publications. Yet reputational surveys, which count for 40 percent of each school's position, are a particularly inadequate proxy for educational quality. Few of those surveyed know enough to make accurate comparative judgments.

Curricula suffer from a number of weaknesses: insufficient practical skills training and lack of opportunities for interactive learning, teamwork, feedback, and interdisciplinary instruction. Ninety percent of lawyers report that law school does not teach the practical skills necessary to succeed in today's economy, a deficiency that has become more acute as legal employers have cut back on training for recent graduates.

A final difficulty with legal education involves the values that it fosters, or fails to foster, concerning professional responsibility. Legal ethics is often relegated to a single course that is narrowly focused on the rules of professional conduct. Failure to integrate issues of professional responsibility throughout the curriculum marginalizes their significance. A related weakness involves pro bono services. Only about 10 percent of schools require participation, and most students graduate without such involvement as part of their education. In one survey of recent law graduates, participants ranked pro bono last on a list of educational experiences that practitioners felt had assisted them significantly in practice. If part of the mission of legal education is to lay the foundations of professional identity, then failure to cultivate a commitment to public service is a significant oversight.

The final chapter summarizes proposals for change and the obstacles that stand in the way. Of critical importance are reducing bar control over regulatory structures, and expanding opportunities for public involvement and accountability. Of still greater importance is motivating a critical mass of lawyers to address fundamental problems in the conditions of practice, diversity in the profession, access to justice, and legal education. We do not lack for reform strategies. The challenge remaining is to convince lawyers that they have a stake in that agenda for change.

2

The Conditions of Practice

"AMERICAN LAW FIRMS CONFRONT a Less Gilded Future" ran the title of an *Economist* profile.[1] This pessimism reflects the prevailing view among commentators, and the mood among lawyers tends toward wistful resignation. Many lament the passing of some hypothesized happier era when law was more a profession than a business.[2] In the current legal marketplace, competition and commercialization are on the rise, while civility and collegiality appear headed in the opposite direction.[3] Yet while the stresses of practice seem likely to increase, the bar has shown little sign of being able to alter those dynamics or reshape its future.

This chapter explores the causes and consequences of recent trends in the American legal profession. It gives particular focus to lawyers in midsize and large firm practice, because they are the leading edge of the bar, and they exercise the greatest influence over the conditions of its workplace. However, many of the dynamics described have broader application and pose challenges for the profession as a whole. Not all of these trends in legal practice are unique to law. Some are a function of broader market and societal forces. But whatever the causes, lawyers have a stake in exercising greater control over the conditions that affect their professional lives.

The Drivers of Change

Size

One of the most significant changes in the contemporary legal profession is the increase in its size and scale of practice. In 1960, the largest firm had 169 lawyers. Today it has over 4000.[4] Between 1978 and 2008, the average size of one of the nation's 250 largest firms increased by a factor of five, growing from 102 to 535 attorneys.[5] Over the past four decades, the number of lawyers has approximately quadrupled.[6] The result has been an increase in competition, a fraying of collegial bonds, and a mismatch between supply and demand. The number of new law graduates substantially outstrips the entry-level jobs available.[7] But as Chapter 3 notes, this oversupply of lawyers coexists with an undersupply of service for middle-class and low-income Americans. At the low end of the market, lawyers cannot afford to provide assistance at a price that many consumers can afford to pay.[8] At the higher end of the market, the demand for legal services has not kept pace with the supply of providers. As one commentator notes, "There are simply many many more high-priced lawyers today than there is high-priced legal work. . . . In fact, the more you talk to partners and associates at major law firms these days, the more it feels like some grand psychological experiment involving rats in a cage with too few crumbs."[9]

Competition

The increase in size is not the only force that has increased competition. Supreme Court decisions on advertising have reduced anticompetitive constraints.[10] Consumer demand has limited the bar's ability to preempt competition by nonlawyers for certain law-related services. Accounting firms have made especially threatening inroads on the profession's traditional turf. Globalization has brought more foreign competitors to American financial centers. It has also encouraged clients to outsource business to offshore legal service providers.

Other dynamics have reduced the need for lawyers and intensified competition for the legal work that remains. Technology is displacing demand for many lawyers' services.[11] For attorneys serving individual clients, document preparation services such as LegalZoom are acquiring an increasing share of the legal market. For attorneys in virtually all areas of legal practice, Richard Susskind has argued that the traditional "artisan" model of lawyering is being replaced by commoditized legal work and that the broader economy's relentless pressure toward "more for less" will intensify this trend.[12] Technology-driven legal service providers "aren't just eating Big Firm's lunch; they are eying breakfast and dinner as well."[13] So too, corporate clients, who are facing increased pressures in their own markets, have responded by curtailing legal costs. Businesses have moved more routine work in-house and parceled out more projects based on short-term competitive considerations rather than long-term lawyer–client relationships. Although few leaders would put it as crudely as a Finley Kumble managing partner, "Stealing lawyers and clients from other firms" has become "a keystone of . . . progress."[14]

Stealing clients from other partners has also become more common as competition inside law firms has intensified. Tensions have been exacerbated by "eat what you kill" compensation structures that reward business-getting and therefore encourage hoarding and fights over who made the kill. At large firms, only half of surveyed partners feel supported by other partners.[15]

The economic recession compounded all of these competitive pressures. Clients increasingly pursued cost-cutting measures, such as refusing to pay for training junior associates. Law firms responded with hiring freezes, layoffs, and de-equitizing unproductive partners. Some commentators are optimistic that the situation will improve as the economy rebounds, baby boomers retire, and the population increases.[16] However, pressures have persisted even as the economy recovers and most lawyers believe that these changes in the legal marketplace are permanent.[17]

The Priority of Profits

Causes and Consequences of Institutional Priorities

At the root of many of these problems is the priority of profit. Because money is at the top of almost everyone's concerns, it is easier to reach consensus on financial rewards than on other values such as shorter hours, associate training, or substantial pro bono commitments. Firms that sacrifice compensation for other workplace satisfactions also risk losing talented members who prefer greater earnings and have portable clients. Once high pay scales are established, they can readily become self-perpetuating; downward mobility is a painful prospect. Even lawyers who entered law school with other aspirations often become trapped in these reward cycles. If they cannot afford to do the kind of public interest work they would really like, they want at least to be very well paid for what they are doing. Media ranking systems that rate law firms on profits per partner, together with transparency of lawyer compensation, have also led firms to pursue short-term profits at the expense of other values.

The greater the firm's size, geographical dispersion, and lateral turnover, the more difficult it becomes to sustain a common culture and to set priorities that compete with short-term profits.[18] Since 2000, partner movement between large firms has also grown by 50 percent.[19] In this culture, the bonds of institutional loyalty, trust, and collegiality have become more frayed. The problem is compounded by skewed incentive structures that encourage lawyers to focus on rainmaking and billable hours at the expense of activities like mentoring that further collective interests.[20] Partners are spending more time marketing their services and have less opportunity and incentive to train junior colleagues, most of whom are likely to leave.

The pursuit of profits per partner has had other adverse consequences. Particularly in large firms, it has made partnerships less accessible and in some ways less attractive. Many firms have decreased the percentage of equity partners, lengthened the path to partnership, and created other statuses such as income partners, of counsel, or permanent associates. Fewer lawyers gain equity partnership, and it no longer promises lifetime security or saner schedules.[21] As chances for advancement dwindle, more associates experience La Rochefoucauld's insight that it is not enough to succeed; others have to fail. And any success is only provisional. Partners who lack sufficient business can lose their status. To many attorneys, the struggle for promotion looks increasingly like a "pie-eating contest where the prize is more pie."[22]

Billable Hours

The priority of profit also encourages the tyranny of billable hours. Thirty years ago, most partners billed between 1200 and 1400 hours per year and most associates between 1400 and 1600 hours. Many firms today would consider these ranges acceptable only for lawyers who had died partway through the year.[23] On average, associates bill close to 1900 hours a year, and the figure is considerably higher in large firms.[24] To bill honestly at that level requires 50- to 60-hour weeks. In some ways, technology has made a bad situation worse by accelerating the pace of practice and placing lawyers perpetually on call. Legal life lurches from deadline to deadline, and lawyers remain tethered to the workplace by e-mail and cell phones. Although these technologies have had an upside by making it more possible for lawyers to work from home, they have also made it less possible to not work from home. Personal lives get lost in the shuffle.[25] It is not uncommon to hear of a client who e-mails on New Year's Eve and fires a firm for being insufficiently responsive on a Sunday morning. One law firm associate relates a common experience of having a partner "come into the office and ask if you had any plans for the weekend. The correct answer was 'no.'" The first time the associate was asked the question, he made the mistake of actually answering it and mumbling something about having hoped to go to Vermont. The partner looked at him with a "combination of incredulity and sympathy. . . . 'It's a rhetorical question. . . .'"[26]

Law firms often blame soul-crushing schedules on client demands. But there is reason to believe that other factors are also at work. Clients do not get efficient services from bleary-eyed, burned-out lawyers. The main problem is that the hourly billing system pegs profits more to the quantity of time spent than to the efficiency of its use, and profits have become the dominant concern. High billable hour quotas also screen out individuals with competing values. A willingness to work long hours functions as a proxy for commitment. Those most often excluded are lawyers with substantial family responsibilities, typically women. But this consequence is dismissed as a necessary, though regrettable, byproduct of a competitive practice culture. The result has been a civilian arms race with escalating personal costs. Although lawyers as a group would benefit if schedules were saner, most practitioners are unwilling to risk a unilateral withdrawal from the competition.

Satisfaction with Practice

Rates of Satisfaction

After reviewing recent trends in legal practice, Stanford Law School Dean Larry Kramer asked, "Does anyone actually want this?"[27] Equally to the point, how happy are lawyers with their professional lives?

This turns out to be a surprisingly complicated question, and the answer depends on whom you ask and how you ask it. Is the inquiry about short-term satisfaction or long-term fulfillment? Does the survey include only current practitioners, which of course excludes those most likely to be dissatisfied: those who have left the law entirely. Discontented individuals may also be less likely to respond to questionnaires, which skew satisfaction rates upward.[28] Experts also note that direct questions about job satisfaction often yield overly positive results; people don't want to admit to a stranger, or even to themselves, that they are unhappy and have not taken steps to remedy the situation. More revealing measures of satisfaction often come from less direct questions, such as whether lawyers plan to leave their jobs or whether they would make the same career choice again for themselves or for their children.

Granting these difficulties, some of the best available data come from a meta-analysis of surveys done over a quarter century. It finds that roughly 80 percent of lawyers indicate that they are very satisfied, somewhat satisfied, or satisfied with their jobs.[29] In the American Bar Association's large-scale longitudinal study, 76 percent of young lawyers were moderately or extremely satisfied with their decision to become a lawyer.[30] A National Opinion Research Center comparative study of occupations finds that about half of lawyers (52 percent) are very satisfied, a figure slightly higher than Americans generally (47 percent).[31] But things could be better. Law does not rank among the top twelve professions for satisfaction.[32] In a rating of jobs on characteristics such as projected job growth, median salary, employment rate, stress level, and work-life balance, law ranked 51.[33] Lawyers rate their jobs about the same as accountants, civil engineers, and car salespeople, and significantly below dentists, engineers, physicians, police officers, and real estate agents.[34] In one *American Bar Association Journal* survey, although four-fifths of legal practitioners are proud to be a lawyer, only about half that number would recommend their career to a young person.[35] In other surveys, 60–70 percent of attorneys would choose a different career.[36] One in-depth survey of lawyers who said they were satisfied with their work found that they had substantial misgivings about some aspects of their jobs, including its social value and work-life balance; half would not choose to attend law school again.[37]

Lawyers' discontent is reflected in other measures, such as high rates of attrition and psychological difficulties. Almost half of associates leave law firms within three years; three-quarters leave within five years.[38] An estimated one-third of lawyers suffer from depression or alcohol or drug addiction. They have about three times the rate of depression and almost twice the rate of substance abuse as other Americans, and have the highest rate of depression of all occupational groups.[39] About half of lawyers report high levels of fatigue and stress.[40] The consequences are costly for all concerned. Although the economic model of most law firms presupposes substantial attrition, the current hemorrhaging of associates is anything but cost-effective. Most junior lawyers leave before generating substantial profits.[41] Each departure imposes between $200,000 and $500,000 in expenses to recruit and train a replacement, and creates harder-to-quantify losses in disrupted client and collegial relationships.[42] Moreover, the lawyers who leave are not necessarily the ones firms want to lose; dissatisfaction rates are highest among those with the best credentials.[43] Further costs result from attorneys who cope with discontent through drugs and alcohol; they generate a highly disproportionate share of the profession's discipline and performance problems.[44] High levels of fatigue impair judgment and decision making.[45]

Satisfaction rates vary across practice areas. In general, lawyers in public sector practice are happier than those in private practice, and those in large and midsize firms are least satisfied.[46] In an American Bar Foundation study tracking the careers of young lawyers, those most dissatisfied were graduates of elite law schools working in large firms. Only a quarter of those attorneys were extremely satisfied with their decision to become a lawyer, and 60 percent said that they expected to leave their jobs within the next two years. Graduates from lower-ranked schools reported higher satisfaction in all practice settings. Forty-three percent were extremely happy with their choice of career and only 40 percent planned to change jobs in two years.[47] Researchers explained the variation in terms of expectations; graduates from higher-ranked schools had a greater sense of entitlement so were disproportionately disaffected when their jobs didn't measure up.

Race, gender, ethnicity, and age also play a role. Overall, women and minorities are not less satisfied with their career decisions, although they are more dissatisfied with some aspects of practice.[48] In the American Bar Foundation study of recent graduates, African Americans were most satisfied with their decision to become lawyers and with the substance of their work but the least satisfied with the social conditions and opportunities for professional development and influence.[49] Women were more satisfied than men with the substance of what they did and less satisfied with its context and opportunities; they were also more likely to leave their position, particularly if it was in a large firm.[50] In a recent *American Lawyer* survey of mid-level associates, women were significantly less satisfied than men on virtually all dimensions of practice and were more likely to leave to achieve a better work-life balance.[51] In other studies, women of color were the least satisfied of all groups with almost all aspects of their workplaces.[52] Women and minorities also have higher rates of mobility, which suggests higher rates of job dissatisfaction.[53] In general, experienced lawyers are more satisfied than younger attorneys, in part because they eventually find jobs that most closely match their preferences, and those most dissatisfied drop out of the profession.[54]

Sources of Satisfaction

What would make lawyers happier? Professional satisfaction reflects a combination of genetic traits, working conditions, and personal effort. Experts generally believe that people have a genetically determined set point for happiness, and that at least 50 percent of the variation in satisfaction reflects this physiological baseline.[55] Changes in circumstances, such as health, finances, and personal relationships, move people up or down in happiness levels, but over time, people typically return to their set point. Some research also suggests that law attracts a disproportionate number of individuals with lower set points and personality traits that work against satisfaction. Pessimism, combativeness, and competitiveness often bring professional rewards, but not the outlook and collegial relationships that foster satisfaction.[56] However, lawyers' characteristics cannot explain the difference in satisfaction levels across practice specialties. And even researchers who stress the importance of genetic predisposition also note the potential for individual improvement. People need not let their "genetic steersman have his way. . . . [W]ithin wide latitude, they can control their destination. . . ."[57] The nature and conditions of work are also important. Job satisfaction depends on how well a position meets basic psychological needs for self-esteem, control, competence, security, and relationships with others.[58]

In general, people are happiest when they feel that they are being effective, exercising strengths and virtues, meeting life's challenges, and contributing to socially valued ends that bring meaning and purpose.[59] Research on highly successful individuals finds four domains of success: "happiness (feelings of pleasure or contentment); achievement (accomplishments that compare favorably against similar goals that others have strived for); significance (the sense of positive impact); and legacy (ways to help others find future success)."[60] Enduring success involves finding a balance among all four of those domains, and achieving "just enough" in each.[61] As that research suggests, individuals benefit from benefiting others. Volunteer work is correlated not only with greater satisfaction but also with greater physical and mental health and self-esteem.[62] For lawyers, pro bono activities enhance career development; they are a way to build skills, reputation, and contacts, while advancing causes to which these individuals are committed.[63]

Causes of Dissatisfaction

In too many respects, the structure of contemporary practice works against satisfaction. One cluster of problems involves the substance of legal practice and the gap between expectations and realities. Individuals often choose law as a career with little knowledge of what lawyers actually do. Law as it appears on prime-time media offers some combination of wealth, power, drama, and heroic opportunities. Law in real time is something else, particularly for those at the bottom of the pecking order. No one makes films titled *Adventures in Document Production*, or *The Man Who Did Due Diligence*.[64] The sheer drudgery of some legal matters exacts a heavy price. It is not surprising that recent graduates from the most prestigious schools, although working in the most prestigious firms, express greatest dissatisfaction with their careers; they expected more from their credentials.[65]

Psychologist Martin Seligman identifies further problems with the substance of legal work. He emphasizes the adversarial, zero-sum, and uncivil aspects of practice, as well as the pressure without control that characterizes much of junior associate life.[66] Voluntary civility codes have proven ineffectual in curbing abuse, and the increasing size of the bar has eroded the power of informal sanctions. All too often, practitioners see incivility rewarded in practice. Jo Jamail, known for his use of obscenities and personal insults in litigation, has been honored with not one but two statues at his alma mater, the University of Texas.[67]

Other researchers note that lawyers often see clients in times of stress and are the bearers of unwelcome messages about legal processes. When lawyers function as "merchants of misery" and as scapegoats for acrimony not of their own making, they are bound to feel disaffected.[68]

Practicing lawyers stress other factors. In their accounts, career advancement issues, as well as work-life balance, play more important roles than the substance or adversarial aspects of legal practice.[69] More than four-fifths of lawyers in an ABA national survey found their work to be intellectually stimulating.[70] The greatest source of disappointment with practice, according to other ABA studies, is the "lack of connection to the social good."[71] Only 16 percent of lawyers report that their ability to contribute to the social good has matched their expectations when they began practicing law.[72] As one career guide puts it, the results clients are fighting for generally "are not going to make the world a better place."[73] Individuals who chose legal careers partly out of concerns for social justice have often shared Archibald MacLeish's inability to care very much "whether $900,000 belongs this way or that."[74]

One obvious response to this disaffection is pro bono work. Yet many legal employers endorse such involvement more in principle than in practice. When a recent joint study by the National Association of Law Placement and the American Bar Foundation asked relatively new entrants to the profession to rate their satisfaction with sixteen aspects of practice, they ranked pro bono opportunities second to last.[75] In my own survey, about half of lawyers reported dissatisfaction with the amount and quality of pro bono activities.[76] As Chapter 3 notes, only about a third of lawyers average at least an hour a week, and what counts as charity includes bar association work; favors for other lawyers, clients, and families; and supervising attorneys' "pet organizations."[77] Only a quarter of lawyers are in workplaces that fully count pro bono work toward billable hours and almost two-thirds feel that such work is a negative or unimportant factor in promotion and compensation decisions.[78]

What is, however, highly rewarded is a willingness to work extended hours and inflexible schedules. A *New Yorker* cartoon captures the prevailing ethic: it features a well-heeled professional advising a younger colleague that "all work and no play makes you a valued employee."[79] Yet these norms are a major cause of dissatisfaction and attrition, particularly among women, who bear a disproportionate share of family responsibilities.[80] Only a fifth of mothers with full-time schedules are satisfied with the amount of time that they have for child care.[81] Women who temporarily opt out of the labor market to address that problem often fail to find a satisfactory position when they are ready to return.[82] Most surveyed lawyers report that they do not have sufficient time for themselves and their families.[83] Only a third to a half believe that their employers support balanced lives and flexible workplace arrangements.[84] According to one associate, her firm's solution to the problem was to hold seminars offering advice on how to "outsource your life."[85] Yet excessive hours carry a substantial cost. Overwork is a leading cause of lawyers' disproportionately high rates of stress, substance abuse, reproductive dysfunction, and mental health difficulties.[86]

Misplaced Priorities

Why do so many lawyers put up with these adverse aspects of practice, and why do so many legal employers fail to make adjustments that would improve not only satisfaction, but also recruitment, retention, and performance? The explanations are interrelated. If too few disaffected lawyers vote with their feet, employers have too little incentive to respond. By the same token, if too few workplaces are implementing effective reforms, too few attorneys see somewhere else to go.

Part of the problem is that people are surprisingly inaccurate judges of what will make them happy, and lawyers are no exception. Psychologists identify a number of factors that interfere with rational choices. One is that focusing on highly salient events or other extrinsic rewards inflates their importance relative to the happiness they actually bring.[87] So, for example, lawyers may overestimate the well-being that will flow from making partner or scoring a large bonus. Desires, expectations, and standards of comparison tend to increase as rapidly as they are satisfied. People become trapped on a "hedonic treadmill": the more they have, the more they need to have.[88] As psychologist David Myers notes, it is better to let "our best experiences be something we experience fairly often than to sacrifice daily sources of pleasure in pursuit of occasional but elusive brass rings."[89] Satisfaction is less a matter of getting what you want than of wanting what you have.[90]

Money

In particular, money plays a much smaller role in promoting personal satisfaction than most people, including lawyers, commonly assume. When asked what single thing would be most likely to make them happier, a majority of Americans answer "more money."[91] Yet most researchers find that for individuals at lawyers' income levels, differences in compensation bear little relationship to differences in satisfaction.[92] Individuals earning $200,000 are not significantly happier than those earning half that much.[93] There is no relationship between compensation and fulfillment across different fields of legal practice. As noted earlier, discontent is least pronounced among relatively low-earning public interest and public sector employees.[94]

One reason for this disconnect between wealth and satisfaction is that most of what high incomes can buy does not yield enduring happiness. As Daniel Gilbert puts it, "We think money will bring lots of happiness for a long time and it actually brings a little happiness for a short time."[95] The novelty of new purchases or circumstances quickly wears thin, and the transitory pleasure that they bring is less critical in promoting well-being than other factors, such as individuals' relationship with families, friends, and communities, and their sense of contributing to larger societal ends.[96] A second reason for the limited effect of money is that satisfaction is most affected by relative not absolute income, and increases in wealth are generally offset by changes in reference groups.[97] To a large extent, pay is a "positional good"; individuals' satisfaction with their pay depends on its position relative to others.[98] As H. L. Mencken once put it, "A wealthy man is one who makes $100 more than his wife's sister's husband."[99]

Yet the increasingly public nature of lawyers' salaries has made the competition for relative income easier to play and harder to win. Steven Brill, the former editor of the *American Lawyer,* noted that once legal periodicals began comparing law firm salaries, "Suddenly all it took for a happy partner making $250,000 to become a malcontent was to read that at the firm on the next block a classmate was pulling down $300,000."[100] This kind of arms race has few winners and many losers. There is, in fact, no room at the top.[101] The problem is compounded when lawyers compare their circumstances to wealthy clients.[102] Attorneys who look hard enough can always find someone getting something more.

Other dynamics help trap lawyers into overvaluing income. One is the difficulty of downward economic mobility. Attorneys who initially chose well-paying jobs in order to gain training and prestige or to pay off student loans often become accustomed to the lifestyle that such positions make possible. So, too, the work required to generate high income creates needs that fuel financial demands. Attorneys working sweatshop hours feel entitled to goods and services that will make their lives easier and more pleasurable. This pattern of compensatory consumption can become self-perpetuating. Luxuries can readily become necessities, and many attorneys feel unable to afford a more satisfying balance of personal, professional, and public service pursuits.

The desire for status and the equation of money with merit push in equally counterproductive directions. For many individuals, including lawyers, income is a key measure of achievement and self-esteem, and a marker of social position. The desire to impress and display is deeply rooted in human nature, and in America's increasingly materialist culture, self-worth is linked to net worth.[103] Yet lawyers pay a high price for these priorities. As Patrick Schlitz concludes:

> Money is at the root of virtually everything that lawyers don't like about their profession: the long hours, the commercialization, the tremendous pressure to attract and retain clients, the fiercely competitive marketplace, the lack of collegiality and loyalty among partners, the poor public image of the profession, and even the lack of civility.[104]

The Rationale for Reform

A growing body of evidence suggests that lawyers, and the institutions that employ them, would do better to focus less on income and more on other conditions that promote individual happiness and workplace satisfaction. Overwork impairs health and performance, and the need for a better work-life balance is a major cause of associate attrition.[105] Happy individuals perform better and live longer, healthier lives.[106] And happiness is related to job satisfaction.[107] Humane schedules, alternative work arrangements, and other family-friendly policies are cost-effective. Such initiatives improve recruitment and retention, and help reduce stress, sleep deprivation, and other health-related disorders. Some estimates suggest that every dollar invested in policies concerning quality of life results in two dollars saved in other costs.[108] Other surveys find that part-time employees are generally more efficient than full-time counterparts, particularly those clocking sweatshop hours; any additional overhead expenses are more than offset by reduced attrition.[109] In short, balanced lives boost bottom lines.

The same is true of pro bono opportunities. They enable lawyers to develop new skills, areas of expertise, and potential client contacts, as well as to enhance their reputations and self-esteem.[110] As one attorney notes, such activity can be "an enormous morale booster for the entire firm. Everyone feels that they touched a life . . . no office picnics or parties can give you that."[111] Pro bono service can also enhance the reputation of the profession as a whole. In one representative public opinion poll that asked what could improve the image of lawyers, the response most often chosen was free legal services to the needy. Two-thirds of those surveyed indicated that it would improve their opinion of the profession.[112] In a world in which competition for talent is increasing, and the status of lawyers and number of law school applicants are declining, the bar could clearly benefit from more pro bono initiatives.[113]

Strategies for Reform

In an influential essay, "The Importance of What We Care About," philosopher Harry Frankfurt argues that people are most fulfilled when they engage in work that they find meaningful and reflect at the deepest level about what meets this definition.[114] It is, in essence, important to remind ourselves what we care most about, and to refuse to settle, at least in the long term, for workplaces that fall short. Although not all the downsides of legal practice are easily avoided, lawyers could do much more, both individually and collectively, to reduce the gap between expectations and experience in their professional lives. What most needs to change is the belief that change is impossible.

Individual Strategies

At the individual level, lawyers need to be more proactive in finding work that lies at the "intersection of their values, pleasures, and strengths."[115] That, in turn, will require individuals to become more informed and self-reflective in their career choices. One step to that end is taking advantage of rankings and databases, like Building a Better Legal Profession, and the *American Lawyer* A-List, which grade selected law firms on factors such as diversity, work-life programs, associate satisfaction, and pro bono activities.[116] Lawyers, bar associations, and law schools should demand more such information about all legal workplaces, including how their formal policies function in actual practice. For example, how does part-time status or substantial pro bono involvement affect promotion and compensation decisions? How much control do lawyers exercise over their schedules and over the kinds of assignments and pro bono opportunities available?

Once employed, practitioners also need to press for such control. That is particularly important for women, who are socialized not to appear pushy or aggressive. The title of a path-breaking book on negotiating behavior put the problem directly: *Women Don't Ask*.[117] But when it comes to professional development and work/family tradeoffs, lawyers of both sexes need to ask; they must actively pursue what is necessary for fulfillment. In one study on career advancement, the most effective strategy was impatience; individuals benefited from seizing every opportunity and leaving a position when a more promising opportunity became available.[118] So, too, professionals committed to improving their current situation often find strength in numbers. Organizing colleagues both within and across workplaces can significantly improve diversity and policies for balancing work and family.[119]

Institutional Strategies

In too many workplaces, attorneys face unwelcome tradeoffs. In *The Happy Lawyer*, Nancy Levit and Douglas Linder note that happiness requires both job security and time for family, friends, and other activities that give meaning and pleasure in daily life. They advise lawyers both to make their jobs more secure by meeting or exceeding employer expectations, and to find a "comfortable work/life balance."[120] To many lawyers, those goals seem incompatible. That has to change.

Legal employers must do more to address sources of discontent and to evaluate the adequacy of their responses. A commitment to quality of life needs to be reflected in workplace priorities, policies, and reward structures. That, in turn, will require systematic evaluation of lawyers' satisfaction, and of practices that affect it. Employers should conduct anonymous surveys that ask for feedback on how happy their lawyers are with various aspects of practice and what changes they would most like to see. Decision makers must track whether underrepresented groups such as women and minorities are advancing in numbers equal to white male counterparts, and whether all groups feel equally well supported in their professional development. Do lawyers working reduced hours find that their schedules are respected, that their pay and benefits are proportionate to their performance, and that they retain opportunities for advancement and desirable assignments? How do lawyers assess their training and mentoring? Do participants in formal mentoring programs feel that their assigned mentor has sufficient time, interest, incentives, and knowledge to provide the necessary support? Do lawyers get regular, constructive, and candid feedback on their performance? Could lawyers be given more control over their schedules, assignments, and working environments? Too many employers now lack answers to these questions, and rely on formal policies that poorly serve their intended beneficiaries.[121]

Too many legal organizations are also insufficiently supportive of pro bono work. Chapter 3 notes the societal importance of greater public service involvement in increasing access to justice. The discussion in this chapter makes clear the value of pro bono work in meeting lawyers' own needs for professional satisfaction. To address that need, employers must make a visible commitment to public service that is reflected in resource allocation and reward structures. At a minimum, workplaces should provide full credit for pro bono work toward billable hour requirements, value pro bono work in promotion and compensation decisions, ensure adequate training and supervision, and develop an effective system for matching participants with work that they find meaningful.[122]

Reforms are also necessary in the structure of practice. One promising initiative involves law firm tracks that allow different hours and compensation tradeoffs without second-class status.[123] Another option is for organizations to match attorneys with projects that fit their substantive and scheduling preferences; often this work is done from home or client offices to maximize flexibility and minimize overhead expenses.[124] Axiom is an example of a legal employer that successfully operates with this model.[125] Alternative fee arrangements that reduce reliance on hourly billing can also help reward efficiency and reduce the financial pressures for overwork.[126]

Of similar importance are reforms that address the causes of excessive attrition, including lack of mentoring and problematic relations with partners.[127] One study found that 43 percent of associates were dissatisfied with the quality of mentoring that they received, and other research finds higher rates of dissatisfaction among women and minorities.[128] Part of the reason is that three-quarters of firms do not credit time spent mentoring toward billable hour requirements.[129] Supervising attorneys need to be adequately trained, evaluated, and rewarded concerning mentoring and treatment of subordinates.[130] Junior attorneys should have an opportunity to rate supervisors in forms that matter in the organization's reward structure.[131]

So too, more lawyers could experiment with ways to reduce the acrimony that frequently accompanies adversarial processes. One example is collaborative lawyering, in which parties commit to cooperative problem solving; if they are unable to reach a negotiated settlement, their lawyers will not provide representation in any subsequent litigation.[132] By removing lawyers' economic incentives to prolong proceedings, the arrangement gives all participants a stake in minimizing conflict.

Clients should also pressure legal employers to address sources of chronic dissatisfaction. Clients seldom get efficient service from lawyers working oppressive schedules, and high rates of attrition involve disruption, inconvenience, and additional training expenses. In addition, as Chapter 4 notes, a growing number of corporate counsel see diversity as both an economic and moral imperative. They want firms that make full use of available talent, and that field teams with a range of backgrounds and perspectives. To that end, many large corporations have pledged to consider diversity in allocating legal work.[133] More clients need to follow suit and to put teeth in their commitments; such pressure could push firms to improve policies that affect women and minorities. Clients should also consider other matters besides diversity, such as the adequacy of pro bono programs, which some government agencies now make a factor in allocating outside work.[134]

Bar associations and state courts could do more to support diversity, pro bono service, and quality of life reforms. For example, some local bar groups have enlisted law firms to endorse goals and timetables for racial and gender equity.[135] Other bar associations have developed initiatives to increase pro bono involvement, and a few state courts have required lawyers to report pro bono work.[136] By raising the visibility of such work, bar associations can pressure employers to support activities that would be rewarding to all concerned.

Legal Education

Law schools have an obvious role to play in responding to issues of professional satisfaction, but it is not one that most law schools have been inclined to assume. Part of the problem is the lack of consensus that there *is* a serious problem that they have any responsibility to address. As Chapter 6 notes, faculty are relatively well insulated from the sources and symptoms of discontent. Their own satisfaction levels are the highest in the profession, partly because they have considerable control in pursuing work that they find meaningful on a schedule that suits their needs.[137] Although law students have disproportionately high levels of stress, substance abuse, and other mental health difficulties, the symptoms are not always obvious, and legal education has failed adequately to address the problem.[138] Issues concerning the conditions of practice are also noticeable for their absence in law school curricula. More than 90 percent of law schools have no courses that address lawyer satisfaction.[139] Only half of students report that their school places substantial emphasis on preparing them to handle the stresses of law practice.[140]

Law schools have also failed to ensure student involvement in pro bono service and to make clear its connection to professional fulfillment. As Chapter 6 notes, a third of graduates do not participate in pro bono activities as part of their educational experience, and many who do participate do so at only token levels.[141] Nor is pro bono typically part of the core curriculum, orientation programs, or even professional responsibility courses.[142]

Yet legal education is also the branch of the profession that is in some respects best situated to address its problems. With that opportunity comes a corresponding obligation. In his celebrated 1934 address on the "Public Influence of the Bar," United States Supreme Court Justice Harlan Stone noted that legal academics were the members of the profession "most detached from those pressures of the new economic order which have so profoundly affected their practicing brethren."[143] That independence gave them a unique capacity for disinterested analysis of the bar as an institution and for "an informed understanding of its problems. . . ."[144] Some 65 years later, Harvard Law professor David Wilkins echoed similar themes in a plenary address to the Association of American Law Schools. As he noted, one of the responsibilities of professional education is to study and teach about the profession:

> At a time when the American legal profession is being radically transformed on almost every dimension . . . the legal academy must become an active participant in developing . . . the knowledge about legal practice that will allow us to construct a vision of legal professionalism fit for the 21st century.[145]

Part of that academic responsibility is to provide an accurate picture of the conditions of practice and the strategies that might improve it. More law professors should teach, study, and write about the realities of lawyering. Legal education also can do more to prepare future generations to address, individually and collectively, the sources of professional discontent. For example, law schools can expose students to different practice settings and the literature on satisfaction through curricular coverage and extracurricular panels and events. Schools could also require employers conducting campus interviews to disclose relevant information concerning quality of life issues. More law faculty should also pursue research that would promote professional fulfillment. We need to know much more about what works in the world. For example, what law school and employer initiatives are most effective in improving health and satisfaction over the long term? What incentives and pressures are most likely to secure those initiatives?

Legal academics take pride in working at the forefront of social change. We like to believe that our teaching and research contribute to more just and efficient governance institutions. We need now to turn more of our efforts toward our own profession, and to promote forms of practice that fulfill lawyers' deepest needs and aspirations.

3

Access to Justice

IT IS A SHAMEFUL irony that the nation with one of the world's high-est concentrations of lawyers does so little to make legal services accessible.[1] According to the World Justice Project, the United States ranks 67th (tied with Uganda) of 97 countries in access to justice and affordability of legal services.[2] "Equal justice under law" is one of America's most proudly proclaimed and routinely violated legal principles. It embellishes courthouse doors, but in no way describes what goes on behind them. Millions of Americans lack any access to justice let alone equal access. More than four-fifths of the legal needs of the poor and a majority of the needs of middle-income Americans remain unmet.[3] The indigent criminal defense system is a national disgrace. The discussion that follows explores the causes of the justice gap and identifies the most promising responses.

Criminal Defense

Institutionalized Injustice: Inadequate Responses to Inadequate
Representation

Fifty years have passed since the United States Supreme Court decided *Gideon v. Wainright*, a landmark decision recognizing a right to counsel for criminal defendants who could not afford it.[4] Yet as Attorney General Eric Holder has noted, that right has "yet to be fully realized." "Across the country, public defender officers and other indigent defense providers are underfunded and under-staffed. Too often when legal representation is available to the poor, it's rendered less effective by insufficient resources, overwhelming caseloads, and inadequate oversight. . . ."[5] The mother of one Georgia defendant had it right: "There's no fair trial unless you can buy one."[6] In many jurisdictions, it is safer to be rich and guilty than poor and innocent; the worst sentences go to those with the worst lawyers, not the worst crimes.[7]

Much of the problem involves resources and the unwillingness of courts to require adequate budgets for indigent defense or to enforce adequate standards of representation. The nation spends more than a hundred billion dollars annually on criminal law enforcement, but only about 2 to 3 percent goes to support lawyers for impoverished defendants.[8] About three-quarters of the roughly one million individuals arrested for felonies each year are poor enough to qualify for court-appointed attorneys, as are a large portion of the eight million individuals arrested for misdemeanors. The adequacy of these attorneys is crucial to the fairness and legitimacy of the criminal justice system. This is particularly true in capital cases, where the stakes in human life and liberty are greatest. Yet experts generally agree that the most important factor in determining whether a defendant will be sentenced to death is not the details of the crime but rather the competence of the defendant's attorney.[9]

Although courts have interpreted the Sixth Amendment to the US Constitution to require effective assistance of counsel, the prevailing standard of effectiveness makes a mockery of constitutional guarantees.[10] Courts have upheld convictions when attorneys have lacked any experience or expertise in trying criminal cases, and when they have failed to do any investigation, cross-examine any witnesses, consult any experts, or present any evidence.[11] What passes for justice in many American criminal courts is a disgrace, particularly to a nation that positions itself as a leader in human rights.

The problem is not that most defense attorneys for the poor are lacking in either competence or commitment. The vast majority are doing the best job possible under challenging circumstances. Rather, the primary problem lies at the structural level: there are too few resources and too few remedies for the minority of lawyers who are incompetent.

For much of the last half century, the indigent defense system has been in financial crisis. Moreover, the problem has been compounded in recent years by the dramatic escalation in criminalization and incarceration. Since *Gideon* was decided, the rate of imprisonment in the United States has more than tripled and is now the highest in the world.[12] Funding for indigent defense has not kept pace with that increase and recent budgetary cutbacks have made a bad situation worse.[13] As one expert has noted, "You could take a dart and throw it at a map of the United States and hit a failing indigent defense system."[14] More than 90 percent of poor criminal defendants plead guilty without trial and typically without any significant investigation of their case.[15]

Jurisdictions rely on three methods of providing indigent defense. One is public defender services. Although a few jurisdictions have model programs that can match prosecutorial resources, they are the exception; impoverished systems for impoverished individuals are the rule. Public defender offices have had to cope with layoffs, furloughs, and crushing caseloads.[16] ABA standards recommend a maximum annual caseload of 150 felonies or 400 misdemeanors per attorney, yet many jurisdictions are dramatically over those limits.[17] Only nine states limit the maximum caseload of public defenders.[18] Defense attorneys have had to juggle as many as 2000 misdemeanors and 500 felonies a year.[19] Lawyers in New Orleans average only seven minutes a case on misdemeanor clients; some lawyers in New York never personally meet their clients.[20]

The problem can be even worse in jurisdictions that rely on a second system for indigent defense: competitive bidding. In this system, lawyers bid to provide representation for a fixed fee for a specified percentage of the courts' total caseload, regardless of the number or complexity of cases. Where, as is common, the jurisdiction has no meaningful system of quality control, this process encourages a race to the bottom. The winners are attorneys who can turn over high volumes of cases, often after only brief hallway conversations with clients, and never, God forbid, an actual trial.[21]

Defendants do not necessarily fare better in a third system, which pays attorneys by the hour but caps fees at often ludicrous levels.

A 2013 survey found the average compensation rate in thirty states to total just $65 an hour, with some states paying as little as $40 per hour.[22] Many jurisdictions also cap the total overall expenditure for a given case at unrealistic levels, which means that after a certain point, lawyers are working as volunteers for their clients. Where jurisdictions have unrealistic ceilings on fees, thorough preparation is a sure route to financial ruin.

Under all of these systems, lack of funding encourages counsel to "meet 'em, greet 'em, and plead 'em."[23] Rarely do many lawyers file motions, consult experts, interview witnesses, or investigate facts.[24] In defending his perfunctory approach, one lawyer explained to reporters that he simply could not afford to put "too much time or money into these cases." He then added that if his clients "want Clarence Darrow, they should hire Clarence Darrow."[25] The lawyer representing Eddie Joe Lloyd on appeal never met with him or even accepted any of his phone calls. "I don't get paid for his long-distance phone calls from Jackson prison," the lawyer explained. "I did the best I could given what I had."[26] The appeal failed. Lloyd served seventeen years in prison before a national advocacy group took his case and had him exonerated by DNA evidence.

In some jurisdictions, defendants languish in jail for months before they obtain even minimal contact with counsel. It is not uncommon for those charged with misdemeanors to wait longer to get a lawyer than they would serve if they received the maximum penalty for their alleged offense.[27] A Mississippi woman accused of shoplifting spent 11 months in jail before the court appointed counsel.[28] Defendants who are found innocent can lose their jobs or homes as a result of such delays.[29] Extended backlogs in some public defender offices mean that almost half of their clients will finish serving their sentences before their appeals are filed and resolved.[30]

Even in capital cases, inadequate representation is all too common. One survey, aptly titled "Lethal Indifference," found that those sentenced to death in Texas faced a "one in three chance of being executed without having the case properly investigated by a competent attorney or without having any claims of innocence or unfairness heard."[31] In many jurisdictions, states are also unwilling to provide reimbursement for necessary experts.[32]

Given the current structure of indigent defense, it should come as no surprise that ineffective representation is a leading cause of wrongful convictions and reversals on appeal.[33] What is striking, however, is the lack of serious concern that this arouses among judges, legislatures, and bar disciplinary agencies. In theory, criminal defendants who receive inadequate representation have three remedies: disciplinary complaints, civil malpractice claims, and reversals of their convictions. In fact, the first two are almost never available, and the third only rarely. Bar disciplinary agencies generally will not consider claims of "mere negligence," and even egregious neglect and incompetence go largely unsanctioned.[34] Moreover, the remedies typically available in bar disciplinary proceedings, such as private reprovals, public censures, or suspensions, do nothing to assist the defendants who file complaints. Malpractice remedies are equally unhelpful because prevailing doctrine denies recovery unless defendants can show that but for their counsel's incompetence, they would in fact have been acquitted. In effect they must prove their innocence.[35] Because convicted criminals are unsympathetic claimants, and have difficulty meeting this standard, they can rarely find lawyers to file their claims.

From the standpoint of individual defendants, the most desirable remedy for ineffective representation is reversal of a conviction or invalidation of a guilty plea. However, here again, the obstacles are usually insurmountable. Defendants must show that counsel's performance fell outside the wide range of professionally competent assistance in the community and that but for their counsel's incompetence, the result would have been different.[36] This task is made especially difficult because defendants must make that showing based on a record made by an ineffective advocate. As a consequence, surveys of ineffective assistance claims have found that fewer than 5 percent are successful.[37] Part of the problem is that the community standard of representation is often abysmally low. A further difficulty is that the vast majority of cases involve plea bargains, which lack a record of what the attorney did, or, more often, did not do.

Even when attorneys' performance is inarguably inadequate, it may be impossible to prove that the outcome was affected. Death sentences have been upheld even when lawyers lacked any prior trial experience or were drunk, asleep, on drugs, or parking their car during key parts of the prosecution case.[38] Even capital cases can end up with lawyers who have never tried a case before and never should again.[39] Defense counsel has slept with sufficient frequency that an entire jurisprudence has developed to determine how much napping is constitutionally permissible. In these cases, courts have applied a three-step test. Did the lawyer sleep for repeated and prolonged periods? Was the lawyer actually unconscious? Were crucial defense interests at stake while the lawyer was dozing?[40] In one case rejecting claims of inadequate representation, a Texas appellate court reasoned that the decision to sleep might have been a "strategic" ploy to gain sympathy from the jury. And a judge reviewing that decision maintained that the "Constitution says that everyone is entitled to an attorney of their choice. But the Constitution does not say that the lawyer has to be awake."[41] In another case, a Houston attorney missed the statute of limitations for filing review petitions for three defendants sentenced to death, and has yet to be held responsible. At last count he was juggling more than 350 felony cases.[42] Yet as one Texas judge noted, "Competent counsel ought to require more than a human being with a law license and a pulse."[43]

Strategies for Reform

Responses to this shameful state are obvious but elusive. Most of all, the system needs a massive infusion of resources, but lacks the political traction to make that possible. Poor defendants are a singularly powerless and unpopular group. For example, about three-quarters of Americans believe that too many criminals get off on technicalities.[44] Therefore, courts need to put pressure on legislatures by recognizing constitutional flaws in systems plagued by inadequate funding and excessive caseloads.[45] Courts also need to uphold public defenders' right to refuse cases when failing to do so would result in ineffective advocacy. Examples include a Missouri Supreme Court decision holding that a defender should not be appointed in violation of an administrative rule limiting caseloads, and a Florida Supreme Court ruling that public defenders could refuse new cases if their workload precludes them from providing adequate representation.[46] The judiciary should also revisit the standard for ineffective assistance of counsel and replace it with a more realistic test that focuses on concrete duties of adequate representation and presumes prejudice when lawyers fall short.[47]

So, too, state legislatures should "get smart on crime" by reclassifying petty criminal offenses. As one group of experts noted,

> Any solution to the indigent defense crisis in America must focus on the front end of the system, as much as the back end. There are simply too many cases coming into the indigent defense system. Overreliance upon criminal prosecution for petty, nonviolent offenses, for which people seldom receive jail sentences, drives defender caseloads to unmanageable extremes, to the detriment of all accused persons and at enormous costs to the public.[48]

The cost savings from reclassification can be considerable. A Texas law that mandated probation for low-level possession of certain drugs saved the state an estimated $51 million over two years.[49]

A related strategy, endorsed by "smart on crime" advocates, is the diversion of minor offenders from the criminal courts. More jurisdictions should follow the example of states that have implemented specialized "holistic," "therapeutic," or "community" courts to address matters such as minor domestic violence, homelessness, drug possession, and juvenile offenses. Judges in these systems receive special training, resources, and access to social service providers. The goal is to address root causes of problems and not just their legal symptoms.[50] By removing low-level offenders from the criminal justice system, this approach also frees attorneys to focus on more serious matters.[51] Given their cost-effectiveness, diversion and reclassification can be sold as bipartisan fiscal issues.[52]

Further progress is possible through performance standards, guidelines, and oversight of counsel for indigent defendants. Such guidelines can include caseload limits and experience requirements. They can also clarify what is necessary for effective representation in terms of factual investigation, communication with clients, and related matters.[53] Procedures should be available for removing attorneys from the list of counsel eligible for court appointment when they have consistently neglected basic responsibilities.[54] Bar disciplinary agencies should also impose significant sanctions on attorneys who take cases for which they the lack the necessary time or expertise. An independent body should be available to monitor lawyers' performance to ensure that they have appropriate qualifications and that their representation meets minimum standards of effectiveness. Where necessary, judges can appoint supervisors to oversee compliance.[55]

Another strategy worth trying is to use trained nonlawyers for certain defense functions, such as representing defendants at bail hearings. As the discussion below indicates, lay advocates have proven effective in a wide range of civil contexts, and there is no reason to believe that their performance would be inadequate in minor criminal defense settings.[56]

Finally, the bench and the bar need to do more to educate the public about problems in indigent defense and the public's own stake in addressing them. Few Americans are aware of the assembly line pleas and ineffective lawyering that have become routine occurrences. Popular perceptions are shaped by well-publicized cases and fictional screenplays in which zealous advocacy is the norm. But a wide gap remains between law in prime time, and law in real time. The public needs to better understand not only the circumstances confronting impoverished defendants, but also its own interest in reform. The prospect of vigorous challenge by defense counsel creates incentives for law enforcement officials to do their jobs effectively and to respect individual rights. Providing adequate representation even for defendants who appear guilty is the best way to protect those who are not.

Ineffective representation is, of course, only one of the problems that plague America's criminal justice system. Other concerns include racial and ethnic bias, mass incarceration, sloppy or suggestive investigative techniques, police and prosecutorial misconduct, excessive sentences, politicized judicial elections, and unmanageable court caseloads. Some commentators have argued that a focus on better lawyering deflects attention from these broader issues.[57] But ineffective representation is a problem that compounds all others because it forecloses the possibility of legally challenging them. Denying an adequate defense to defendants who cannot afford it compromises our most basic commitments to equal justice under law.

Barriers in the Civil Justice System

Similar problems plague the civil justice system. In principle, America is deeply committed to individual rights. In practice, few Americans can afford to enforce them. The barriers have financial, structural, doctrinal, and political dimensions.

Financial Barriers

Money may not be the root of all evil, but it is surely responsible for much of what ails the current legal aid system. Americans do not believe that justice should be for sale, but neither do they want to pay for the alternative. Even before recent budgetary cutbacks, there was only one legal aid lawyer per 6415 low-income individuals.[58] In some jurisdictions, poor people must wait two years before seeing a legal aid lawyer for matters not considered an emergency, and other jurisdictions exclude such cases altogether.[59] The United States federal government spends only about a dollar per person per year for legal aid.[60] At this funding level, not much due process is available. Compared with other advanced economies, America spends less per legal aid case and has fewer institutions such as advice agencies and ombudspersons to assist with routine needs.[61] As a consequence, more individuals are priced out of the legal system than in other comparable countries. For example, one survey reported that in the United States, 38 percent of poor and 26 percent of middle-income individuals took no action in response to a legal problem, compared with 5 percent in England and 10 percent in the Netherlands.[62] According to the most recent national research, only a quarter of

American civil justice problems are taken to a lawyer, and only 14 percent are taken to a court or another hearing body.[63]

Moreover, the recent economic downturn has made a bad situation worse. High rates of unemployment, bankruptcies, foreclosures, and reductions in social services have created more demands for legal representation at the same time that many of its providers have faced cutbacks in their own budgets.[64] The federal budget for legal aid has been cut by almost a fifth since 2010 and private foundation funding has also declined at the same time that the eligible client population has increased.[65] In effect, understaffed and overextended legal assistance programs are often being asked to do more with less. As a result, millions of Americans find that legal protections available in principle are inaccessible in practice. For example, domestic violence victims cannot obtain protective orders, elderly medical patients cannot collect health benefits, disabled children lack educational services, and defrauded consumers lack affordable remedies. The list is long and the costs are incalculable.

Structural Barriers

A second set of problems is structural and involves the absence of any coherent system for allocating assistance and matching clients with the most cost-effective service provider. Researchers at the American Bar Foundation (ABF) recently undertook the first ever state-by-state portrait of funding available for civil legal services. They found considerable inequality within and across states: "Geography is destiny: the services available to people from eligible populations who face civil justice problems are determined not by what their problems are or the kinds of services they may need, but rather by where they happen to live."[66] Georgia offers a representative case of the mismatch between supply and demand that often underlies the inequality. Some 70 percent of the state's lawyers are in the Atlanta area, while 70 percent of the poor live outside it.[67] Six counties have no lawyer and dozens have only two or three.[68] Moreover, as ABF researchers found, "Little coordination exists for civil legal assistance, and existing mechanisms of coordination often have powers only of exhortation and consultation."[69] Priorities about who gets services and what kinds of services they receive are typically set by local legal aid programs. The result is not only resource disparities across jurisdictions, but also resource inadequacies in scaling up promising programs.[70] A related problem is the lack of reliable "empirical evidence . . . about what [form of] assistance would best meet [claimants'] needs, and . . . the coordination and planning that would assure that the right assistance is readily available to those who need it."[71]

The system is also unduly lawyer-centric. Bar organizations, which have been the most powerful voice in the debate over access to justice, have seen the solution as "more lawyers." In 2006, the American Bar Association (ABA) unanimously adopted a resolution urging the provision of "legal counsel as a matter of right at public expense to low income persons in those categories of adversarial proceedings where basic human needs are at stake. . . ."[72] Many state and local bars passed comparable resolutions.[73] These organizations have not been similarly enthusiastic about court simplification and nonlawyer assistance, and have actively fought self-help publications and nonlawyer providers.[74] As New York University law professor Stephen Gillers notes, it has not been "the bar's finest hour."[75] From the profession's perspective, the focus on guaranteeing more lawyers makes obvious sense. But from the standpoint of the public, the objective is more access to justice, not necessarily to lawyers.

In courts that handle housing, bankruptcy, small claims, and family matters, parties without attorneys are often now less the exception than the rule.[76] Yet they must cope with procedures designed by and for lawyers. Although courts have made increasing attempts to accommodate these unrepresented litigants, one national survey found only 11 states with comprehensive programs to help self-represented parties.[77] Many of the services that are available are unusable by those who need help most: low-income litigants with limited computer competence and limited English-language skills.[78] All too often, parties confront procedures of excessive and bewildering complexity, and forms with archaic jargon. The United States lags behind other nations in providing access through less expensive approaches than representation by lawyers.[79] In the United

Kingdom, for example, trained nonlawyer volunteers provide routine assistance at 3400 Citizens Advice Bureaus.[80] Legal assistance is also available through government networks of help desks, online services, insurers, banks, unions, consumer organizations, and even grocery stores.[81] In this country, millions of individuals lack such help, and only about half of Americans have reported satisfaction with their own resolution of legal problems.[82] The experience of one lawyerless litigant was all too common. When told by a trial court that he lacked a draft order that would authorize a referral to counseling, the man began asking questions about how to prepare the order. The judge responded, "I'm not your secretary" and shooed the man out of the courtroom.[83]

Moreover, for some cases, such as uncontested divorces, lawyers may be contributing more to the problem than the solution. In one survey of parents represented by counsel, 71 percent felt that the legal process exacerbated hostility.[84] Parents also felt that the role of attorneys contributed to conflict by replacing direct communication with discussion filtered only through counsel.[85] Other research finds that divorcing parties prefer simpler, less adversarial procedures, and that many do not hire lawyers for fear of intensifying conflict.[86]

Doctrinal Barriers

At the doctrinal level, a fundamental problem arises from courts' inherent power to regulate the practice of law, and their exercise of that power to ban the unauthorized practice of law (UPL) by nonlawyers without respect to its quality or cost-effectiveness. A second problem involves courts' restrictive standards for determining when court-appointed counsel is available. The result has been to place on unrepresented litigants an unrealistic burden of showing that the absence of a lawyer makes a legal proceeding fundamentally unfair.

A common feature of statutory and common-law prohibitions on unauthorized practice of law is their broad and ambiguous scope. A number of jurisdictions simply prohibit without defining the practice of law by nonlawyers.[87] Others take a circular approach: the practice of law is what lawyers do.[88] Some list conduct that is illustrative, such as legal advice, legal representation, and preparation of legal documents, and then conclude with some amorphous catch-all provision, such as "any action taken for others in any matter connected with the law."[89] On their face, these prohibitions encompass a wide range of common commercial activities. Many individuals, including accountants, financial advisors, real estate brokers, insurance agents, and even newspaper advice columnists, could not give intelligent advice without reference to legal concerns. Moreover, the ban on personalized assistance stands as a powerful barrier to competent low-cost providers. So, for example, form-processing services may provide clerical help, but are prohibited from correcting obvious errors or answering simple questions about where and when papers must be filed.[90] A few decisions have even held that online document assistance constitutes the unauthorized practice of law because the services go beyond clerical support.[91] Court clerks are also banned from giving advice to unrepresented parties.[92] Some courthouses even have signs stating that clerks "can't answer questions of a legal nature."[93] Yet as one California judge noted, those are the only questions that clerks generally encounter, other than, "Where is the restroom?"[94]

Such expansive prohibitions ill serve the public interest. Although courts repeatedly insist that broad prohibitions on unauthorized practice serve to protect the public, support for that claim is often lacking.[95] In my recent review of ten years of reported UPL cases, only a quarter analyzed whether actual harm occurred or could occur from the unauthorized practice in question.[96] In my national survey of officials involved in UPL enforcement, two-thirds could not recall a specific case of injury in the past year.[97] So, too, other research similarly casts doubt on the frequency of client injury. The vast majority of UPL lawsuits filed against online services are brought not by consumers but by lawyers or unauthorized practice committees, and generally settle without examples of harm.[98]

Other nations permit nonlawyers to provide legal advice and assist with routine documents, and the evidence available does not suggest that their performance has been inadequate.[99] In a study comparing outcomes for low-income clients in the United Kingdom on matters such as welfare benefits, housing, and employment, nonlawyers generally outperformed lawyers in terms of concrete results and client satisfaction.[100] After reviewing their own and other empirical studies, the authors of that study concluded that "it is specialization, not professional status, which appears to be the best predictor of quality."[101] Ontario allows licensed paralegals to represent individuals in minor court cases and administrative tribunal proceedings, and a five-year review reported "solid levels of [public] satisfaction with the services received."[102]

In the United States, research on lay specialists who provide legal representation in bankruptcy and administrative agency hearings finds that they generally perform as well as or better than attorneys.[103] Extensive formal training is less critical than daily experience for effective advocacy.[104] Yet existing unauthorized practice doctrine focuses only on whether the nonlawyer is providing legal assistance, not the quality of that assistance or the evidence of public injury.

Further doctrinal problems arise from the restrictive standards that courts have established to determine rights to counsel in civil proceedings. The most recent authoritative case is the Supreme Court's decision in *Turner v. Rogers*. The case involved Michael Turner, who had been jailed repeatedly for civil contempt for his failure to make child support payments to Rebecca Rogers, the mother of his child. Turner was unrepresented at his civil contempt hearings, and while serving a one-year sentence, he found a pro bono attorney to challenge the failure of the South Carolina state court to appoint counsel for him. In a unanimous decision, the Supreme Court held that the Due Process Clause did not entitle Turner to counsel. The Court applied a balancing test articulated in *Mathews v. Eldridge*, which requires consideration of the "(1) the nature of the 'private interest that will be affected,' (2) the comparative 'risk' of an 'erroneous deprivation' of that interest with and without 'additional or substitute procedural safeguards,' and (3) the nature and the magnitude of any countervailing interest in not providing 'additional or substitute requirement[s].'"[105] On balance, the Court concluded that despite the defendant's strong liberty interest, the facts tipped against appointment of counsel. In so holding, the Court stressed that the critical issue of the defendant's ability to pay support was "sufficiently straightforward" and uncomplicated to be resolved without counsel. Moreover, since Rogers was not represented, appointing counsel only for Turner could create an asymmetry that might unduly slow payment and make the proceedings "less fair overall."[106] The majority also believed that there was an alternative set of protections that could "significantly reduce the risk of an erroneous deprivation of liberty" without appointing counsel.[107] These protections included giving notice that ability to pay child support is a key issue; asking defendants to fill out financial disclosure forms; allowing defendants to respond to questions about their finances; and making express findings regarding ability to pay. Because Turner had received neither a lawyer nor these alternative safeguards, the Court overturned his conviction.

The decision is problematic on several grounds. One is the absence of empirical evidence to support the court's assertions about the complexity of procedures and fairness of alternatives. Some commentators suggested that the Court's analysis revealed a "breathtaking disconnect from the real world."[108] "I don't think the Court understands what it's like to go into court without a lawyer," noted Georgetown law professor Peter Edelman. "It would be good for the whole lot of them to go and spend the day in landlord-tenant court and see if they have the same view."[109] How would an unrepresented litigant be able to establish that alternative procedures would lack fundamental fairness or present an unacceptable risk of error?[110] Critics also noted that Turner faced more jail time for civil contempt than he would have served for criminal contempt, which would have required appointment of counsel.[111]

Yale law professor Judith Resnik found still more fundamental problems with the *Mathews* balancing test that *Turner* applies. "Neither judges nor litigants can identify with any rigor the actual costs of various procedures, let alone [gauge] the impact in terms of [errors] . . . produced by the same, more or different processes . . ."[112] A further problem is how unrepresented litigants could ensure that the court will in fact supply essential alternative safeguards.[113] As Resnik notes, the trial judge in *Turner* "spent less than five minutes . . . made no findings on the record . . . and sent Turner to jail for twelve months," which suggests the inadequacies of the court that that would be responsible for ensuring those alternative protections.[114] Absent some "public accounting and lawyer involvement, few mechanisms exist to police the fairness that Turner calls for. . . . "[115]

Moreover, the balancing test endorsed in *Turner* is not only flawed in theory; it has proven unworkable in practice. Vulnerable litigants in need of assistance have almost never succeeded in persuading federal courts to provide it.[116] State courts and legislatures have mandated counsel only in extremely limited categories of cases, typically involving certain family, medical, and civil commitment issues.[117] Judging from the caseloads of civil legal aid programs, about 98 percent of cases that directly involve low-income parties are not entitled to counsel.[118] So, too, the selection of cases in which counsel is guaranteed sometimes seems idiosyncratic. Why should individuals challenging voluntary vaccination orders or school attendance get a lawyer but not individuals dealing with survival needs such as food, housing, medical benefits, or protection from domestic violence?[119] Even where lawyers are available, requirements of adequate experience, training, and compensation are "more often than not . . . neither imposed nor satisfied."[120]

The denial of assistance to undocumented immigrants imposes particular hardship. Their frequent lack of language skills and understanding of American legal processes makes it difficult for them to proceed without legal assistance. Yet only about a third of aliens and 10 percent of those in detention have legal representation in immigration proceedings.[121] Programs funded by the federal Legal Services Corporation are prohibited from representing undocumented aliens.[122] Although leading federal decisions authorize the appointment of counsel to prevent erroneous judgments, surveys find not a single immigration case in three decades where a noncitizen has been granted a court-appointed lawyer.[123]

Political Barriers

A final set of barriers in the justice system is political. The public is uninformed and unorganized on issues concerning access to justice, and prefers options that the organized bar has reasons to oppose.[124] Although the vast majority of Americans support provision of legal services to those who cannot afford it, four-fifths also incorrectly believe that the poor are entitled to counsel in civil cases.[125] Two-thirds think that low-income individuals would have no difficulty finding legal assistance, a perception wildly out of touch with reality.[126] On the rare occasions when its opinion has been solicited, four-fifths of the public also agreed that "many things that lawyers handle . . . can be done as well and less expensively by nonlawyers."[127] Yet ordinary citizens lack adequate incentives to mobilize for reforms permitting access to such service providers. Unlike health care, which is a crucial and continuing need, most Americans' demand for legal assistance is much more episodic and less life-threatening.

The obstacles to reform are especially formidable, given the organized bar's incentives and capacity for resistance. No other occupation enjoys such prominence in all three branches of government. As a result, the bar has traditionally been well positioned to block changes that might benefit the public at the profession's expense. The bar has repeatedly fought publication of self-help materials and opposed access to nonlawyer assistance.[128] The ABA is on record as supporting efforts to strengthen unauthorized practice enforcement and over four-fifths of surveyed lawyers favor prosecution of independent paralegals.[129] The bar has also been concerned that "pro se court reform will spread upwards from the poor to the middle class and beyond."[130] And the courts, which enforce unauthorized practice prohibitions and control procedural simplification and pro se assistance programs, have been unduly deferential to the bar on matters that affect its livelihood.[131]

Political opposition from attorneys has also sabotaged efforts to mandate pro bono service. Although bar leaders and ethical codes have long maintained that all lawyers share a professional responsibility to provide legal assistance to those who cannot afford it, proposals to put teeth into that obligation have been unceremonially buried.[132] In the absence of requirements, only about a quarter of American lawyers meet the aspirational standard of 50 hours of service annually that is codified in the ABA Model Rules of Professional Conduct.[133] In the nation's largest firms, only a minority of lawyers contribute even 20 hours a year.[134] Given these participation levels, it is perhaps unsurprising that most attorneys resist campaigns to make service mandatory. Only nine states even require lawyers to report their pro bono hours.[135]

The inadequacy of bar involvement reflects a missed opportunity for the profession as well as the public. Lawyers themselves benefit, both individually and collectively, from participation in public service. It can enhance their skills, contacts, reputation, and psychological well-being, as well as the profession's public image.[136]

Civil Justice Reform

Despite these obstacles, there is reason to hope that some progress is possible on access to justice. First, the increasing public interest in do-it-yourself publications and services and the increasing volume of pro se litigants has created corresponding pressure for reform. As law professor Russell Engler notes, attitudes toward the role of judges and court clerks concerning unrepresented parties have "undergone a sea change over the past fifteen years. . . ."[137] About half the states have access to justice commissions, and a consortium of law professors recently formed to support research and teaching initiatives on access issues.[138] The state of Washington has enacted a licensing system for independent paralegals who can provide certain routine services, New York has approved a system of trained nonlawyer "navigators" who can assist pro se litigants in certain courts, and California is considering similar reforms.[139] Bar efforts to crack down on self-help software have triggered reversal by state legislatures, and market demand for such products has overwhelmed the capacity of bar organizations to respond.[140] The ABA has abandoned its attempt to promulgate a restrictive definition of unauthorized practice after the Justice Department, the Federal Trade Commission, and the ABA's own antitrust division suggested that the revision would be anticompetitive.[141] California and Massachusetts have launched pilot projects to evaluate the cost-effectiveness of guaranteeing the right to counsel in specified circumstances.[142] According to a study of a Massachusetts program, every dollar spent on legal aid would save the state $2.69 in other services such as emergency shelter, foster care, and law enforcement.[143] An ABA Task Force on the Future of Legal Education has recommended a licensing system for paralegals to provide routine legal services.[144] Another ABA Task Force on the Legal Access Job Corps is considering ways to help new entrants to the bar provide assistance to underserved populations.[145] Never has there been a more receptive climate for access to justice issues.

Further progress will require strategies on four levels. First, we need to maximize opportunities for self-help and for legal assistance from less expensive service providers than lawyers. A second strategy should focus on ways to match cases with the most cost-effective providers, and to ensure access to lawyers in cases involving fundamental interests that cannot be effectively addressed in other ways. A third strategy should involve research to assess different methods of assistance and to gain a better understanding of what works best for whom in what circumstances.[146] A final strategy should ensure more education of the public and the profession about the need for reform.

Self-Help and Nonlawyer Service Providers

The first strategy is already well under way. Courts around the country are implementing reform efforts to accommodate unrepresented pro se litigants.[147] These litigants are often particularly vulnerable. They are disproportionately poor and unfamiliar with legal proceedings, and many face barriers of language and computer literacy.[148] They need what Richard Zorza has termed "The Self-Help Friendly Court."[149] This court would seek to reduce complexity, take advantage of technology, and train judges and staff in assisting litigants.[150] Models are increasingly available. The American Judicature Society and the National Center for State Courts have published guides to make legal proceedings more equitable and accessible to parties without lawyers.[151] The Self-Represented Litigation Network has also published materials compiling best practices and innovative approaches.[152] Some court systems have established special magistrate courts for pro se cases, or employed staff attorneys to assist pro se litigants.[153] Others have hotlines, pro se clerks' offices, "lawyers of the day programs," and self-help centers.[154] However, all these strategies assume a commitment to making courts more accessible that has too often been lagging.[155] In many jurisdictions, severe financial constraints and recent budgetary cutbacks have compounded the challenge of funding adequate pro se services.[156] Surmounting those obstacles will require more exposure of inaccessible systems, more resources for innovation, and more ways to hold the courts accountable.

Americans would also benefit from more effective channels of informal dispute resolution, not only in courthouses, but also in neighborhood, workplace, commercial, and online settings. Considerable evidence suggests that well-designed employee and consumer grievance procedures benefit both business and individual participants, and that most people prefer to resolve disputes through informal, out-of-court processes.[157] Such processes may often be more cost-effective than judicial intervention, and may enable participants to craft outcomes that better address their underlying problems. Businesses over a certain size could be given incentives to institutionalize such dispute-resolution processes, and reforms could be mandated for arbitration and mediation procedures that are now skewed against weaker parties.[158]

We also need changes in unauthorized practice doctrine and enforcement. Charges of unauthorized practice should only be brought in cases of demonstrated consumer injury. Judges should follow the lead of courts that have weighed the public interest in determining whether to ban nonlawyer assistance. For example, the Colorado Supreme Court upheld a system enabling nonlawyers to represent claimants in unemployment proceedings; the Court reasoned that lay representation had been accepted by the public for fifty years and "poses no threat to the People of the State of Colorado. Nor is it interfering with the proper administration of justice. No evidence was presented to the contrary."[159] Similarly, the

Washington State Supreme Court, after considering factors such as cost, availability of services, and consumer convenience, concluded that it was in the public interest to allow licensed real estate brokers to fill in standard form agreements.[160] Such a consumer-oriented approach would make for a more socially defensible regulatory structure than conventional bans on nonlawyer practice irrespective of its quality and cost-effectiveness.

Licensing systems could also be developed to allow qualified nonlawyers to offer personalized assistance on routine matters. Consumer protections could be required concerning qualifications, disclaimers, ethical standards, malpractice insurance, and discipline.[161] Many administrative agencies already have power to regulate nonlawyers appearing before them, and no evidence suggests that the performance of these nonlawyers has been inadequate.[162] Under their inherent powers, courts could oversee the development of such licensing systems or could approve legislatively authorized structures as consistent with the public interest. More states should follow the lead of Washington and New York, which have already taken steps in this direction. If the goal is to protect clients from incompetence, rather than lawyers from competition, then regulation—not prohibition—of lay specialists makes sense.

Such a regulatory system would be particularly beneficial in the area of immigration, a field characterized by both pervasive fraud and pervasive unmet needs.[163] Individuals holding themselves out as notaries and immigration consultants have preyed on the ignorance of undocumented consumers who cannot afford attorneys and who are reluctant to approach authorities to complain about fraudulent practices. Many of these consultants capitalize on the status of *notario publicos* in some Latin American countries, where these legal professionals enjoy formal legal training and authority to provide legal assistance.[164] The situation would benefit from a licensing structure similar to that in Australia, Canada, and the United Kingdom, which allow licensed nonlawyer experts to provide immigration-related assistance.[165] Although the United States allows accredited nonlawyers to represent individuals in immigration appeals, it permits only representatives who work for nonprofit organizations and who accept only nominal fees for their efforts.[166] An expanded licensing system that would allow qualified lay experts to charge reasonable fees could expand access to justice for a population in great need of assistance.[167]

In short, the current structure is both underenforced and overinclusive. Bar prohibitions encompass a sweeping array of competent, low-cost services. Yet strong consumer demand for such assistance makes these prohibitions difficult to enforce. As a result, most lay practice goes unregulated, and when abuses occur, as in the immigration context, the public has inadequate remedies. A preferable regulatory structure would provide both less and more protection—less for attorneys and more for consumers.

A Right to Counsel in Civil Cases

Not only do we need to increase less expensive options than attorneys; we also need systems to match clients with appropriate service providers and to ensure provision of lawyers where other options are inadequate.[168] The right to counsel ("Civil *Gideon*") should depend on whether fundamental interests are at issue and whether a lawyer's assistance is critical to ensure basic fairness.[169] In identifying fundamental interests, a starting point for analysis is the American Bar Association's resolution in favor of appointing counsel in areas of "basic human need," defined as shelter, sustenance, safety, health, and child custody.[170] In determining basic fairness, courts and legislatures should consider the complexity of the procedures and the power relations between the parties.

Such a right to counsel is compelling in principle, but challenging in practice. More than eighty years ago, the U.S. Supreme Court recognized that an individual's "right to be heard [in legal proceedings] would be, in many cases, of little avail if it did not comprehend the right to be heard by counsel."[171] Access to an attorney will often be critical to the rule of law and social justice. The United States lags behind the 49 countries in the Council of Europe, as well as other nations such as Canada, Japan, India, and Australia, which have recognized a right to counsel in at least some civil cases.[172]

What stands in the way is money. America's experience in attempting to fund a right to counsel in criminal cases is not encouraging. As noted earlier, in many jurisdictions, staggering caseloads and shamefully inadequate fees have made effective representation impossible.[173] Given the current constraints on state and local budgets, there is no reason to expect that funding for a civil right to counsel would be better. In jurisdictions that now appoint lawyers for defendants in child support cases, inadequate time and resources often prevent effective assistance.[174] A related concern is that extending the civil right to counsel "will compete with other rights to counsel, spreading funding ever thinner."[175]

The only principled response to such concerns is for courts to put pressure on state and federal legislatures to provide adequate funding for legal assistance, and for the bar to require pro bono service by lawyers. It is national disgrace that civil legal aid programs now reflect less than 1 percent of the nation's legal expenditures.[176] It is a professional disgrace that most lawyers cannot manage even an hour a week on pro bono service. We can and must do better.

Legal Services for the Poor

Although the problems of inadequate access are by no means limited to the poor, the distinctive needs of low-income groups deserve special attention. Not only do the poor and near-poor experience more legal difficulties than the average American; their needs take on special urgency. Individuals at the economic margin are much less able to "lump it" when faced with a denial of rights or benefits. Low-income individuals are also less likely to have the education and skills to handle their legal problems effectively without assistance.

Addressing these problems will require government funding adequate to meet the demands of those who need legal assistance but cannot realistically afford it. What constitutes "need" and "affordability" is, of course, open to dispute, but by almost any standard, our current system falls far short. Most European nations guarantee legal assistance for a much broader category of individuals than those entitled to legal aid in the American system, where eligibility is limited to those below or just above the official poverty line. In other countries, the eligibility criteria include

- Does the claim have a reasonable chance of success?
- What would be the benefits of legal assistance or the harms if it is unavailable?
- Would a reasonable lawyer, advising a reasonable client, suggest that the client use his or her own money to pursue the issue?[177]

In assessing financial eligibility, these systems typically operate with sliding income scales. Such an approach permits serving a broader range of clients than are currently served by American legal aid offices. Other nations' more liberal eligibility structures remedy a major limitation of the U.S. model, which excludes many individuals with urgent problems and no realistic means of addressing them. Although such a structure would require more funding, it would also have more political appeal than the current program, which benefits only the poor.

Subsidies for an expanded system could come from various financial sources likely to command greater public support than general tax revenues. Examples include a small progressive tax on law-related revenues, a surcharge on court filing fees based on the amount in controversy, and an expansion of contexts permitting fee awards to prevailing parties.[178] In a nation with more than $240 billion in gross legal revenues, a modest 1 percent tax would make a significant difference.[179]

An equitable and cost-effective legal aid system would also operate without the restrictions on activities that now accompany government subsidies. Legal services programs that receive federal funds may not use that money, and in some instances may not use any other revenue, for a broad range of matters including school desegregation, abortion, political redistricting, welfare reform, and clients who are undocumented aliens or prison inmates. Nor may these programs engage in activities such as lobbying, community organizing, class actions, or representation in legislative and administrative rule-making proceedings.[180] Since these are the very strategies most likely to address the causes of legal problems and to deter future abuses, legal aid programs have faced an unpalatable choice. They can do without federal funds and help far fewer individual clients, but in a more effective fashion. Or they can handle more cases, but only for politically acceptable clients, and in ways less likely to promote real change. This is a choice we should not require. Legislators who have demanded such restrictions are attempting to accomplish indirectly what they have been unable to do directly: curtail rights and social services benefiting the least popular of the poor. This is unworthy of a nation committed to equal justice under law in practice as well as principle.

Pro Bono Service

Another obvious way to increase access to legal counsel is to require pro bono contributions from lawyers. Fifty hours a year, the current aspirational standard, should be mandatory, with a financial buyout option for those who lack the time or inclination for service. Buyout contributions could go to support designated legal aid providers. Such a requirement, calling for less than an hour a week of assistance or the financial equivalent, hardly justifies the overblown descriptions advanced by critics of mandatory service: "latent fascism," "economic slavery," and "involuntary servitude."[181]

The rationale for a pro bono requirement is straightforward. Because access to law so often requires access to lawyers, they bear a particular responsibility to help make legal services available. As courts and bar ethical codes have long noted, the state grants lawyers special monopoly privileges that impose special obligations.[182] As officers of the court, lawyers bear some responsibility for ensuring fundamental fairness in its processes. Because lawyers occupy such a central role in our justice system, there is also particular value in exposing them to how that system functions, or fails to function, for the have-nots. Pro bono work offers many attorneys their only direct contact with what passes for justice among the poor. Giving the bar some experience with poverty-related problems and public interest causes can lay crucial foundations for change. Pro bono programs have often launched social reform initiatives and strengthened support for government subsidies of legal aid.[183]

Mandating pro bono service would benefit the profession as well as the public. Volunteer service offers ways for lawyers to gain additional skills, trial experience, and community contacts. Such career development opportunities, on behalf of causes to which attorneys are committed, are often their most rewarding professional experiences.[184] Many lawyers report that they would like to do more pro bono work but are in institutions that do not support it.[185] ABA surveys find that young lawyers' greatest source of dissatisfaction in practice is its lack of connection to the public good.[186] Pro bono service can supply that connection.

In the absence of a requirement for pro bono service, more efforts could be made to encourage voluntary contributions. More courts and bar associations should require legal workplaces to report their pro bono assistance, and more clients should consider lawyers' involvement when selecting counsel. For example, California legislation requires pro bono contributions as a condition of any state contract for legal services exceeding $50,000.[187] Organizations such as the ABA Standing Committee on Pro Bono and Public Service could publish directories with information concerning employers' pro bono policies and contributions. They could also develop best practices and publicize lists of employers who certify that their lawyers have met the ABA's aspirational standard of 50 hours a year of service. Best practices could include

- adoption of a formal pro bono policy that gives credit for pro bono work toward billable hour requirements;
- a visible commitment by the organization's leadership;
- consideration of pro bono service as a favorable factor in performance evaluations and in promotion and compensation decisions;
- requirements of compliance with the ABA Model Rules standard of 50 hours of service per year or the financial equivalent;
- adequate supervision and training; and
- recognition and showcasing of service.[188]

Greater efforts could also be made to target particular groups of lawyers whose services have been underutilized, such as retired lawyers and legal academics.[189] Bar associations could offer backup assistance, free malpractice insurance, and continuing education credit for pro bono training. The objective should be to ensure a closer match between the profession's rhetorical and actual commitment to public service.

Unbundled Services and Innovative Delivery Structures

Another way of expanding access to counsel for middle-income clients is through unbundled legal services. Under this approach, lawyers provide assistance on discrete legal tasks, such as advice, negotiation, document preparation, or court appearances, rather than full representation.[190] In one ABA poll, two-thirds of potential clients would like to have a conversation about unbundling, and two-thirds said lawyers' willingness to provide unbundled services would be important to their decision about whom to engage.[191] Courts can encourage this trend by allowing lawyers to submit ghostwritten pleadings and to limit their liability for specified tasks as long as the limitation is reasonable and clients give informed consent.[192] To make such representation more accessible, lawyers could follow the lead of initiatives such as the chain Legal Grind, which dispenses brief advice along with cappuccino and self-help materials, and LegalForce, a store that offers advice along with do-it-yourself books and computer kiosks.[193] To increase demand for such services, more state bars could also establish special referral programs that match clients of limited means to lawyers willing to provide reduced-fee assistance.[194]

Research

A major obstacle to increasing access to justice is the lack of research on key issues. For example, we know little about when counsel is necessary to secure fundamental fairness. Methodologically sound studies on the contributions of lawyers in routine cases are scarce and conflicting.[195] Researchers using randomized control groups have come to different conclusions as to whether lawyers improve outcomes.[196] Moreover, short-term outcomes are not the only, or necessarily the most important, measures of impact. We know almost nothing about the long-term consequences of appointing counsel. For example, how much does winning a landlord-tenant case help in terms of stabilizing a party's living situation or producing improvements in building conditions?[197] Are there better uses of lawyers' time? Could they do more to prevent homelessness by focusing more on policy and organizing efforts and less on individual representation? We know little about what cases are most appropriate for unbundled legal services.[198] And we lack adequate data about various self-help strategies such as hotlines, pro se clinics, and document preparation services like LegalZoom.[199] More research is critical to assessing the relative cost-effectiveness of particular forms of assistance.

We also need more evaluation of the quality and social impact of pro bono representation. All too often, lawyers assume that any work done pro bono *is* pro bono; representation is taken as a good in and of itself regardless of cost-effectiveness.[200] In the only recent survey of law firms' pro bono programs, none made any formal efforts to assess the social impact of their work or the satisfaction of clients and nonprofit partners who referred cases.[201] Many firms operate with a "spray and pray" approach: they spread services widely and hope that something good will come of them.[202] Something usually does, but it is not necessarily the best use of resources. Nor do good intentions always ensure good results. On one of the rare occasions when someone asked, almost half of public interest legal organizations reported problems with the quality of pro bono work that they obtained from outside firms.[203]

Ensuring that pro bono resources are used most effectively will require systematic research. Pro bono providers should collect standardized data on the amount and types of services provided, the outcomes obtained, and the satisfaction of clients and public interest partners.[204] Only through such research efforts can we identify the legal needs that fall through the cracks and the quality concerns that should be addressed.

Legal Education

Legal education could do more to promote access to justice both by supporting research and by integrating the issue into curricular and programmatic activities. Currently, the topic is missing or marginal in the traditional core curriculum.[205] Even professional responsibility courses, which are logical forums for such coverage, often focus on the law of lawyering and omit broader questions about the distribution of legal services.[206] In my own national survey, only 1 percent of law school graduates recalled coverage of pro bono obligations in their professional responsibility class or orientation program.[207] Although many legal clinics offer some firsthand exposure to what passes for justice among low-income communities, not all students take these courses. And given the need to provide both skills training and knowledge of relevant substantive and procedural law, not all clinics find time to consider structural problems in the delivery of legal services. To address these gaps, schools should offer at least one course that focuses on access to justice and should encourage integration of the topic into the core curriculum.

Given the profession's aspiration that all lawyers should provide pro bono services, all law schools should lay the foundations for that commitment. A decade ago, a commission of the Association of American Law Schools recommended that every institution "make available for every student at least one well-supervised pro bono opportunity and either require participation or find ways to attract the great majority of students to volunteer."[208] We remain a considerable distance from that goal. Only a small minority of schools require pro bono work, fewer still impose specific obligations on faculty, and in many institutions, the amounts required are minimal.[209] Although other schools have voluntary programs, their scope and supervision sometimes leave much to be desired, and more than a third of students graduate without pro bono work as part of the educational experience.[210] Legal education could do better, and models are available that could be widely replicated. An example is the Roger Williams Law School Pro Bono Collaborative, in which faculty oversee some thirty initiatives involving students, nonprofit organizations, and pro bono attorneys who assist low-income individuals.[211]

The American Bar Association's Council on Legal Education and Admission to the Bar should also do more to support such initiatives. Its standards for accreditation call on law schools to "offer substantial opportunities for . . . student participation in pro bono activities."[212] But enforcement of this standard has had little teeth. The ABA should mandate that schools require pro bono service and include access to justice issues in the core curriculum.[213]

Legal education should also do more to educate the public concerning these issues. As noted earlier, much of the problem of access to justice stems from the lack of public recognition that there *is* a significant problem. Not only do most Americans believe incorrectly that the poor already have a right to appointed counsel, they also think that the nation has too much litigation.[214] Such perceptions make increased budgets for legal services a low priority. Academics need to do more writing for nonacademic audiences in ways that put a human face on legal needs.

The ideal of equal justice is deeply embedded in American legal traditions and routinely violated in legal practice. Our nation prides itself on its commitment to the rule of law, but prices law out of reach of the vast majority of its citizens. Our constitution guarantees effective assistance of counsel in criminal cases but our courts fail to ensure it. Primary control over the legal process rests with the profession that has the least stake in reducing its expense.

More than three decades ago, President Jimmy Carter noted that the United States had "the heaviest concentration of lawyers on earth . . . but no resource of talent and training . . . is more wastefully or unfairly distributed than legal skills. Ninety percent of our lawyers serve 10 percent of our people. We are overlawyered and underrepresented."[215] The situation has not improved. And at least part of the problem is of the profession's own making. Our nation does not lack for lawyers, nor does it lack for ideas about how to make legal services more accessible. The challenge remaining is to learn more about what strategies work best, and to make them a public and a professional priority. If our nation is truly committed to equal justice under law, we must do more to translate that rhetorical aspiration into daily reality.

4

Diversity in the Profession

ONE IRONY OF THIS nation's continuing struggle for diversity and gender equity in employment is that the profession leading the struggle has failed to set an example in its own workplaces.[1] In principle, the bar is deeply committed to equal opportunity and social justice. In practice, it lags behind other occupations in leveling the playing field. According to the American Bar Association, only two professions (the natural sciences and dentistry) have less diversity than law; medicine, accounting, academia, and others do considerably better.[2] Part of the problem lies in a lack of consensus on what exactly the problem is. What accounts for gender, racial, and ethnic inequalities in law firms? Who is responsible for addressing them? Which proposed solutions would be worth the cost?

These are not new questions. But recent economic and client pressures have made clear the need for better answers. Many of the obstacles to diversity and equity in legal practice are symptomatic of deeper structural problems. This chapter focuses primarily on barriers involving gender, race, and ethnicity. Although these are not the only relevant dimensions of diversity, they provide a useful framework because they affect the greatest number of lawyers and have been subject to the most systematic research. However, much of the analysis in this chapter has broader application and would improve the quality of professional life for other groups as well.

The discussion below follows conventional usage in referring to "women and minorities," but that should neither obscure the unique experience of women of color nor mask differences within and across racial and ethnic groups. The point, rather, is to understand how different identities structure the professional experience.

The Gap between Principle and Practice

Gender

Viewed historically, the American legal profession has made substantial progress in the struggle for gender equality. Until the late 1960s, women constituted no more than about 3 percent of the profession and were largely confined to low-prestige practice settings and specialties.[3] Now, close to half of new lawyers are female and are fairly evenly distributed across substantive areas.[4] As Chapter 2 notes, women also express approximately the same overall level of satisfaction with practice as do men.[5]

Yet significant gender inequalities persist. Women constitute more than a third of the profession but only about a fifth of law firm partners, general counsels of Fortune 500 corporations, and law school deans.[6] Women are less likely to make partner even controlling for other factors, including law school grades and time spent out of the workforce or on part-time schedules.[7] Studies find that men are two to five times more likely than women to make partner.[8] Even women who never take time out of the labor force and who work long hours have a lower chance of partnership than similarly situated men.[9] The situation is bleakest at the highest levels. Women constitute only 17 percent of equity partners.[10] Women are also underrepresented in leadership positions such as firm chairs and members of management and compensation committees.[11] Only seven of the nation's hundred largest firms have a woman as chair or managing partner.[12] Gender disparities are similarly apparent in compensation.[13] A pay gap persists even after controlling for factors such as productivity and differences in equity/nonequity status.[14]

So, too, although female lawyers report about the same overall career satisfaction as their male colleagues, women experience greater dissatisfaction with key dimensions of practice such as level of responsibility, recognition for work, and chances for advancement.[15] In attempting to account for this paradox, theorists suggest two explanations. The first involves values. Women may ascribe less significance to aspects of their work environment on which they are disadvantaged, such as compensation and promotion, than to other factors such as intellectual challenge, which evokes greater satisfaction among female than male attorneys.[16] A second theory is that women have a lower sense of entitlement, in part because their reference group is other women or because they "have made peace with second best."[17] In either case, female lawyers' dissatisfaction with key aspects of practice, which is reflected in disproportionate rates of attrition, should be cause for concern in a profession committed to equal opportunity and diversity.

Race and Ethnicity

Progress for racial and ethnic minorities has also been substantial, but slower than for white women. In 1960, lawyers of color accounted for less than 1 percent of the profession.[18] Although blacks, Latinos, Asian Americans, and Native Americans now constitute about a third of the population and a fifth of law school graduates, they still only account for fewer than 7 percent of law firm partners and 9 percent of general counsels of Fortune 500 corporations.[19] In major law firms, only 3 percent of associates and less than 2 percent of partners are African Americans.[20] About half of lawyers of color leave within three years.[21] Attrition is highest for women of color; about 75 percent depart by their fifth year and 85 percent before their seventh.[22] Compensation in law firms is lower for lawyers of color, with minority women at the bottom of the financial pecking order.[23] Few lawyers of color have served in leadership roles.[24]

Satisfaction surveys reflect mixed and sometimes paradoxical results. In a large national study of young lawyers by the American Bar Foundation, blacks were happiest with their decision to become a lawyer and the substance of their legal work; whites and Asian Americans were the happiest in their job settings.[25] Among lawyers in large firms, the ABA's Commission on Women in the Profession found stark differences among racial groups. White men graded their career satisfaction as A, white women and minority men graded theirs as B, and minority women hovered between B minus and C plus.[26]

In short, the legal profession reflects substantial gender, racial, and ethnic differences in both subjective and objective measures of career achievement. But what accounts for those differences and how they can be addressed remain matters of dispute.

Explaining the Gap

Capabilities and Commitment

In a parody of diversity efforts during a celebrated British television series, "Yes Minister," a stodgy white male civil servant explained the folly of such initiatives. By his logic, if women had the necessary commitment and capabilities, they would already be well represented in leadership positions. Since they weren't well represented, they obviously lacked those qualifications. It should come as no surprise that similar views are common among leaders of the American bar. After all, those in charge of hiring, promotion, and compensation decisions are those who have benefitted from the current structure, and who have the greatest stake in believing in its fairness. Although many leaders are willing to concede the persistence of bias in society in general, they are less likely to see it in their own institutions. Rather, they attribute racial, ethnic, and gender differences in lawyers' career paths to differences in capabilities and commitment.[27]

For lawyers of color, the most common explanation for underrepresentation is underperformance, measured by traditional merit standards. Minorities are underrepresented in law schools and on average have lower law school grades than their white counterparts.[28] Because the vast majority of lawyers believe that grades and law school rank are important in hiring, racial disparities appear to be an unintended but inevitable consequence of the merit system.[29]

One in-depth study of attitudes toward diversity found that the standard narrative in large firms ran something like this:

> We understand that most big firms began in an era of overt discrimination. We regret this and for many years have attempted to do something about it. We have tried a variety of things and will continue to work very hard at the problem. However, it is very, very difficult to solve the problem without lowering our standards, which of course we can't do. All of this adds up to a metaphorical shrug.[30]

In other workplaces, the narrative is much the same, with the added twist that they cannot compete with large firms in money or prestige in recruiting "qualified" lawyers of color.[31] In effect, bar leaders "claim to be trapped by a system that they have created and choose to maintain."[32]

My own recent survey of diversity in large firms and Fortune 100 corporate counsel departments found a more nuanced picture. Virtually all managing partners and general counsel mentioned diversity as a high priority in their organization and many were dissatisfied with the progress that they had made. One managing partner expressed widespread views: "[We're] not nearly successful enough, no question about it."[33] Some attributed the low representation of lawyers of color to clogs in the pipeline. But others acknowledged unconscious bias and "diversity fatigue."[34]

By contrast, the "woman problem" is commonly explained in terms not of credentials but of commitment and client development. Because women continue to have disproportionate family responsibilities and are more likely to reduce their schedules or to take time out of the workplace than men, they are assumed to be less available, less dependable, and less worthy of extensive mentoring. In one survey, although women and men reported working similar hours, over a quarter of male lawyers thought their female counterparts worked less and a fifth rated the number of hours these women worked as "fair to poor."[35] So, too, women are often presumed to be less adept in business development and in the self-promotional abilities that underlie it.[36]

These attitudes may help to explain the relatively rosy assessment that many lawyers offer of diversity initiatives. In a survey by Catalyst, only 11 percent of white lawyers felt that diversity efforts were failing to address subtle racial bias, compared with almost half of women of color. Only 15 percent of white men felt that diversity efforts were failing to address subtle gender bias, compared with half of women of color and 40 percent of white women.[37]

The research summarized below, however, suggests that many lawyers underestimate the impact of unconscious bias and overestimate the effectiveness of current responses. The current system is highly imperfect in screening for talent; considerable research suggests that employers grossly overestimate the effectiveness of credentials like grades and law school prestige in predicting performance.[38] There is also no basis for the assumption that women can solve their own problems if they just "lean in," to borrow Sheryl Sandberg's term. As Linda Chanow, executive director of the Center for Women in Law, noted, "Women can 'lean in' as much as they want, so much so that they're on the verge of falling over. But the culture of law firms and their persistent implicit biases can undermine and inhibit women's success."[39] Lawyers who are truly committed to a just and inclusive workplace need a better understanding of what gets in the way. That includes a deeper appreciation of how racial, ethnic, and gender stereotypes affect not just evaluations of performance but the performance itself, and the relative value attached to specific performance measures.

Racial, Ethnic, and Gender Stereotypes

Racial, ethnic, and gender stereotypes play a well-documented, often unconscious role in American culture, and legal workplaces are no exception. The stereotypes vary across groups. For example, African Americans and Latinos bump up against assumptions that they are less qualified. Many report that their competence is constantly questioned and that even if they graduated from an elite law school, they are assumed to be beneficiaries of affirmative action rather than meritocratic selection.[40] Blacks who are assertive risk being viewed as angry or hostile.[41] Asian Americans are saddled with the myths of the "model minority"; they are thought to be smart and hardworking, but also insufficiently assertive to command the confidence of clients and legal teams.[42] The special stigma confronting women of color is apparent in the frequency with which they are still mistaken for secretaries, court reporters, or interpreters.[43]

The result is that talented minorities lack the presumption of competence granted to white male counterparts; up-and-coming whites may be fast tracked based on promise, while minorities need to demonstrate performance.[44] A recent study by a consulting firm demonstrated the persistence of unconscious racial bias. The study's authors inserted 22 errors in a legal memo, ranging from minor spelling and grammatical errors, to errors of fact and analysis. Sixty law firm partners received copies of the memos, which they were told was a "writing analysis study." Half the partners were told that the author was an African American named Thomas Meyer, and the other half were told that that the writer was a white man named Thomas Meyer. The reviewers gave the memo attributed to the white man a rating of 4.1 on a scale of 5, and a rating to the African American of 3.2. While the white man received praise for his potential and analytical skills, the African American was said to be average at best and in need of "lots of work."[45]

Even outstanding capabilities of a lawyer of color may do little to dislodge traditional stereotypes and unconscious biases. Psychologists refer to this as the "flower blooming in winter" effect.[46] A classic example is the description Senator Joseph Biden offered of Barack Obama during the 2008 presidential campaign, as the "first mainstream African-American who is articulate and bright and clean and a nice-looking guy."[47] Although the exceptional lawyer gets a special boost, others aspiring to that status remain trapped by conventional stereotypes.

Gender stereotypes also subject women to double standards and a double bind. Despite recent progress, women, like minorities, often fail to receive the presumption of competence enjoyed by white men.[48] In national surveys, between a third and three-quarters of female lawyers believe that they are held to higher standards than their colleagues.[49] Studies of performance evaluations find some support for those perceptions; similar descriptions of performance result in lower ratings for women than for men.[50] Male achievements are more likely to be attributed to capabilities, and female achievements to external factors, a pattern that social scientists describe as "he's skilled, she's lucky."[51]

Mothers, even those working full-time, are assumed to be less available and committed, an assumption not made about fathers.[52] In one representative study, almost three-quarters of female lawyers reported that their career commitment had been questioned when they gave birth or adopted a child. Only 9 percent of their white male colleagues, and 15 percent of their minority male colleagues, had faced similar challenges.[53] Yet women without family relationships sometimes face bias of a different order: they may be viewed as "not quite normal" and thus "not quite leadership material."[54]

Women are also rated lower than men on qualities associated with leadership, such as assertiveness, competitiveness, and business development.[55] Even though women are more likely to use effective leadership styles, people more readily credit men with leadership ability and more readily accept men as leaders.[56] An overview of more than a hundred studies confirms that women are rated lower when they adopt authoritative, seemingly masculine styles, particularly when the evaluators are men, or when the woman's role is one typically occupied by men.[57] What is assertive in a man seems abrasive in a woman, and female leaders risk seeming too feminine or not feminine enough. Either they may appear too "soft" or too "strident"—either unable to make tough decisions or too pushy and arrogant to command respect.[58]

Self-promotion that is acceptable in men is viewed as unattractive in women.[59] In a telling Stanford Business School study, participants received a case study about a leading venture capitalist with outstanding networking skills. Half the participants were told that the individual was Howard Roizen; the other half were told that she was Heidi Roizen. The participants rated the entrepreneurs as equally competent but found Howard more likeable, genuine, and kind, and Heidi more aggressive, self-promoting, and power-hungry.[60] Even the most accomplished lawyers can encounter such biases. Brooksley Born, now widely acclaimed for her efforts to regulate high-risk derivatives while chair of the Commodity Futures Commission, was dismissed at the time as "abrasive," "strident," and a "lightweight wacko."[61] In commenting on those characterizations, a former aide noted, "She was serious, professional, and she held her ground against those who were not sympathetic to her position. I don't think that the failure to be 'charming' should be translated into a depiction of stridency."[62] Hillary Clinton has been subject to even more vitriolic descriptions: "power-hungry," "castrating," "Hitlerian," and "feminazi."[63] During her presidential campaign, she coped with sales of a Clinton nutcracker, charges that she reminded men of a scolding mother or first wife, and hecklers with signs demanding, "Iron my shirt."[64]

Other cognitive biases compound the force of traditional stereotypes. People are more likely to notice and recall information that confirms their stereotypical assumptions than information that contradicts those assumptions; the dissonant facts are filtered out.[65] For example, when lawyers assume that a working mother is unlikely to be fully committed to her career, they more easily remember the times when she left early than the times when she stayed late. So too, when female and minority lawyers are assumed to be less effective, their failures will be recalled more readily than their achievements. Both women and minorities also receive less latitude for mistakes.[66] That, in turn, may make lawyers reluctant to seek risky "stretch assignments" that would demonstrate outstanding capabilities. Biased assumptions about lawyers' commitment or competence can also affect the allocation of work. The result is to prevent women and minorities from getting opportunities that would demonstrate or enhance their capabilities, which creates a cycle of self-fulfilling prophecies.[67]

In-Group Bias: Mentoring, Sponsorship, Networks, and Assignments

A related set of obstacles involves in-group favoritism. Extensive research has documented the preferences that individuals feel for members of their own groups. Loyalty, cooperation, favorable evaluations, mentoring, and the allocation of rewards and opportunities are greater for individuals who are similar to their superiors in important respects, including gender, race, and ethnicity.[68] As a consequence, women and minorities face difficulty developing "social capital": access to advice, support, sponsorship, desirable assignments, and new business opportunities.[69] Lawyers of color often report isolation and marginalization, while many white women similarly experience exclusion from "old boys" networks.[70] In ABA research, 62 percent of women of color and 60 percent of white women, but only 4 percent of white men, felt excluded from formal and informal networking opportunities; most women and minorities would have liked better mentoring.[71]

Part of the problem lies in numbers. Many organizations lack sufficient women and minorities at senior levels who can assist others on the way up. The problem is generally not an absence of commitment. Recent research finds no evidence for the Queen Bee syndrome, in which prominent women keep other women from getting ahead.[72] In a Catalyst study, almost three-quarters of women who were actively engaged in mentoring were developing female colleagues, compared with 30 percent of men.[73] But the underrepresentation of women in leadership positions, and the time pressures for those juggling family responsibilities, leaves an insufficient pool of potential mentors. Moreover, recent research suggests that women and minorities who push for women and minorities to be hired and promoted are penalized in their own performance reviews, which may help prevent them from gaining positions where they can effectively mentor.[74]

Although a growing number of organizations have formal mentoring programs, these do not always supply adequate training, rewards, or oversight to ensure effectiveness.[75] Nor can these formal programs substitute for relationships that develop naturally and that yield not simply advisors but sponsors—individuals who act as advocates and are in positions to provide opportunities. As participants in one ABA study noted, female mentors may have "good intentions," but are already pressed with competing work and family obligations or "don't have a lot of power so they can't really help you."[76] Concerns about the appearance of sexual harassment or sexual affairs discourage some men from forming mentoring relationships with junior women. Discomfort concerning issues of race and ethnicity also deters some white lawyers from crossing the color divide.[77] In cross-racial mentoring relationships, candid dialogue may be particularly difficult. Minority protégés may be reluctant to raise issues of bias for fear of seeming oversensitive. White mentors may be reluctant to offer candid feedback to minority associates for fear of seeming racist or of encouraging them to leave. The result is that midlevel lawyers of color can find themselves "blindsided by soft evaluations": "your skills aren't what they are supposed to be, but you didn't know because no one ever told you."[78]

Assumptions about commitment and capabilities also keep mentors from investing in female or minority subordinates who seem unlikely to stay or to succeed.[79] Such dynamics also put pressure on these lawyers to assimilate to prevailing norms. As one attorney of color put it, the "only way to succeed in a large firm is to make them forget you're Hispanic."[80] If a minority lawyer "just doesn't fit in," the assumption is that the problem lies with the individual, not the institution.[81]

In-group favoritism is also apparent in the allocation of work and client development opportunities. Many organizations operate with informal systems that channel seemingly talented junior lawyers (disproportionately white men) to leadership tracks, while relegating others to "workhorse" positions.[82] In the ABA Commission study, 44 percent of women of color, 39 percent of white women, and 25 percent of minority men reported being passed over for desirable assignments; only 2 percent of white men noted similar experiences.[83] Other research similarly finds that women and minorities are often left out of pitches for client business.[84]

Lawyers of color are also subject to "race matching"; they receive certain work because of their identity, not their interests, in order to create the right "look" in courtrooms, client presentations, recruiting, and marketing efforts. Although this strategy sometimes opens helpful opportunities, it can also place lawyers in what they describe as "mascot" roles in which they are not developing their own professional skills.[85] Linda Mabry, the first minority partner in a San Francisco firm, recounts an example in which she was asked to join a pitch to a company whose general counsel was African American. "When the firm made the pitch about the firm's relevant expertise, none of which I possessed, it was clear that the only reason I was there was to tout the firm's diversity, which was practically nonexistent. In that moment I wanted to fling myself through the plate-glass window of that well-appointed conference room. . . ."[86] Race matching is particularly irritating when lawyers of color are assumed to have skills and affinities that they in fact lack. Examples include a Japanese American asked to a meeting to solicit a Korean client, and a Latina who was assigned documents in Spanish even after she explained that she wasn't fluent in the language.[87] "Oh, you'll be fine," she was told. "Look [anything unfamiliar] up in a dictionary."[88]

Workplace Structures and Gender Roles

Escalating workplace demands and inflexible workplace structures pose further obstacles to diversity and inclusion. Hourly demands have risen significantly over the last quarter century, and what hasn't changed are the number of hours in the day. Technology that makes it possible for lawyers to work at home makes it increasingly impossible not to. Constant accessibility has become the new norm, with attorneys electronically tethered to their workplaces. The cost is disproportionately borne by women, because they are disproportionately likely to assume primary family responsibilities.

The problem is compounded by the inadequacy of structural responses. Despite some efforts at accommodation, a wide gap persists between formal policies and actual practices concerning work/life conflicts. Although more than 90 percent of American law firms report policies permitting part-time work, only about 6 percent of lawyers actually use them.[89] Many lawyers believe, with good reason, that any reduction in hours or availability would jeopardize their careers.[90] Part-time status and time out of the workforce generally result in long-term losses in earnings as well as lower chances for partnership.[91] In one survey of University of Michigan law school graduates, just a single year out of the workforce correlated with a third lower chances of making partner and an earnings reduction of 38 percent.[92] Stories of the "faster than a speeding bullet" maternity leave are all too common. Stories of women in hospital delivery rooms drafting documents while timing contractions are also depressingly common. If you're billing at six-minute intervals, why waste one? Those who opt for a reduced schedule after parental leave often find that it isn't worth the price. Their schedules aren't respected, their hours creep up, the quality of their assignments goes down, their pay is not proportional, and they are stigmatized as "slackers."[93]

Although these are not only "women's issues," women suffer the greatest cost. Despite a significant increase in men's domestic work over the last two decades, women continue to shoulder the major burden.[94] It is still women who are most likely to get the phone call that federal district judge Nancy Gertner received on the first day that she was about to ascend the bench: "Mama, there's no chocolate pudding in my [lunch]."[95] In the American Bar Foundation's survey of young lawyers, women were about seven times more likely than men to be working part-time or to be out of the labor force, primarily due to child care.[96] In the University of Michigan study, only 1 percent of fathers had taken parental leave, compared with 42 percent of women.[97] Part of the reason for those disparities is that the small number of fathers who opt to become full-time caretakers experience particular penalties. Male lawyers suffer even greater financial and promotion consequences than female colleagues who make the same choice.[98]

The problems are likely to increase. "Millennial" lawyers have expectations inconsistent with prevailing norms.[99] Growing numbers of men as well as women are expressing a desire for better work-life balance, and examples of lawyers of all ages who insist on it are increasingly visible. A *New York Times* article titled, "He Breaks for Band Recitals," reported that President Barack Obama was willing to leave key meetings in order to get home for dinner by 6 or attend a school function of his daughters.[100]

Although bar leaders generally acknowledge the problem of work-life balance, they often place responsibility for addressing it anywhere and everywhere else. In private practice, clients get part of the blame. Law is a service business, and expectations of instant accessibility reportedly make reduced schedules difficult to accommodate. Resistance from supervisors can be equally problematic. In a competitive work environment, they have obvious reasons to prefer lawyers at their constant beck and call.[101] In my recent survey of large law firms and corporate counsel offices, many managing partners and general counsel commented on the problem:

> Everyone feels stressed. . . . It's the profession we've chosen.
>
> We run a 24/7 business. . . . We have a difficult and time-committed job.
>
> It's a real tough [issue]. We do programs on the subject but I'm not sure people have time to attend.[102]

Yet the problems are not as insurmountable as is often assumed. The evidence available does not indicate substantial resistance among clients to reduced schedules. They care about responsiveness, and part-time lawyers generally appear able to provide it.[103] In one recent survey of part-time partners, most reported that they did not even inform clients of their status and that their schedules were adapted to fit client needs.[104] Accounting, which is also a service profession, and anything but indifferent to the bottom line, has developed a business model that more than offsets the costs of work/family accommodation by increasing retention.[105] Considerable evidence suggests that law practice could do the same, and reap the benefits in higher morale, lower recruitment and training expenses, and less disruption in client and collegial relationships.[106] Although some leadership positions may be hard to reconcile with substantial family demands, many women could be ready to cycle into those positions as caregiving obligations decrease. The challenge lies in creating workplace structures that make it easier for lawyers of both sexes to have satisfying personal as well as professional lives, and to ensure that those who temporarily step out of the workforce or reduce their workload are not permanently derailed by the decision.

Backlash

A final obstacle to diversity and gender equity initiatives involves backlash; the concern is that addressing these issues might add more to the problem than the solution. Leaders who appear to support "special" treatment of women and minorities have to worry about resentment among their white male counterparts. In a study by the Minority Corporate Counsel Association, white men often agreed that "diversity should take a back seat to performance and capability."[107] In their view, too much "reverse discrimination" causes backlash, and "stretch hires of minorities who are not qualified sometimes does much to undermine . . . acceptance of diversity and inclusion."[108] As one white male lawyer put it, "Taking opportunities . . . from those with merit and giving [them] . . . to people based upon race, gender, or sexual identity is forcing us apart not bringing us together. . . . I can think of few things worse for an ostensibly color blind and meritocratic society."[109] In a letter to the editor of the *National Law Journal*, a self-described "young, white straight male attorney who happens to be politically progressive" similarly protested employment layoff decisions partly attributable to "meeting an important client's newly asserted diversity demands." From his perspective, "Surely firing people even partially on the basis of an immutable characteristic is as unjust when done in the name of increasing diversity as it is when done to maintain homogeneity."[110] Many white lawyers appear to agree. In one ABA survey, only 42 percent supported affirmative action.[111]

By contrast, 92 percent of African Americans expressed support.[112] And a strong case can be made that the insistence on color blindness comes generations too early and centuries too late. As Harvard Law professor David Wilkins argues, diversity initiatives remain necessary to "detect and correct the myriad of subtle, but nevertheless pervasive, ways that . . . current practices differentially disadvantage certain [groups based on color]."[113]

The Limits of Law

Although antidiscrimination law provides some protection from overt bias, it is ill suited to address contemporary racial, ethnic, and gender obstacles. Close to fifty years' experience with civil rights legislation reveals almost no final judgments of discrimination involving law firms.[114] The frequency of informal settlements is impossible to gauge, but the barriers to effective remedies are substantial. Part of the problem is the mismatch between legal definitions of discrimination and the social patterns that produce it. To prevail in a case involving professional employment, litigants generally must establish that they were treated adversely based on a prohibited characteristic, such as race, ethnicity, or sex.[115] Yet as the preceding discussion suggested, many disadvantages for women and minorities do not involve such overtly discriminatory treatment.

Nor is it often possible for individuals to know or to prove whether they have been subject to bias, given the subjectivity of evaluation standards. Evidentiary barriers are often insurmountable, both because lawyers generally are smart enough to avoid creating paper trails of bias, and because colleagues with corroborating evidence are reluctant to provide it for fear of jeopardizing their own positions.[116] Even those who believe that they have experienced discrimination have little incentive to come forward, given the high costs of complaining, the low likelihood of victory, and the risks of informal blacklisting.[117] Many women and minorities do not want to seem "too aggressive" or "confrontational," to look like a "bitch," or to be typecast as an "angry black."[118] Lawyers who express concerns are often advised to "let bygones be bygones," or to "just move on."[119] Channels for candid dialogue are all too rare. Most law firms do not give associates opportunities to offer feedback about their supervisors, and of lawyers who provide such evaluations, only about 5 percent report changes for the better.[120] The message in many law firm cultures is that "complaining never gets you anywhere. . . . [You are perceived as] not being a team player."[121]

Lawyers who persist in their complaints are putting their professional lives on trial, and the profiles that emerge are seldom entirely flattering. A gay associate who sued the Wall Street firm Sullivan and

Cromwell for bias in promotion was characterized in press accounts as "smarmy," and a "paranoid kid with a persecution complex."[122] In an equally notorious sex discrimination suit, Philadelphia's Wolf, Block, Schorr, & Solis-Cohen denied a promotion to Nancy Ezold, whom firm leaders believed lacked both analytic abilities and other characteristics that might compensate for the deficiency. According to one partner, "It's like the ugly girl. Everybody says she has a great personality. It turns out that [Ezold] didn't even have a great personality."[123] What she did have, however, was sufficient evidence to prevail at trial. At the time she was rejected for partnership, the firm's litigation department had just one woman out of fifty five partners; nationally, by contrast, about 11 percent of partners at large firms were female.[124] Ezold had positive evaluations by the partners for whom she had worked, and male associates who had been promoted were subject to performance concerns at least as serious as those raised about her. Characterizations of those men included "wishy washy and immature," "more sizzle than steak," and "not real smart."[125] The record also revealed gender stereotypes, such as some partners' belief that Ezold was too "assertive" and too preoccupied with "women's issues."[126] Despite such evidence, the court of appeals found for the firm. In its view, the performance concerns of the two-thirds of partners who voted against Ezold were not so "obvious or manifest" a pretext to show discrimination.[127] Yet, given the damage to the firm's reputation and recruiting efforts, the victory was hardly a full vindication. In reflecting on the decision not to settle the matter, one firm leader concluded, "This may have been a case that wasn't worth winning."[128]

Evidentiary difficulties also confront women who take reduced schedules and find themselves out of the loop of challenging assignments and career development opportunities. In dismissing a class-action complaint brought by mothers against Bloomberg News, the district court expressed widely prevailing views. The law "does not mandate work-life balance." In an organization "which explicitly makes all-out dedication its expectation, making a decision that preferences family over work comes with consequences."[129] Attorneys who experience such consequences seldom see options other than exit. One mother who returned from leave after three years at a firm found her situation hopeless: "I was simply dropped from all my work with no questions or discussion. . . . It was as if I had fallen off the planet."[130]

Not only does current antidiscrimination law provide insufficient remedies for individuals, it also offers inadequate incentives for institutions to address unintended biases. The case law on diversity is in flux and suggests that race-conscious hiring, especially by governmental employers, requires special care.[131] Columbia law professor Susan Sturm's research also suggests that fear of liability can discourage organizations from collecting information "that will reveal problems . . . or patterns of exclusion that increase the likelihood that they will be sued."[132]

Yet while law has supplied inadequate pressures for diversity initiatives, other considerations are pushing strongly in that direction. Both the moral and business case for diversity should inspire leaders in law to do more to build inclusiveness in their institutions and in their own ranks as well.

The Case for Diversity

Beginning in the late 1980s, bar leaders launched a series of initiatives designed to increase minority representation and influence in the profession. Drawing on arguments gaining influence in the corporate sector, they stressed the business case for diversity. As the Minority Corporate Counsel Association put it,

> Law firms commit to becoming diverse because their future, market share, retention of talent, continuation of existing relationships with corporate clients, and performance depend on understanding and anticipating the needs of an increasingly diverse workforce and marketplace.[133]

A 2010 report by the ABA Presidential Initiative Commission on Diversity similarly emphasized that "it makes good business sense to hire lawyers who reflect the diversity of citizens, clients, and customers from around the globe. Indeed, corporate clients increasingly require lawyer diversity and will take their business elsewhere if it is not provided."[134] Comments from managing partners and general counsel in my recent survey stressed that diversity was not just the "right thing to do," but was also critical to organizations' economic success:

> A diverse team is a more effective team: it has a broader base of experience . . . and the client gets a better product.
> We're in the human capital business. [Diversity is a way to get] the best people and the best decision making.[135]

Advocates of gender equity take a similar approach. A widely recognized 2009 *Manifesto on Women in Law* elaborated the business case. Its core principles stated,

A. The depth and breadth of the talent pool of women lawyers establishes a clear need for the legal profession to recruit, retain, develop, and advance an exceptionally rich source of talent.
B. Women increasingly have been attaining roles of influence throughout society; legal employers must achieve gender diversity in their leadership ranks if they are to cultivate a set of leaders with legitimacy in the eyes of their clients and members of the profession.
C. Diversity adds value to legal employers in countless ways—from strengthening the effectiveness of client representation to inserting diverse perspectives and critical viewpoints in dialogues and decision making.[136]

In support of these claims, advocates rely on a variety of evidence. For example, some social science research suggests that diverse viewpoints encourage critical thinking and creative problem solving; they expand the range of alternatives considered and counteract groupthink.[137] Some studies also find a correlation between diversity and profitability in law firms as well as in Fortune 500 companies.[138] Other research has drawn on signaling theory to argue that diversity conveys a credible commitment to equal opportunity and responsiveness to diverse stakeholders.[139]

It is, however, important not to overstate the business case for diversity. Not all social science research finds strong performance benefits from diversity.[140] If poorly managed, it can heighten conflict and communication problems, or cause outsiders to suppress divergent views.[141] Nor do all studies find a correlation between diversity and profitability.[142] In those that do, it is unclear which way causation runs. Financial success may sometimes do more to enhance diversity than the converse; organizations that are on strong financial footing are better able to invest in diversity initiatives and sound employment practices such as mentoring and work/life accommodations that promote both diversity and profitability.[143]

On balance, however, there are strong reasons to support diversity initiatives. As the ABA Presidential Initiative Commission noted, increasing numbers of corporate clients are making diversity a priority in allocating work. More than a hundred companies have signed the "Call to Action: Diversity in the Legal Profession," in which they pledge to "end or limit . . . relationships with firms whose performance consistently evidences a lack of meaningful interest in being diverse."[144] A growing number of clients impose specific requirements, including reports on diversity within the firm and in the teams working on their matters, as well as relevant firm policies and initiatives.[145] Wal-Mart, which has been the most public and detailed in its demands, specifies that firms must have flexible time policies and include as candidates for relationship partner for the company at least one woman and one lawyer of color. It has also terminated firms that have failed to meet its diversity standards.[146] The Gap also inquires into flexible time policies and sets out expectations for improvement with firms that fail to meet its goals.[147] Microsoft provides incentives for firms to hit its diversity targets.[148]

Again, it is important not to overstate the reach of these initiatives. Almost no research is available to assess the impact of these policies, to determine how widely they are shared, or to ascertain how often companies that have pledged to reduce or end representation in appropriate cases have actually done so. In my recent study of large firms, only one reported losing business over the issue and many were frustrated by clients who asked for detailed information on diversity and then failed to follow up or to reward firms that had performed well.[149] Still, the direction of client concerns is clear, and in today's competitive climate, the economic and symbolic leverage of prominent corporations should not be discounted.

Moreover, there are other benefits of diversity initiatives. As noted earlier, some policies, such as those involving work/family accommodations, make business sense. So does fostering diverse perspectives and effectively managing any conflict that results. Many practices that would improve conditions for women and lawyers of color serve broader organizational interests. Better mentoring programs, more equitable compensation and work assignments, and greater accountability of supervising attorneys are all likely to have long-term payoffs, however difficult to quantify with precision. Skeptics of the business case for diversity often proceed as if the business case for the current model is self-evident. Few experts on law firm management agree.[150]

The fact that data are lacking on some benefits of diversity is a reason to avoid exaggerating their significance but not to dismiss their relevance. In a world in which the talent pool is half women and one-fifth lawyers of color, it is reasonable to assume that firms will suffer some competitive disadvantage if they cannot effectively recruit and retain these groups. Part of the reason that such disadvantages have been hard to quantify is that comparative data on diversity traditionally have been hard to come by. Now, with the emergence of more complete and accessible databases, job candidates and clients who care about racial, ethnic, and gender equity can make more informed decisions. Their decisions are likely to be significant, particularly if diversity is at least a potential tiebreaker in today's increasingly competitive legal market.

The question then becomes how organizations can help institutionalize diversity and build cultures of inclusiveness. And equally important, what can women and minorities do to enhance their own career options?

Strategies for Individuals

To improve their chances for success, women and minorities should be clear about their goals, seek challenging assignments, solicit frequent feedback, develop mentoring relationships, build professional contacts, and cultivate a reputation for effectiveness. Succeeding in those tasks also requires attention to unconscious biases and exclusionary networks that can waylay careers.

So, for example, aspiring female lawyers need to strike the right balance between "too assertive" and "not assertive enough." Survey research underscores the importance of developing a leadership style that fits the organization and that "men are comfortable with."[151] That finding is profoundly irritating to some lawyers. At an ABA Summit on Women's Leadership, many participants railed against asking women to adjust to men's needs. Why was the focus always on fixing the female? But as others pointed out, this is the world that women inhabit, and it is not just men who find overly authoritative or self-promoting styles off-putting. To maximize effectiveness, female lawyers need ways of projecting a decisive and forceful manner without seeming arrogant or abrasive. Experts suggest being "relentlessly pleasant" without backing down.[152] Strategies include frequently smiling, expressing appreciation and concern, invoking common interests, emphasizing others' goals as well as their own, and taking a problem-solving rather than critical stance.[153] Successful lawyers such as Sandra Day O'Connor have been known for that capacity. In assessing her prospects for success in the Arizona state legislature, one political commentator noted that "Sandy . . . is a sharp gal" with a "steel-trap mind . . . and a large measure of common sense. . . . She [also] has a lovely smile and should use it often."[154] She did.

Formal leadership training and coaching can help in developing interpersonal styles, as well as capabilities such as risk taking, conflict resolution, and strategic vision. Leadership programs designed for women or minorities provide especially supportive settings for addressing their special challenges.[155] Profiles of successful lawyers can also provide instructive examples of the personal initiative that opens professional opportunities. These lawyers have not waited for the phone to ring. Michele Mayes, one of the nation's most prominent African American general counsels, recalls that after receiving some encouragement from a woman mentor, she approached the chief legal officer at her company and "told him I wanted his job."[156] After the shock wore off, he worked up a list of the skills and experiences that she needed. He also recruited her to follow him to his next general counsel job. She never replaced him, but with his assistance, she prepared for his role in other Fortune 500 companies. Louise Parent, the general counsel of American Express, describes learning to "raise my hand" for challenging assignments and being willing to take steps down and sideways on the status ladder in order to get the experience she needed.[157] Terry McClure, the general counsel of United Parcel Service, was told she needed direct exposure to business operations if she wanted to move up at the company. After accepting a position as district manager, she suddenly found herself as a "lawyer, a black woman, [with] no operations experience walking into a . . . [warehouse] with all the truck drivers."[158] Her success in that role was what helped put her in the candidate pool for general counsel.

Setting priorities and managing time are also critical leadership skills. Establishing boundaries, delegating domestic tasks, and giving up on perfection are essential for those with substantial family commitments: "done is better than perfect."[159] What lawyers should not sacrifice is time spent developing relationships with influential mentors.[160] To forge those strategic relationships, lawyers need to recognize that those from whom they seek assistance are under similar time pressures. The best mentoring generally goes to the best mentees: those who are reasonable and focused in their needs and who make sure the relationship is mutually beneficial.

Lawyers who step out of the labor force should find ways of keeping professionally active. Volunteer efforts, occasional paying projects, continuing legal education, and reentry programs can all aid the transition back.

Finally, and most important, lawyers need to choose the right partner. As Linda Addison, managing partner of Norton Rose

Fulbright puts it, "If your career is not as important to your partner as it is to you, you don't stand a chance."[161]

Strategies for Organizations

The most important factor in ensuring equal access to professional opportunities is a commitment to that objective, which is reflected in organizational policies, priorities, and reward structures.[162] That commitment needs to come from the top. An organization's leadership needs not simply to acknowledge the importance of diversity, but also to establish structures for promoting it, and to hold individuals accountable for the results. The most successful approaches generally involve task forces or committees with diverse members who have credibility with their colleagues and a stake in the results.[163] The mission of that group should be to identify problems, develop responses, and monitor their effectiveness.

As an ABA Presidential Commission on Diversity recognized, self-assessment should be a critical part of all diversity initiatives.[164] Leaders need to know how policies that affect inclusiveness play out in practice. That requires collecting both quantitative and qualitative data on matters such as advancement, retention, assignments, satisfaction, mentoring, and work/family conflicts. As earlier discussion indicated, many firms have official policies on flexible and reduced schedules that are viewed as unworkable in practice. Periodic surveys, focus groups, interviews with former and departing employees, and bottom-up evaluations of supervisors can all cast light on problems disproportionately experienced by women and minorities. Monitoring can be important not only in identifying problems and responses, but also in making people aware that their actions are being assessed. Requiring individuals to justify their decisions can help reduce unconscious bias.[165]

Whatever oversight structure an employer chooses, a central priority should be developing effective systems of evaluation, rewards, and allocation of leadership and professional development opportunities. Women and minorities need to have a critical mass of representation in key positions such as management and compensation committees.[166] Supervisors need to be held responsible for their performance on diversity-related issues, and that performance should be part of self-assessments and bottom-up evaluation structures.[167] Performance appraisals that include diversity but that have no significant rewards or sanctions are unlikely to affect behavior.[168] Nor are organizations well served by initiatives like the memorandum from King and Spaulding that proposed ways for attorneys to "become more involved" in diversity efforts. Among the suggestions were to invite "diverse" attorneys to lunch or a weekend social event, or to "take 20 minutes and ask a female attorney and/or a diverse attorney, 'Where do you want to go from here?'" Lawyers were also reminded to bill the time spent on these collegial interchanges. The memorandum circulated on the Internet under the title, "Is this the Most Offensively Misguided Diversity Memo You've Ever Seen?"[169]

However, we know too little about strategies that work. What has helped firms deal with powerful partners who rate poorly on diversity? Are incentives like mentoring awards and significant bonuses effective in changing organizational culture? More experimentation and sharing of information could help organizations translate rhetorical commitments into institutional priorities.

We particularly need to know more about training. Some surveyed lawyers have been "lukewarm" about the usefulness of diversity education, and some experts who have studied its effectiveness are even less enthusiastic.[170] In a large-scale review of diversity initiatives across multiple industries, training programs did not significantly increase the representation or advancement of targeted groups.[171] Part of the problem is that such programs typically focus only on individual behaviors, not institutional problems; they also provide no incentives to implement recommended practices, and sometimes provoke backlash among involuntary participants.[172] Yet findings from my recent survey of managing partners and general counsel offer a more optimistic picture; they reported largely positive responses to unconscious bias training. Lawyers "don't know what they don't know," and well designed educational programs can be helpful in "opening dialogue and making people aware."[173]

Another common strategy involves networks and affinity groups for women and minorities.[174] These vary in effectiveness. At their best, they provide useful advice, role models, contacts, and development of informal mentoring relationships.[175] By bringing lawyers together around common interests, these networks can also forge coalitions on diversity-related issues and generate useful reform proposals.[176] Yet the only large-scale study on point found that networks had no significant positive impact on career development; they increased participants' sense of community but did not do enough to put individuals "in touch with what or whom they ought to know."[177]

One of the most effective interventions involves mentoring, which directly addresses the difficulties of women and minorities in obtaining the support necessary for career development. Many organizations have formal mentoring programs that match employees or allow individuals to select their own pairings. Well-designed initiatives that evaluate and reward mentoring activities can improve participants' skills, satisfaction, and retention rates.[178] However, most programs do not require evaluation or specify the frequency of meetings and goals for the relationship.[179] Instead, they permit a "call me if you need anything" approach, which leaves too many junior attorneys reluctant to become a burden.[180] Ineffective matching systems compound the problem; lawyers too often end up with mentors with whom they have little in common.[181] Formal programs also have difficulty inspiring the kind of sponsorship that is most critical. Women and minorities need advocates, not simply advisors, and that kind of support cannot be mandated. The lesson for organizations is that they cannot simply rely on formal structures. They need to cultivate and reward sponsorship of women and minorities, and to monitor the effectiveness of mentoring programs. Identifying and nurturing high performers should be a priority.[182]

Organizations can also support efforts to expand the pool of qualified minorities through scholarships and other educational initiatives. The ABA's Pipeline Diversity Directory describes about 400 such programs throughout the country.[183] A prominent example is the $10 million pledge by Skadden Arps for a ten-year program offering law school preparation to students from disadvantaged backgrounds.[184] In commenting on that example, one ABA official noted, "This is the kind of money we need to make a difference. . . . Now we need just 500 other firms to take action."[185]

To make all these reforms possible, they must be seen not as "women's" or "minority" issues, but as organizational priorities in which women and minorities have a particular stake. As consultants emphasize, "Inclusion can be built only through inclusion. . . . Change needs to happen in partnership with the people of the organization, not to them."[186] The challenge remaining is to create that sense of unity and to translate rhetorical commitments into organizational priorities.

5

Regulation of the Profession

WITH MUCH FANFARE, THE American Bar Association created the Commission on Ethics 20/20 to recommend modifications in bar ethical rules in light of changes in technology and globalization. In making its recommendations, the Commission was to follow three principles: "protecting the public; preserving the core values of the profession; and maintaining a strong, independent, and self-regulated profession."[1] The project was constrained by its fundamentally conservative mission—"preserve" and "maintain"—and by a ratification process ill suited to innovation or reform.[2] The Commission was made up entirely of lawyers. Proposed modifications required approval by the ABA House of Delegates and then by state supreme courts after review by state bar associations. All of these groups are controlled by lawyers or former lawyers who by training and disposition tend to resist change.[3] That resistance is particularly intense when the profession's own status and financial interests are at risk.[4] As a result, none of the Commission's work resulted in major reform.[5] The most significant proposal that it considered, nonlawyer investment in law firms, was abandoned. A third of the members of the House of Delegates attempted even to prevent debate on the issue. They supported a resolution that stated, without supporting facts or arguments, that any nonlawyer involvement was inconsistent with the "core values" of the legal profession.[6]

This process is emblematic of the obstacles confronting any fundamental reform efforts. From a regulatory standpoint, the American bar is in some sense a victim of its own success. In no country has the legal profession been more influential and more effective in protecting its right to regulatory independence. Yet that success, and the structural forces that ensure it, have shielded the profession from the accountability and innovation that would best serve societal interests. The problem is compounded by a mismatch between professional and public objectives for the regulatory process. From the public's perspective, the process should provide protection from incompetent and unethical services, promote access to cost-effective assistance, and ensure lawyers' independence from governmental overreaching. From the profession's perspective, the process should also promote the bar's economic and social status, and preserve its regulatory autonomy. The American bar's governance system has been dominated by the profession and, unsurprisingly, it has done much more to advance its own interests than those of the public.

This chapter explores problems in bar regulatory processes involving multijurisdictional and multidisciplinary practice, nonlawyer investment in law firms, continuing legal education (CLE), and lawyer discipline. All suffer from the insularity of the bar's regulatory structure and all point to the need for fundamental reform.

The Structure of Regulation

Lawyer regulation suffers from two structural problems: the profession's unchecked control over its own governance, and its state-based system of oversight. Both stem from the judiciary's inherent and exclusive power to regulate legal practice, which state courts began asserting around the turn of the twentieth century.[7] That authority, rooted in constitutional requirements of separation of powers between the judicial, executive, and legislative branches, has largely foreclosed legislative intervention.[8] That insularity is reinforced by the courts' inaccessibility to influence by the public and by their willingness to let the organized bar call "the major shots and most of the minor ones" on governance issues.[9]

Although the inherent powers doctrine has played a valuable role in guaranteeing the independence of the profession from governmental interference, the cost has been substantial. The effect has been to insulate the profession from public accountability. As Cornell law professor Charles Wolfram has put it, the doctrine "stands as a powerful barrier shielding the legal profession from any of its critics. . . . The legal profession has in that way both identified and 'protected' the interest of clients and the public without permitting them to participate in any way in those processes."[10] This lack of participation has led to an unduly self-interested regulatory framework.[11] Judges share the background and worldview of those they claim to regulate. The profession's distinctive norms, behaviors, and ways of thinking construct an institutional identity that shapes decision making.[12] Moreover, as Tennessee law professor Benjamin Barton notes, most state judges are elected and depend on lawyers for endorsements, rankings, and campaign contributions.[13] Even in states where judges are selected through merit processes, state and local bars exercise substantial influence.[14] The judiciary is also dependent on support from the organized bar concerning salaries and budgets, and is readily accessible to informal lawyer lobbying at conferences, annual meetings, and social gatherings.[15] By contrast, consumer interests rarely have such opportunities for influence.

A further problem is the public's lack of information and incentives to mobilize on issues involving bar governance. Few voters are aware of the judiciary's role in regulating the profession, and no powerful groups have sought to make such issues relevant in judicial elections.[16] Help Abolish Legal Tyranny (HALT), the only national consumer organization that focuses on reforming the legal profession, claims only about 20,000 members.[17] Its resources and influence cannot compare to those of local and national bar associations that represent close to a million lawyers.[18] Nor have consumer protection agencies been willing to intervene and level the playing field.[19]

Equally problematic is the dominant role of the ABA in drafting the Model Rules of Professional Conduct, which state courts have adopted with little modification.[20] Not only is the ABA a highly self-interested body; its decision-making process leaves much to be desired. As one veteran of ABA rule making noted, "I can't think of a more cumbersome and difficult way of writing ethics rules than presenting them to a group of 400 lawyers and trying to convince them in two- or three-minute speeches that it's a sensible thing to do."[21]

A second structural problem in the regulatory process involves its state-based framework, which has failed to adapt to the increasingly national and transnational character of legal practice. Many lawyers' work has mirrored the multijurisdictional nature of their clients' businesses. The result is that state-based regulatory regimes have grown increasingly out of touch with daily realities.

Multijurisdictional Practice

In general, the bar's rules of professional conduct prohibit lawyers who are not licensed in a state from providing any legal services in that state.[22] Traditionally, attorneys who wished to represent a client outside of the jurisdiction in which they were admitted to practice had to affiliate local counsel, or, if the matter involved litigation, request the court to admit them temporarily, *pro hac vice*. Courts are not constitutionally obligated to extend *pro hac vice* admission, and may impose requirements such as affiliation of local counsel.[23] Some jurisdictions have permitted in-house lawyers to provide legal services on behalf of their employer from an office outside the state if they register and submit to the local bar's regulatory authority.[24]

For most of this nation's history, state licensing of lawyers made sense, because legal matters were typically confined to a single state, and lawyers' knowledge of local law was of particular importance.[25] However, the traditional approach ill suits contemporary practice. Many legal matters and attorney communications by phone, e-mail, fax, and Internet websites do not remain within jurisdictions where the attorneys are licensed to practice law. Nor, in an age of virtual law offices, are all attorneys even tethered to a physical domicile.[26] Moreover, as New York University law professor Steve Gillers points out, "Specialized knowledge will often define the borders of a lawyer's competence with greater assurance than will the geographical borders of his licensing jurisdiction. . . . [A] UCC expert in Ohio will know more about the UCC in Indiana than will the products liability expert in Indiana."[27]

Summarizing these trends, an ABA Commission on Multijurisdictional Practice observed,

> Testimony before the Commission was unanimous in recognizing that lawyers commonly engage in cross-border legal practice. Further, there was general consensus that such practice is on the increase and that this trend is not only inevitable, but necessary. The explosion of technology and the increasing complexity of legal practice have resulted in the need for lawyers to cross state borders to afford clients competent representation. . . .
>
> The existing system of lawyer regulation is and should be a matter of serious concern for many lawyers. Even in contexts where jurisdictional restrictions clearly apply, as in state-court proceedings, problems are caused by the lack of uniformity among the *pro hac vice* provisions of different states, unpredictability about how some of the provisions will be applied by the courts in individual cases, and, in some cases, the provisions' excessive restrictiveness. Of even greater concern, however, is that, outside the context of litigation, the reach of the jurisdictional restrictions is vastly uncertain as well as, potentially, far too restrictive. . . . The existing system of lawyer regulation has costs for clients. For example, out of concern for jurisdictional restrictions, lawyers may decline to provide services that they are able to render skillfully and ethically. . . .[28]

In response to growing concerns, the ABA approved recommendations by its Commission on Multijurisdictional Practice that amended the Model Rules of Professional Conduct. As revised, Model Rule 5.5 provides certain "safe havens" from unauthorized practice prohibitions for an out-of-state lawyer who provides legal services on a temporary basis. One exception involves services that are "undertaken in association with a lawyer who is admitted to practice in this jurisdiction and who actively participates in the matter."[29] But adding a lawyer substantially increases the expense to the client and may provide nothing of value apart from compliance with protectionist regulations designed to benefit home-state attorneys.

Another important exception is for services that arise out of or are reasonably related to the lawyers' practice in a jurisdiction in which the lawyer is admitted to practice. Similarly, a safe haven is available for services reasonably related to a "pending or potential arbitration, mediation, or other alternate dispute resolution proceeding" if the services arise out of or are reasonably related to the lawyer's practice and are not services for which the forum requires *pro hac vice* admission. Finally, the lawyer may provide assistance to the lawyer's employer or its organizational affiliates.

Many commentators believe that even with such exceptions, the approach of Model Rule 5.5 is unduly complex and restrictive. As law professor Eli Wald notes, it allows for only "temporary . . . [or] incidental national practice that has a strong factual or legal nexus to the state where a lawyer is licensed."[30] The rule persists because local bars, which are a powerful force in regulatory policy, have much to lose from liberalizing restrictions on out-of-state attorneys.[31] Although large-firm lawyers would benefit from liberalization, they have little incentive to push for it because they face little risk of enforcement. "Sneaking around" jurisdictional boundaries is widely tolerated.[32] Bar disciplinary authorities rarely have sufficient information or resources to enforce prohibitions on out-of-state practice. And when out-of-state attorneys feel the need to affiliate local counsel, they pass those expenses on to clients.

From a societal standpoint, however, this regime imposes significant costs. To the extent that the rule is flouted, it breeds disrespect for law. And to the extent that lawyers comply, it stifles competition and imposes additional expenses for clients when local attorneys are affiliated.[33]

Attorneys who attempt to avoid unauthorized practice by obtaining admission in multiple jurisdictions bump up against substantial obstacles. Some states require passage of their own bar exam, however experienced the attorney. Some require residency, including a local office, and others will waive exam requirements only for lawyers from jurisdictions that extend the same privileges to the states' own lawyers. Such reciprocity rules are difficult to justify from any consumer protection perspective. If experienced out-of-state attorneys are competent to practice in the jurisdiction, why should it matter how their local bars treat competitors?

The most obvious corrective, a national bar exam and system of admission, has been dismissed out of hand as inconsistent with state courts' inherent regulatory power. And attorneys worry that the centralized bureaucracy necessary to administer the system would be vulnerable to political capture and would pose an undue risk to the independence of the profession.[34] A more promising variation on this approach, which would avoid a national licensing authority, would be to follow the approach of Australia. There, lawyers are admitted by a state or territory, but under uniform standards, so that their admission is recognized nationally.[35] In this country, state supreme courts could retain power to admit lawyers but base admission on a national exam with a uniform cutoff score.

Another alternative is an open border system, in which a license to practice law would be similar to a driver's license. The attorney's state of residence would test for competence, and other jurisdictions would honor its judgment as long as the attorney's presence was temporary.[36] States could still discipline attorneys for local misconduct, including failure to become familiar with local rules. If some additional protection proved necessary, states could require nonresident attorneys to pass an exam testing mastery of those rules. To prevent a "race to the bottom," in which applicants would flock to the states with the most permissive admittance standards and then seek to practice elsewhere, attorneys could be required to have a minimum period of practice in the home jurisdiction.[37]

A related proposal is to follow the approach of the fifteen-member European Community. Provisions in the Treaty of Rome allow a lawyer licensed in one member country to offer legal services in another country, except for activities specially reserved to members of that country's bar, such as in-court representation. Under European Council Directives, an attorney licensed in one member country may be admitted to the bar of another after practicing the law of that country and the European Union for more than three years. A lawyer admitted in only one country may also provide temporary legal services in another, subject to certain requirements.[38] Attorneys must limit their practice to occasional activity, agree to comply with local ethics rules and enforcement processes, and maintain legal malpractice insurance.[39]

In the United States, Colorado has taken the lead in establishing an open-border policy. It allows lawyers who are licensed in another jurisdiction to practice in the state up to the point of litigation, as long as they don't become domiciled there or open an office.[40] Those attorneys must comply with local ethics rules and submit to state disciplinary processes.[41] In testimony before the ABA's Ethics 20/20 Commission, the chief deputy counsel in the state's office of attorney regulation maintained that the rule has "worked well."[42] Former ABA president Carolyn Lamm responded that advocating such an approach would impair the Commission's credibility and would "not go over in the ABA House of Delegates."[43] That objection underscores the problems of vesting so much authority over regulatory policy in the organized bar, which is anything but disinterested concerning issues affecting professional competition. The current framework cries out for reform, but it is difficult to see where the impetus will come from in a system held so hostage to protectionist impulses.

Multidisciplinary Practice

Another issue on which reform is socially desirable but politically problematic involves the bar's prohibition on multidisciplinary practice that involves fee sharing with nonlawyers.[44] That ban has grown increasingly controversial as clients' interest in multidisciplinary services has grown increasingly apparent. Other Western industrialized nations generally permit nonlawyers to provide out-of-court law-related services and to employ or form partnerships with lawyers.[45] As a consequence, large accounting firms dominate the global legal market. They have a presence in 138 countries and are making increased inroads in the United States. Federal law provides that tax advice and representation in tax court does not constitute the practice of law. This exception to traditional unauthorized practice prohibitions enables lawyers to provide services for clients of accounting firms as long as the work can be defined as tax, not legal, assistance. Over the past decade, accounting firms have taken increasing liberties with the definition, and have expanded their in-house legal staff to provide much the same service as law firms on matters such as tax, financial and estate planning; intellectual property; alternative dispute resolution; and litigation support. The American legal profession faces growing difficulties competing with these accounting organizations, which generally offer a wider range of services, greater economies of scale, and more effective marketing and managerial capacities. As law professor Geoffrey Hazard puts it, accountants are "eating our lunch."[46]

Supporters of multidisciplinary practice (MDP) stress the advantages to clients of "one-stop shopping" and the advantages to lawyers of being able to attract additional capital and expertise, making them more competitive with other well-financed service providers. The benefits would extend not just to large firms and business clients, but to small firms and sole practitioners whose individual clients have needs cutting across multiple fields. So, for example, a law firm specializing in elder law might find advantages in affiliating with medical and social workers.[47]

Opposition to Multidisciplinary Practice

By contrast, opponents worry that lawyers will become accountable to nonlawyer supervisors who come from a different tradition with less rigorous standards governing confidentiality, conflicts of interest, and pro bono service. In critics' view, as disciplinary boundaries blur and thin, law will become just another business, and clients will pay the price as professional judgments are driven by the bottom line.[48] To some commentators, the misconduct in cases like Enron reflected conflicts of interest between accountants' auditing and consulting functions and demonstrated why lawyers should not participate in partnerships providing such services.[49]

In 1999, an ABA Commission on Multidisciplinary Practice issued a report acknowledging these ethical concerns but proposing strategies short of prohibition. The Commission recommended holding nonlawyers in multidisciplinary firms to the same ethical standards governing conflicts of interest and confidentiality as those applicable to the bar generally. In addition, the Commission recommended special audit provisions to prevent nonlawyers from interfering with lawyers' professional judgments. Under this framework, the attorney–client privilege either could be extended to cover nonlawyers, or clients could be warned about its unavailability.[50]

The ABA House of Delegates twice rejected the Commission's recommendations. House members initially voted against relaxing prohibitions on multidisciplinary partnerships "unless and until additional study demonstrates that such changes will further the public interest without sacrificing or compromising lawyer independence and the legal profession's tradition of loyalty to clients." However, as the Commission responded, it will be impossible to assess the public interest in such arrangements until the "taint of illegality" is removed. Nonetheless, the Commission took additional testimony from business clients and consumer groups, all of whom urged the Association to permit MDPs. Not a single user of legal services voiced any opposition.[51] Lawyers who had worked in both law firms and MDPs testified before the Commission that there were not significant differences in the ethical cultures of the two kinds of organizations, apart from the rules governing conflicts of interest. Many of the MDPs that presented testimony also pointed to records of pro bono service that rivaled those of law firms. Despite this positive response, the House of Delegates disbanded the Commission and rejected any fee sharing with nonlawyers as inconsistent with the "core values of the legal profession."[52] The entire debate took less than an hour and underscored problems with the ABA as a decision-making body. As one delegate described the deliberations,

> In the discussion in the ABA meeting, . . . the focus was almost entirely on how MDP will affect lawyers, their practice, their integrity, and their grip on the provision of legal services. There was almost no consideration [of] how limitations of the provision of legal services would affect clients and their needs. . . .[53]

Responses to Objections

The dispute over multidisciplinary practice has triggered what is variously perceived as a turf battle or holy war. Opponents of MDPs paint the struggle in apocalyptic terms. At stake are the independence and core values of the profession, now threatened by an invasion of profit-maximizing infidels subject to less rigorous standards governing confidentiality, conflicts of interest, and pro bono service. Supporters of MDPs see the struggle in less lofty terms. From their perspective, the stakes are status and money. Professionalism is window dressing for protectionism; lawyers unable or unwilling to compete are attempting to miscast prudential interests as public values.

Part of the difficulty in resolving these disputes involves the lack of systematic information about the extent of ethical problems in multidisciplinary organizations compared with other organizations, and the effectiveness of proposed responses. It is, however, worth noting that American lawyers already face pressures that limit professional independence and that these are not qualitatively different from those that would arise in multidisciplinary settings. In-house lawyers, government lawyers, and lawyers working for accounting firms or prepaid legal service plans need to please nonlawyer management.[54] Even if it could be established that conflicts of interest and confidentiality problems were somewhat more likely to arise in multidisciplinary partnerships than in law firms, total prohibition is not necessarily the best response. Why not give clients the option of weighing the risks and benefits of MDPs and tailor ethical restrictions to address demonstrated abuses?[55]

However these issues are resolved, multidisciplinary collaborations of some form are likely to increase. There is a strong market demand and legitimate societal need for integrated legal and nonlegal advice. Where state bars prohibit multidisciplinary partnerships, multidisciplinary practice may take other forms. For example, New York permits, and some American law firms are developing, "strategic alliances" with professional services firms. Under these arrangements, the firms agree to share clients and sometimes capital and marketing capacities.[56] In other jurisdictions, lawyers and nonlawyers are providing integrated services through collaborative arrangements that do not involve fee sharing.[57] Whether these arrangements can address client needs as effectively as fully integrated MDPs remains to be seen. If they cannot, the bar's approach should be revisited.

Nonlawyer Investment

Another context in which ABA rulemaking has proven particularly problematic involves nonlawyer investment in law firms.[58] Such investment is permitted in some form in Australia, England, Wales, Scotland, Germany, the Netherlands, New Zealand, and parts of Canada.[59] However, in 2012, the ABA's Ethics 20/20 Commission tabled a modest proposal for similar nonlawyer investment in the United States. The proposal would have required that firms engage only in legal practice, that nonlawyer investment be capped at 25 percent, that nonlawyers be actively engaged in the enterprise, and that they pass a fit-to-own test similar to the character and fitness test required for entrance to the bar.[60] Once again, ABA decision making proved hostage to professional rather than public interests.

Opposition to Nonlawyer Investment

Opposition to such investment rests on three concerns. The first is that shareholder preoccupation with profits would pose a threat to professional independence.[61] The American Bar Association's Model Rule 5.4, which prohibits sharing fees with nonlawyers, justifies the prohibition as necessary "to protect the lawyer's professional independence of judgment."[62] According to the Reporter for the Ethics 20/20 Commission, opponents believe that nonlawyers who are not subject to the bar's code of ethics might push lawyers "to chase the dollar rather than abid[e] by the rules of professional conduct."[63] Symbolic and status concerns are also at stake. According to some commentators, nonlawyer investment would mean "diluting the essence of what it means to be a lawyer."[64] If Wal-Mart could own law firms, Lawrence Fox predicts that "it will be the end of the profession. . . . We will become just another set of service providers."[65]

Other objections involve confidentiality and conflicts of interest. Corporations in the United States are generally required to report income, major clients, and details of work to equity investors.[66] Yet sharing such information could constitute a violation of lawyers' duties of confidentiality and a waiver of the attorney–client privilege. A further concern is the conflicts of interest that could arise from strategic equity purchases. A large investor could purchase shares in multiple firms in order to claim a conflict of interest when a competitor or adversary attempted to hire one of those firms.[67]

The Rationale for Nonlawyer Investment

Missing from these arguments is any evidence of such problems in the jurisdictions that permit nonlawyer ownership. The ABA's Ethics 20/20 Commission reviewed the experience of the District of Columbia, which has permitted nonlawyer ownership interests in law firms for more than two decades, and found no record of disciplinary concerns.[68] Nor did the Commission identify any ethical difficulties in Australia or England, which have more recently permitted nonlawyer investment in "alternative business structures." Both countries require appointment of a legal director or head of practice to ensure compliance with ethical obligations.[69] Both countries also subject alternative business structures to the same ethical rules as those governing legal professionals, and nonlawyer owners are obligated not to cause a lawyer to breach any professional duties.[70] Slater and Gordon, the Australian law firm that was the first in the world to become a publicly traded company, made clear in its prospectus that obligations to courts and clients take precedence over the interests of shareholders.[71] According to its executive director, going public has not only preserved professional independence, but the additional revenue has given lawyers more distance from business pressures than traditional partnerships.[72] Thomas Gordon, the legal and policy director of Consumers for a Responsive Legal System, points out that "concerns about financial pressure . . . are not unique to firms with outside investors. Sole practitioners are under pressure to pay their bills and lawyers at large firms are under pressure to make their hours."[73] As other commentators also have noted, there are already many American contexts in which nonlawyers are involved in a managerial capacity. In these contexts, strategies have emerged to preserve professional independence and confidentiality. Examples include government agencies, insurance defense, group legal service plans, public interest organizations, and in-house corporate legal departments.[74] To some opponents, however, such examples were beside the point. In one heated exchange, a vocal critic was asked whether his mind could be changed by any empirical research showing that nonlawyer owners of firms did not interfere with the professional judgment of lawyers. His response was "no."[75]

Not only did opponents fail to consider evidence concerning the absence of harms; they also failed to acknowledge the benefits that might follow from the infusion of capital and talent. Equity financing holds a number of advantages over traditional approaches, which rely on the capital contributions of partners or outside borrowing. As Georgetown law professor Milton Regan notes, a "partnership's capital base is limited to the wealth of its partners, and its assets are mobile."[76] In an era of increasing lateral movement, partners who are uncertain about their own or their colleagues' future plans may be reluctant to invest in firms' long-term needs. These partners may be equally wary of assuming loan obligations that will leave them liable for firm debt if others depart. Excessive reliance on loans is one of the precipitating causes of law firm dissolution.[77] At the same time, demand for alternative sources of capital is growing in light of globalization, nationalization, and technological advances. The need to service clients in multiple locations has fueled expansion that depends on additional resources. So, too, developing information technology to assist in diagnosing legal issues, providing basic assistance, and generating documents is highly capital-intensive.[78] Innovative legal service providers generally rely on nonlawyer financing.[79] Prohibition of lay investment cuts legal organizations off from the sources of funds that fuel innovation elsewhere in the economy: angel investors, venture capital, private equity, and public capital markets.[80]

Law firms could also benefit from involvement by other professionals in marketing, finance systems, engineering, project management, and similar occupations.[81] Research on innovation finds that it most often comes through interactions with those in related fields.[82] As Richard Susskind notes, just as librarians did not create Google, lawyers may not create tomorrow's breakthroughs in the delivery of legal services.[83] The desire to attract and retain outside investors may also "tend to impose financial . . . discipline on law firms whose members have not experienced serious pressure to exercise it."[84] Nonlawyer ownership could also help businesses bundle multiple types of services, including law, in ways that increase convenience and efficiency. For example, these businesses may be able to save on shared overhead costs or joint advertising campaigns.[85]

The need for outside capital and expertise is particularly acute in the marketing of routine assistance. The prospect of legal services at Wal-Mart, however distasteful to lawyers, is likely to be appealing to many consumers.[86] The chain already offers a variety of professional services, including medical, dental, and eye care. Law would be a logical next step. A similar evolution has already begun in England. WHSmith, a London-based chain, offers legal advice on divorce, wills, real estate transactions, and basic contracts through legal kiosks run in partnership with QualitySolicitors.[87] Co-operative Legal Services, an offshoot of a supermarket, offers legal assistance often packaged with other related services.[88] As law professor Renee Knake puts it, outside investment may "democratize" the delivery of legal services in ways that expand access to justice for underserved consumers.[89] That is the claim underlying a recent lawsuit challenging the ban on outside investment. There, Jacoby & Meyers argues that it needs external capital to finance its efforts to realize economies of scale in delivering affordable routine assistance.[90]

In short, the ban on nonlawyer investment requires rethinking. Invoking "core values" is not, as Gillers notes, "a substitute for reasoned dialogue, although unfortunately it seems at times to serve as one."[91] Although further research is necessary to assess the full implications of nonlawyer investment, the evidence to date suggests insufficient justification for banning the option.[92] Given the

potential benefits of such investment and the availability of regulatory safeguards to minimize its risks, a more disinterested forum
would allow the practice.

Continuing Legal Education[93]

Question: How can lawyers get tax deductions and employer reimbursement for

a week at Club Med in Mexico;

a European cruise;

a Giants baseball game;

courses in cardiovascular health, overeating, and Tibetan relaxation
methods?

Answer: Call it "continuing legal education."

In principle, CLE is hard to oppose. All but five states require such
instruction, and who could object to having lawyers make modest
efforts to stay current in their field?[94] In practice, however, the system leaves much to be desired. In order to gain support from lawyers, CLE requirements have been minimal and highly user-friendly.
States typically require only ten to twelve hours a year of passive
attendance, and course credit is available for an "ethical afternoon at
the movies," a sports law seminar complete with baseball game and
complimentary hot dogs, and a week at a luxury resort Club Med
discussing legal developments with Superior Court judges.[95]

The Rationale for Mandatory Continuing Legal Education

Arguments in support of mandatory continuing legal education
(MCLE) often start and sometimes end with the premise that "education for all lawyers is valuable, and no one seriously argues it is
not."[96] Although acknowledging the absence of studies establishing
the value of CLE, a Michigan state bar president nonetheless maintained that "no studies are needed. We know that education is good

and makes people better at what they do. How can lawyers reject that fundamental principle?"[97]

These comments miss the point. What opponents are rejecting is not education per se; it is MCLE in its current form. If its value were as self-evident as supporters claim, compulsion would not be required. It is precisely because many lawyers have not seen the benefit of CLE that state bars have pushed for minimum requirements. Rates of attendance at voluntary programs vary widely, but it is clear that many lawyers would not participate without the threat of sanctions.[98]

A second premise of MCLE is that attendance, even if compelled, will enhance competence. Particularly for new lawyers starting a small or solo legal practice, "the seminars can fill the void of a mentor who would teach them some of the practical aspects of practicing law."[99] For more senior lawyers, CLE is a way to keep abreast of recent developments, hone their specialties, or explore new practice areas. Even lawyers who are "anti-MCLE" will assertedly "run the risk of learning something. . . . MCLE certainly will not hurt competence and may even help improve it."[100] But the issue is whether it will do so enough to justify the cost. On that point, supporters are often silent, although an occasional claim is that the cost passed on to clients is "insignificant."[101]

A further justification for MCLE is that it enhances public trust.[102] As one commentator acknowledged, "To deny that public relations is a part of any MCLE program is to ignore the obvious."[103] One variation on this argument is that because other states have a continuing education requirement, lawyers in a state without mandatory CLE are at "risk [of losing] public confidence."[104] A similar variation is that because other professions are subject to continuing education mandates, the bar would jeopardize its own public standing if it failed to follow suit.[105] A California bar report detailed the obligations imposed on other licensed occupations, including not only doctors and accountants, but also acupuncturists, barbers, cosmetologists, and real estate appraisers. The report then concluded "that it would be cavalier, if not shocking, were California lawyers excused from the obligation to continue to learn, while all those other California professionals, and most lawyers across the land, are required to discharge it."[106]

The Problems with Mandatory Continuing Legal Education

The central problem with MCLE is that there is no research "demonstrating that lawyers who participate in CLE deliver better services than lawyers who do not."[107] There is, moreover, reason to doubt that compelled passive attendance at CLE courses is an effective strategy for addressing the causes of incompetence. To state the obvious, "Presence is not evidence of learning."[108] Anyone familiar with MCLE will recall the sight of participants reading newspapers, e-mails, and other non-course-related materials.[109] For many adult learners, Plato's wisdom remains apt: "Knowledge which is acquired under compulsion obtains no hold on the mind."[110]

Moreover, the format of most CLE courses is inconsistent with adult learning principles. "What is heard in the classroom, without advance preparation, classroom participation, review, and application is unlikely to be retained."[111] One survey of Indiana participants reported

> scant evidence that the court's minimum continuing legal education standards have promoted competence or professional development in a meaningful way. We found lawyers who attend CLE programs acquire new knowledge but do not retain it and seldom apply the newly acquired knowledge in their work. . . . Almost half of those surveyed reported that they seldom practice what they learn at CLE programs and twenty percent reported that they did not know whether they ever practice what they learned. While survey respondents reported that the training sessions provided useful information and techniques, most did not report lasting changes in their skills and knowledge. Most attorneys do not have enough practical application and follow up to create lasting change.[112]

In a survey of Pennsylvania attorneys, only about a quarter of participants thought that what they learned in MCLE would help improve their practices.[113] Almost never do CLE programs provide the kind of environment that experts find conducive to adult learning, which involves preparation, participation, evaluation, accountability, and opportunities to apply new information in a practice setting.[114] As studies on continuing education in medicine make clear, lectures are a particularly inadequate tool.[115] Effective training is a process, and the one-shot lectures and panels that are common in MCLE fall short.

Nor do those programs address the root causes of most client grievances, which involve not lack of technical knowledge, but problems of neglect, inadequate preparation, overcharging, failure to communicate, and so forth.[116] In criminal cases, where ineffective assistance of counsel is of greatest concern, the problems are largely attributable to excessive caseloads, which CLE does nothing to address.[117]

It is equally doubtful that mandatory continuing education is an effective public relations strategy. There is no evidence that the public "pays attention to our CLE endeavors. After more than 20 years of mandatory CLE . . . people still love to hate all lawyers except their own."[118] A search of newspaper archives "shows that this issue makes nary a blip on the public radar. . . . If the mandate dies, civic grief counseling will not be necessary."[119] If the public did pay attention, it is unclear how much their confidence would be enhanced by seeing some of the tax-deductible and employer-reimbursed boondoggles that can qualify for CLE credit. As other commentators note, public relations seems an "especially flimsy hook on which to hang *mandatory* CLE. One could just as easily and effectively proclaim to the public that . . . lawyers *voluntarily* participated in x-thousands of CLE hours in the most recent calendar year."[120]

As to the quality of continuing legal education, a mandatory system with captive audiences may not create as much incentive for cost-effectiveness as a voluntary program.[121] Under a pure market system, "the programs with substance and reasonable fees . . . will return and will multiply. These natural selective forces are severely restrained in a mandatory system."[122] As a consequence, inadequate quality is a pervasive problem.[123] Many state bars do not have the resources to monitor quality.[124] Nor can they oversee compliance with self-study, which permits attorneys to certify that they have watched videos, listened to audiotapes, or completed online programs. Since no exams are required, bar officials cannot verify whether any significant "study" occurred, or whether participants were even sober or awake, let alone engaged in the learning process.

Reform Strategies

Mandatory CLE requires rethinking. Despite the weakness of the case for requirements, abolition would be politically difficult. In most states, the train has left the station. Mandatory CLE offers too many benefits to bar associations, not only in course fees but in attendance at bar conventions where CLE credit is available. It is also likely that terminating requirements would be seen as a public relations problem. It proved difficult enough to resist imposing mandates in the first instance; it may be harder still to suggest that they are no longer necessary.

What does seem possible, however, is to make continuing education programs more meaningful. One possibility is to require both less and more. States could demand fewer hours but impose greater quality controls. Bar officials could require passage of an exam or at least crack down on boondoggles that bear little demonstrated relationship to performance in practice. More incentives and bar support should be available for courses that meet best practice standards suggested by adult learning research and that supply opportunities for interaction, application, feedback, and follow-up. An example is the New York City Bar's pilot New Lawyer Institute, which offers mentoring as well as a year-long curriculum including programs targeted to practical skills, nuts-and-bolts practice management, and career development.[125]

Alternatively, states could combine required and voluntary approaches. CLE could be mandatory for new lawyers and for other practitioners who are subject to disciplinary, judicial, or malpractice sanctions. Attorneys who complete voluntary CLE courses and pass a basic exam could receive a certification of their coursework. That credential could become part of a broader certification structure.

For example, lawyers who achieved such recognition could use that status in attracting clients and reducing their malpractice insurance premiums. States could encourage this trend by expanding specialization programs that require CLE and publicizing their value to consumers.[126]

Another possibility would be to give credit to lawyers who provide free legal services as part of designated pro bono programs that include training and supervision. For example, New York allows three MCLE credit hours per year for pro bono work.[127] An expanded system of training and credit might provide a constructive alternative for lawyers who view current course options as mindless busywork.

As an abstract concept, continuing education is hard to oppose. Its potential value is self-evident for a profession confronting changing laws, evolving practice technologies, and significant ethical challenges. But as currently administered, the system falls far short of its potential. Legal education should be a continuing commitment, not the token gesture that many lawyers now experience.

Discipline

The American disciplinary process has never lacked for critics.[128] Over the last four decades, both bar commissions and independent scholars have identified serious problems in the profession's responses to misconduct. UCLA law professor Richard Abel summarized their consensus: "Too little unethical behavior is named, blamed, claimed, and punished."[129] Most Americans agree. Only about a third of the public believes that the bar does a good job disciplining lawyers.[130] "Too slow, too secret, too soft, and too self-regulated" has been a widespread complaint.[131]

The Flawed Structure of Professional Oversight

The basic problem is structural. As Columbia law professor John Coffee puts it, self-regulation permits "the continued government of the guild, by the guild, and for the guild."[132] What that has meant for bar discipline is too little focus on consumer protection and too much focus on lawyers' reputational concerns. Many disciplinary authorities do not even handle garden-variety misconduct—"mere" negligence and overcharging—because of resource limitations and the often erroneous assumption that other civil liability remedies are available. But virtually all authorities sanction misconduct committed outside of professional relationships in what is too often a misdirected effort to preserve lawyers' public image.

Here again, the problem is rooted in the inherent powers doctrine. State supreme courts have claimed authority to regulate lawyers but have lacked sufficient time, interest, or capacity to exercise that authority effectively.[133] Most of these courts face crushing caseloads, and their justices have neither the resources nor the expertise to ensure adequate disciplinary oversight.[134] Nor do they have much inclination or incentive to challenge the organized bar on matters that hold great importance for lawyers but are not priorities for the general public.

A related problem is that the individual clients and third parties most vulnerable to lawyers' misconduct lack political leverage and incentives to demand reform.[135] Most are "one-shot players" who use lawyers infrequently and episodically. The few sporadic efforts that have been made to create more publicly accountable disciplinary structures have proceeded with little consumer support and have folded in the face of opposition by the profession.[136] As a consequence, courts have delegated day-to-day oversight authority to bar organizations or to bodies that are nominally independent but that are closely aligned with bar interests. Lawyers can appeal disciplinary sanctions to the state supreme courts, but consumers have no effective recourse for decisions or processes that are unresponsive to their interests.

Bar oversight processes are almost entirely reactive and generally address only complaints of serious professional misconduct or criminal convictions.[137] Although almost all jurisdictions have ethical rules requiring lawyers to report evidence of other attorneys' misconduct, these mandates are widely ignored and rarely enforced. Only about 10 percent of the complaints to disciplinary bodies come from the profession.[138] Yet despite lawyers' notorious unwillingness to inform on other lawyers, the most comprehensive survey found only four disciplinary actions over two decades for failure to report ethical violations.[139]

The resulting reliance on client grievances leads to underinclusive remedies. The system fails to respond when clients benefit from misconduct, as in abusive litigation practices or complicity in fraud, or when victims lack information or incentives to file complaints. Sophisticated corporate clients typically find that withdrawal of business and nonpayment of fees are more effective remedies than those available from the disciplinary system. Even less powerful consumers who lack such options often doubt that bringing the matter to the bar will produce a satisfactory response. They are generally correct. The vast majority of grievances are dismissed without investigation because they fail to state a plausible claim within agency jurisdiction; for the remaining claims, inadequate resources often limit the effectiveness of responses.[140] Only about three percent of cases brought to disciplinary authorities result in public sanctions.[141] Even where the bar finds significant misconduct, sanctions are often lenient and clients are not guaranteed adequate compensation.[142] Lying under oath and destroying documents has earned as little as six months' suspension; an extended history of client neglect and misuse of an escrow account has earned only three months' suspension.[143] For cases involving minor grievances of neglect, negligence, and fee disputes that authorities decline to handle, malpractice litigation is too expensive. Moreover, the lawyers most likely to generate complaints frequently lack malpractice insurance.[144] Although a growing number of states have alternative dispute resolution systems for minor grievances and fee disputes, few of these programs are mandatory, and the only available research on their performance finds substantial client dissatisfaction.[145] Many states also lack remedial approaches that respond to the causes of ethical violations. Attorneys too often receive reprimands rather than the training and oversight that will assist them in avoiding future problems.[146]

The problem is compounded by the absence of transparency. Except in four states, bar disciplinary agencies will not disclose the existence of a complaint unless they have found a disciplinary violation or probable cause to believe that a violation has occurred. Lawyers with as many as twenty complaints under investigation have received a clean bill of health when a consumer asked for information about their records, and it has sometimes taken as many as forty-four complaints over a decade to get a practitioner disbarred.[147] Even where sanctions are imposed, the public lacks a ready way of discovering them. Not all states publish information concerning disciplinary sanctions, and many do not do so online or in forms that consumers can readily access.[148] Because the vast majority of complaints never result in public sanctions, and the vast majority of malpractice actions never result in published opinions, consumers lack crucial knowledge about lawyers' practice histories.

The profession and the public also lack information that would enable them to assess the adequacy of disciplinary processes. Few states publish aggregate data concerning the nature of grievances, characteristics of attorneys, and sanctions imposed.[149] The lack of transparency concerning the treatment of complaints, and the lack of proactive oversight of corporate lawyers whose clients seldom file grievances, feeds practitioners' suspicion that the disciplinary system is biased against small firms, solo practitioners, and racial and ethnic minorities.[150] The studies to date have not been adequate to evaluate that concern.[151] Nor do the twenty states that have diversion programs publish statistics on the effectiveness of these programs in preventing misconduct and addressing clients' concerns.[152]

One consequence of the profession's failure to develop adequate regulatory processes is that other decision makers have supplemented or supplanted bar oversight. For example, lawyers' complicity in some of the major financial scandals of the early twenty-first century led to no disciplinary actions but major new legislation.[153] Congress required, over the ABA's vehement objections, that counsel in publicly traded companies make internal reports of potential fraud to corporate leadership.[154] Other federal and state agencies have imposed ethical standards beyond what bar rules require, and prosecutors have brought criminal proceedings where disciplinary authorities have failed to act.[155] Rutgers law professor John Leubsdorf summarizes the trend: "More and more regulators have sought to regulate the bar . . . [and] have become increasingly unwilling to defer to either bar associations or courts."[156] Clients and commercial organizations have also entered the arena. Retainer agreements by large companies have included ethical mandates, insurance companies have insisted on additional ethics-related safeguards as a condition of malpractice coverage, and lawyer directories and websites have included information on disciplinary history and/or client reviews.[157]

Yet these initiatives have fallen short. State courts' assertion of inherent regulatory powers has limited the scope of comprehensive administrative and legislative intervention.[158] And insurance companies' leverage has been limited by the unwillingness of all but one state bar to require that lawyers have malpractice coverage.[159] Moreover, on some matters, such as the bar's oversight of nonprofessional misconduct, there have been no external efforts to intervene, despite the inherent problems in current enforcement practices.

The Undisciplined Scope of Disciplinary Review: Nonprofessional Misconduct

Whatever its inadequacies in responding to misconduct that occurs within a lawyer–client relationship, the bar has often been highly vigilant in its responses to criminal offenses occurring outside it. That should come as no surprise. Such cases are relatively easy to pursue, because the hard investigative work has already been done by prosecutors, and offenders are often highly unsympathetic to both the public and the profession. Virtually all states have a version of the ABA's Model Rules of Professional Conduct that authorizes discipline for a criminal act that reflects adversely on the lawyer's honesty, trustworthiness, or fitness as a lawyer, or for conduct that involves "dishonesty, fraud, deceit or misrepresentation," or is "prejudicial to the administration of justice."[160] ABA standards identify eleven aggravating circumstances and sixteen mitigating circumstances that can be relevant in determining sanctions, which permits widely varying responses to similar offenses across and even within jurisdictions.[161]

Part of the difficulty lies in the absence of evidence linking particular conduct to the justifications for bar discipline. Courts have articulated two main rationales for professional oversight of nonprofessional offenses. One is to protect the public and the administration of justice from future violations of ethical standards. The other is to preserve popular confidence in the integrity of lawyers and the legal system. In principle, both seem uncontroversial; in practice, both have proven highly problematic.

The public protection rationale assumes that those who break rules in nonprofessional settings are also likely to do so in professional settings. Yet a vast array of psychological research makes clear that ethical decision making is highly situational, and depends on circumstantial pressures and constraints.[162] Except in extreme cases, efforts even by mental health experts to predict dishonesty, deviance, or other misconduct based on past acts are notoriously inaccurate.[163] Untrained disciplinary officials and judges are unlikely to do better, particularly when the factors contributing to nonprofessional misconduct differ vastly from those encountered in lawyer–client relationships. But many decision makers dismiss or discount the circumstances that distinguish personal from professional misconduct.

A case in point involves Laura Beth Lamb. Trapped in an abusive marriage, Lamb lost her law license for ten years after taking the bar exam for her husband.[164] At the time of the exam, she was seven months pregnant and suffering complications from chronic diabetes. Her husband, who had previously failed two exams, had bouts of rage and depression during which he threw heavy objects, and threatened to kill Lamb and her unborn child if she did not take the test in his place. She agreed, disguised herself as her husband, and scored ninth out of some 7,000 applicants. After an anonymous tip revealed the matter to the state bar, she pleaded guilty to felony impersonation and deception. She received a $2,500 fine, probation, and a sentence of 200 hours of community service. She also divorced her husband and received psychological treatment. Despite her therapist's conclusion that Lamb "was unlikely to 'do anything remotely like this again,'" the California Supreme Court reasoned that her deceitful acts were of "exceptional gravity" and warranted disbarment.[165] In the court's view, the "legal, ethical, and moral pressures of daily practice come in many forms. Besides raw avarice and self-aggrandizement, they may include the sincere but misguided desire to please a persuasive or overbearing client. . . ."[166] Yet for the court to equate the pressure of an insistent client to that of an abusive, mentally unstable spouse suggests a profound insensitivity to the risks of domestic violence facing a pregnant woman.[167]

In a recent Massachusetts case, another victim of battering had her license suspended for conduct unlikely to recur in any professional setting.[168] Fawn Balliro, an assistant district attorney, was assaulted by a man in Tennessee with whom she was romantically involved. A neighbor alerted the police, which led to misdemeanor assault charges. The defendant pressured Balliro to drop the charges because he was on probation for drug offenses; if he was convicted, he would be incarcerated and no one would be available to support his two minor daughters. Balliro was unsuccessful in preventing the prosecution, and, when called as a witness, testified falsely that her injuries occurred while falling. The case was dismissed, and the Tennessee prosecutor informed the Massachusetts District Attorney's Office that employed her of the suspected perjury. The Office put Balliro on leave until she agreed to undergo counseling and report her conduct to disciplinary authorities. She did so, and the bar recommended a public reprimand, partly on the basis of psychiatric testimony indicating that she was highly unlikely to commit such an act again.[169] The Massachusetts Supreme Court, however, concluded that false testimony under oath could not be condoned, "irrespective of the circumstances," and suspended her from practice for six months.[170] In so ruling, the court noted the perceived inequity of giving her a greater penalty than the two-month suspension previously imposed on a lawyer who had assaulted his estranged wife.[171] In the justices' view, however, lying under oath was a more serious offense than battery, despite the mitigating circumstances.

In most published decisions involving nonprofessional conduct, courts do not even bother to consider the likelihood of its replication in a professional relationship. It is enough that the conduct threatens the reputation of the profession. A representative example involves Albert Boudreau, a Louisiana lawyer convicted of importing several magazines and a video of child pornography.[172] Boudreau purchased the items in the Netherlands, where the magazines were lawful and the models were of legal age to be photographed nude. They were underage by American definitions, however.[173] The Louisiana Supreme Court agreed with the disciplinary board that the actions constituted a "stain upon the legal profession," and clearly reflected on the lawyer's "moral fitness to practice law."[174] Despite the absence of any prior disciplinary record, or any relationship between personal and professional conduct, the court ordered disbarment.[175]

If the goal of such sanctions is to ensure public confidence, a better strategy would be to make the oversight process more responsive to professional misconduct, and less idiosyncratic in its responses to nonprofessional offenses. It can scarcely enhance respect for bar discipline when lawyers guilty of such offenses receive wildly different treatment, and the focus is the profession's reputation rather than the public's protection. Sanctions for drug offenses, tax evasion, and domestic violence now range from reprimand to disbarment, and decision makers often disagree about the appropriate response in the same case.[176] As former Supreme Court Justice Robert H. Jackson noted in a related context, a standard like moral turpitude, which permits decisions to turn on reactions of "particular judges to particular offenses," invites caprice and clichés.[177] A profession concerned about the legitimacy of its own regulation should aspire to do better.

Reform Strategies

A more effective disciplinary process would strengthen its oversight of professional performance, and narrow its concern with nonprofessional offenses. The jurisdiction of disciplinary agencies should be broadened to include neglect, negligence, and fees. Bar resources should be increased to ensure adequate investigation and remedial responses. Rather than relying almost exclusively on client complaints, supplemented by felony convictions, regulatory officials should initiate investigations based on judicial sanctions and malpractice judgments. Mandatory dispute-resolution processes should be available for minor misconduct. Lawyers should be required to carry malpractice insurance and remedies should include client compensation. Support services and diversion programs for lawyers with mental health, substance abuse, office management, and short-term financial difficulties should help these practitioners establish an appropriate remedial plan and supervise their compliance.[178] More efforts should also be made to track program effectiveness and to deal with recidivists.

The process also needs to become more transparent. Lawyers should be required to provide information to clients or to centralized databases concerning their disciplinary and malpractice records.[179] Four-fifths of surveyed Americans express a desire for such resources, and replicable models involving physicians are widely available.[180] Disciplinary complaints should also be made public if the relevant oversight body finds probable cause for investigation. Although lawyers have opposed this proposal on the ground that disclosure of unfounded complaints would unjustly prejudice their reputations, no evidence has demonstrated those harms in the minority of states with open processes. If civil complaints and police arrests are matters of public record, why should grievances against lawyers be subject to special protection?[181] Because consumer surveys find deep suspicion about closed-door proceedings, even the ABA's own disciplinary commission has recommended disclosure of nonfrivolous complaints.[182]

Concerns of public protection should also figure more prominently in the review of nonprofessional misconduct. Given the difficulties of predicting future offenses from unrelated past misconduct, the most defensible approach would be to limit bar oversight to matters involving fraud, dishonesty, and other acts relevant to professional work.[183] If that limitation is politically implausible, another possibility would be guidelines comparable to standards applicable in other licensing contexts. At the very least, the profession should strive for more consistent treatment of similar conduct, and make public protection rather than public image the dominant concern.

Alternative Regulatory Models: Lessons From Abroad

Given the flaws in the US professional regulatory structure, it is useful to look at alternatives developed in other nations with comparable legal systems. Great Britain and Australia offer instructive models.

Great Britain

In 2003, the Lord Chancellor of Great Britain gave the following charge to Sir David Clementi, an accountant and former deputy governor of the Bank of England:

- To consider what regulatory framework would best promote competition, innovation, and the public and consumer interest in an efficient, effective, and independent legal sector.
- To recommend a framework which will be independent in representing the public and consumer interest, comprehensive, accountable, consistent, flexible, transparent, and no more restrictive or burdensome than is clearly justified.[184]

That charge was a response to widely perceived problems in the bar's handling of disciplinary complaints and its insulation from competition.[185] Just prior to Clementi's appointment, the Office of Fair Trade had issued a White Paper that was highly critical of the bar's practices.[186] Clementi's report was similarly critical. Its recommendations paved the way for fundamental reforms through the Legal Services Act of 2007.

What is most instructive for comparative purposes are the consumer-oriented goals that Clementi identified for his review, and those that underpinned the subsequent Legal Services Act. Clementi's report identified six objectives for the regulation of legal services:

maintaining the rule of law;
access to justice;
protection and promotion of consumer interests;
promotion of competition;
encouragement of a confident, strong, and effective legal profession;
promoting public understanding of . . . citizens' legal rights.[187]

Consistent with those goals, the Act permitted alternative business structures with nonlawyer investment. Advantages for consumers included additional choice, greater price and quality competition, more nonlawyer expertise and resources, and increased access and convenience from one-stop shopping and economies of scale.[188] Because alternative business structures would typically have built a strong reputation in providing nonlegal services, they would have a strong incentive to maintain that reputation when offering legal assistance.[189]

For those in the United States concerned with issues of access to justice, cost-effective services, and responsive disciplinary processes, there is much to admire in the Legal Services Act reforms and the process that produced them. The Act establishes an independent Legal Services Board, with a majority of lay members and a lay chair, which has responsibility for oversight of legal services in England and Wales. The Board approves a frontline regulator for each type of licensed legal providers. The regulators retain disciplinary responsibility for complaints that allege serious professional misconduct, but must create a largely independent body to exercise oversight.[190] In addition, the governance body of the largest regulator, the Solicitors Regulation Authority, has a majority of lay members.[191] If an approved regulator is too slow or ineffective in exercising its authority, the Board may fine the regulator, make remedial orders, or withdraw its oversight powers.[192]

Less serious complaints involving performance issues are addressed by the legal ombudsman. Created by the Office for Legal Complaints, under the authority of the Legal Services Act, the legal ombudsman considers complaints by individuals and small businesses about the quality of the legal services that they have received. The ombudsman determines an outcome between the lawyer and the client that is "fair and reasonable," taking into account how a court would perceive the relationship between the lawyer and client, the applicable rules of conduct, and what the "ombudsman considers to have been good practice at the time of the act/omission."[193] The ombudsman may require the lawyer to pay compensation for financial losses or "inconvenience/distress," and may also take action "in the interests of the complainant" to put right "any specified error, omission or other deficiency."[194] The legal ombudsman may also require the lawyer to refund or waive fees.[195]

Australia

In Australia, widely publicized scandals also prompted state governments to create more accountable and consumer-oriented regulatory processes. In 2004, a Standing Committee of Attorneys General established Model Provisions for the Legal Profession that eventually were translated into Legal Profession Acts by all but one state and territory.[196] Although the Acts vary in certain respects, they share a commitment to increased transparency and responsiveness in oversight processes. For example, in New South Wales, an independent Legal Services Commissioner receives all complaints and refers them either to consumer-oriented mediation or to the bar's own regulatory bodies. Complainants who are unsatisfied with the results may seek review by the Commissioner, who has the power to substitute a new decision. The Commissioner also oversees the process for handling complaints and may take over a particular investigation or recommend more general changes.[197] Queensland has an independent Legal Services Commission headed by a nonlawyer.[198] Its disciplinary system includes a Client Relations Center, which resolves minor disputes, and a Legal Practice Tribunal, composed of a Supreme Court Justice, one nonlawyer, and one practitioner as advisors. Problems of competence and diligence can be subjects for discipline, and all disciplinary actions are published on the Legal Services Commission website.

All but one Australian state and territory also allow incorporated legal practices (ILPs), which permit ownership interests by nonlawyers. The regulatory framework for these practices is being extended to other law firms. It requires firms to have at least one practitioner responsible for implementing appropriate management systems that ensure compliance with professional conduct rules. In New South Wales, which has the most well-developed oversight structure, ILP proactive management systems must address ten objectives in areas that often give rise to complaints, such as competence,

communications, supervision, trust funds, and conflicts of interest.[199] All ILPs must conduct a self-audit to assess their compliance
with each of these objectives.[200] ILPs that rate themselves as not
fully compliant must work with the Office of the Legal Service
Commissioner to improve their practice management systems.[201] In
cases where the ILP's self-audit or client complaints raise concerns,
the Commissioner can initiate an independent audit.[202] A comprehensive study of the New South Wales framework found that requiring ILPs to go through the process of self-assessment resulted in
frequent internal reforms and that the result was a client complaint
rate about one-third that of other firms.[203] Almost two-thirds of surveyed lawyers agreed that the process was a "learning exercise that
enabled [their] firm to improve client service"; only 15 percent dis-
agreed with that statement.[204]

Queensland is another model of regulatory innovation. It is developing external audit processes that will ensure adequate oversight
without intrusive or burdensome requirements. Among these processes are web-based surveys of ILP practitioners and staff concerning matters such as ethical culture, billing practices, and complaint
management systems.[205] Results will enable the ILPs to bench-
mark their performance against that of peers, and will help the
Commissioner assess the effectiveness of different regulatory processes. Success with this framework could lead to adoption for traditional firms as well as those with alternative practice structures.[206]

Such a proactive management-based regulatory structure could
readily be adapted to the United States. As Arizona law professor Ted Scheneyer has noted, Rule 5.3 of the ABA's Model Rules
of Professional Conduct requires a partner in a law firm to "make
reasonable efforts to ensure that the firm has in effect measures giving reasonable assurance that all [of its] lawyers . . . conform to
the Rules of Professional Conduct."[207] Enforcement of that Rule has
been rare.[208] State supreme courts could require such proactive management systems as a way to comply with the Model Rule, or adopt
other aspects of the Australian framework. Such reforms would offer
an obvious improvement over America's reactive complaint-driven
process, which has proven so inadequate to the oversight task.

Rethinking the Regulatory Structure

In no other country does the legal profession exert so much influence over its own regulatory process. One consequence of that regulatory power has been to insulate the bar from public accountability and from disinterested perspectives about how best to respond to market forces. The flaws are readily apparent in the bar's approach to multi-jurisdictional and multidisciplinary practice, nonlawyer investment, continuing legal education, and lawyer discipline. The obvious solution is to move in the direction of Great Britain and Australia, toward a co-regulatory model in which the bar shares authority with an independent oversight body controlled by nonlawyers.

However attractive in theory, such a system is likely to be difficult to achieve in practice. It would take a forward-thinking state court that was willing to withstand the opposition of the organized bar. If that proves too much to ask, it may at least be possible to convince courts to accord less deference to the bar when considering changes to the Rules of Professional Conduct or to bar disciplinary processes.

In an influential history of the profession prepared under ABA auspices, Harvard law professor Roscoe Pound assured his sponsor that it was not the "same sort of thing as a retail grocer's association."[209] If he was right, it was for the wrong reason. Lawyers, no less than grocers, are motivated by their own occupational interests. What distinguishes the American bar is its ability to present self-regulation as a societal value. Courts and consumers should see through that pretense, and demand regulatory approaches that serve public rather than professional interests.

6

Legal Education

"AMERICAN LEGAL EDUCATION IS in crisis," announced a *New York Times* op-ed.[1] A chorus of other commentators agrees.[2] To many critics, "Law school is not a fixer-upper, it's a tear-down. Its problems have gone unattended for decades."[3] Even legal education's most loyal defenders acknowledge that it is operating in a difficult climate, characterized by rising costs, declining enrollments, reduced job placements, and disaffected students.[4]

This chapter explores challenges confronting law schools. It argues that part of the problem is a lack of consensus over what the problem is. Faculty and regulators are developing well-intended but inadequate responses to the symptoms, not the causes, of law school woes. The focus on the cost of legal education has deflected attention from broader concerns about its structure and priorities. As law professor William Henderson notes, our profession is failing to "take serious issues seriously."[5]

Finances

Accreditation

American legal education has come a considerable distance from Thomas Jefferson's view that "All that is necessary for a law student is access to a library and directions in what order the books are to be read."[6] The Council of the American Bar Association Section of Legal Education and Admissions to the Bar prescribes a vast range of expensive requirements for accreditation, including three years of post-graduate study; job security for faculty; an extensive library and physical plant; and limits on the number of courses that can be taught online or by adjuncts.[7] Even applying for accreditation is a costly process. An irony that did not escape notice by one low-budget applicant was that seven of its administrators had to fly from Tennessee to Puerto Rico to make a brief presentation at the Ritz Carlton, where the Council was meeting.[8]

The result has been a "stultifying sameness" among law schools.[9] Rigid accreditation standards discourage innovation and different models of legal education that could significantly lower its cost.

Rankings

According to many legal educators, rankings are an even more important influence on costs than accreditation.[10] *U.S. News and World Report,* the "mother of misguided metrics," has significantly distorted law school priorities.[11] One of the easiest ways for schools to rise in this competition is to spend more in areas rewarded by the *U.S. News* formula. One example is expenditures per student, which have risen dramatically in the decades since the rankings went into effect.[12] Another factor is students' median GPA and LSAT scores; schools have incentives to spend more on merit scholarships to attract high-scoring applicants. Because those individuals also are likely to perform the best academically, and to obtain the highest-paying jobs, the practice amounts to a reverse Robin Hood transfer; tuition payments by poorer students subsidize scholarships for richer ones.[13] Schools also attempt to boost their rankings by spending that is designed to enhance their reputations, including subsidies for faculty scholarship and glitzy publications.[14] Yet reputational surveys, which count for 40 percent of each school's position, are a particularly inadequate proxy for educational quality.[15] Few of those surveyed know enough to make accurate comparative judgments. Most participants rely instead on word-of-mouth reputation and prior rankings, which makes the process self-perpetuating. Past recognition creates a halo effect that results in high scores even when the evaluator knows nothing about a school's current performance. This explains why Princeton and MIT law schools do so well in surveys, even though they do not exist.[16] Moreover, the ranking system excludes many factors that materially affect a student's educational experience, such as access to clinical courses, pro bono opportunities, and a diverse faculty and student body.[17]

The rankings have had other adverse effects on law school decision making. In some cases, schools have fudged the facts or used "Enron-type accounting standards" in calculating per-pupil expenditures.[18] In other cases, schools have hired their own graduates for short-term positions to boost their placement rates.

This is not to suggest that rankings are entirely without value. Some relevant characteristics can be objectively assessed, and schools should be accountable for their performance. In the absence of comparative data, law school applicants would encounter an educational Lake Woebegon, in which every institution claimed to be above average. But the *U.S. News* system is deeply flawed and unduly influential. It assigns arbitrary weights to incomplete measures, uses uninformed reputational surveys as proxies for quality, and forces schools to compete in an academic arms race that inflates costs. Yet more than four-fifths of pre-law students said that law school ranking was important or very important in their decision of where to apply.[19] It is similarly influential with donors, employers, and faculty.[20] Washington University law professor Brian Tamanaha puts it bluntly: "The rankings have law schools by the throat."[21]

Rising Costs and Declining Jobs

Taken together, rankings and accreditation requirements have encouraged a rapid increase in tuition. The lifting of caps on student borrowing has pushed in similar directions.[22] Over the last three decades, the price of legal education has increased approximately three times faster than average household incomes.[23] From 1989 to 2009, when the cost of a college education grew 71 percent, law school tuition rose 317 percent.[24] Now the average debt for law school graduates tops $100,000.[25] Only 57 percent secure full-time legal jobs, and those who do and report income often earn too little to cover their debts.[26] According to calculations by former

Northwestern Law School dean David Van Zandt, more than 40 percent of American law school graduates start at salaries inadequate to service average debt levels.[27] Unsurprisingly, debt burdens are unevenly spread and amplify racial and class disadvantages.[28]

Student loans are generally not dischargeable in bankruptcy and often cause substantial hardship. A representative example is the graduate of Loyola Law School in Chicago who abandoned her plans to become a prosecutor because of a $200,000 debt load that she still could not pay off while working for a midsize corporation. As she told the *New York Times,*

> Right now, loans control every aspect of my life. Where I practice, the number of children I'll have, where I live, the type of house I can live in. I honestly believe I'll be a grandparent before I pay off my loans. I have yet to make even a dent in them.[29]

Although the federal government and most law schools offer some loan repayment assistance to graduates who take public interest jobs, law school programs are often insufficiently funded and the federal programs do not provide full discharge until after 10 years of public interest employment.[30] Nor do these programs address the fundamental problem of lack of jobs, public interest or otherwise, that makes law school a questionable investment. In recent years, only about half of new graduates obtain full-time long-term employment for which a law degree is preferred.[31] A graduate of Thomas Jefferson School of Law described the difficulties finding sufficient employment to meet obligations on a $150,000 loan:

> For eight years, I have never had a steady job, just on-and-off document review. . . . After sending out literally thousands of resumes over the years, I have given up. In the "good" years, I used to work 80 hours a week, and half my salary would go to student loans. In the last couple of "bad" years, I haven't been able to pay my loans, and the work has been so unsteady that I have been evicted from my apartment and have had to resort to food stamps. Furthermore, despite eight years having gone by, my loan balance has decreased

by just 10 percent. I will never get out of this debt trap, will never own my own home, nor will I ever be able to afford children. I have contemplated suicide. . . .[32]

As more debts become delinquent, the current system becomes less sustainable, politically and financially.[33] The sense of betrayal among those with crushing debt burdens is apparent in blogs running under titles such as "Shilling me Softly," "Jobless Juris Doctor," and "Exposing the Law School Scam."[34]

Concerns about oversupply and underemployment of lawyers are, however, nothing new and not always permanent. In 1927, the dean of Stanford Law School declared,

We have more lawyers today than there is any legitimate need for. The truth is that we are simply being swamped with aspiring young lawyers, most of whom will necessarily and within a few years after admission, drift into real estate, insurance and related lines, and that is not a process calculated to help the reputation of our profession.[35]

Some commentators believe that the current situation will improve due to a tripling of retirement rates as baby boomers age, the population increases, and the law grows more complex.[36]

However, most commentators see the current difficulties for graduates as more serious and persistent than in preceding years, due to structural changes in the market for legal services.[37] More employers are relying on paralegals, technology, outsourcing, and contract attorneys to do work previously performed by recent graduates, and cash-strapped public sectors are unable to expand hiring even in the face of significant needs.[38]

Applications

As debt burdens are rising and employment prospects are declining, fewer individuals are taking the LSAT and applying to law schools. Applications have declined 38 percent since 2010 and have hit a thirty-year low.[39] For many law schools, this presents an uncomfortable choice between accepting applicants with lower qualifications, which will adversely affect their *U.S. News* rankings, or cutting the size of entering classes, which will decrease tuition revenues. Two-thirds of accredited law schools opted to cut their classes in 2013.[40]

Still, demand for legal education exceeds the jobs available, and in defiance of market trends, fifteen new schools have opened in the last decade even as existing ones have struggled to fill their classes.[41] This raises the question of why so many students have made the high-risk decision to attend law school. Part of the problem has been the lack of transparency in law school disclosures about placement and salaries, which has triggered class-action lawsuits and tighter ABA standards.[42] Other applicants, subject to biases toward optimism, have engaged in "magical thinking."[43] Their assumption has been that they, unlike their classmates, will find well-paying jobs despite adverse market conditions. In one survey, a majority of prospective law students reported that they were "very confident" that they would find a legal job after graduating, but only 16 percent were "very confident" that the majority of their classmates would do the same.[44] But as Brian Tamanaha notes, even the most rational students will have difficulties assessing the long-term value of investment in law school, given disputes and uncertainties over how to calculate economic return.[45]

Social Costs

Whatever the causes, the inability of many students to pay back loans may have societal as well as individual consequences. A substantial default rate will encourage Congress to reconsider providing easy credit to law students.[46] And a tightening of credit markets could further reduce the applicant pool and make a bad situation for law schools worse.

There are other social costs of the high price of legal education. Rising tuitions have limited who can afford to attend law school and what kinds of jobs graduates can afford to take. The decline of need-based scholarships and increased emphasis on GPAs and LSAT scores in order to boost rankings have impeded efforts to recruit minority applicants and diversify the profession. High debt burdens have priced many graduates out of the market where demand for services is greatest. As Chapter 3 noted, it is ironic that the nation with one of the world's highest concentrations of lawyers fails so miserably at making their assistance available to those who need it most. Bar surveys have consistently found that more than four-fifths of the legal needs of low-income individuals, and a majority of those of middle-income individuals, remain unmet.[47] Yet after three years of expensive legal education, graduates are unable to generate sufficient income from this kind of work to pay off their debts and sustain a legal practice. The perverse result is an oversupply of lawyers and an undersupply of legal services.

Structure

Part of the reason for this asymmetry in supply and demand involves the structure of legal education mandated by accreditation standards. The American Bar Association adopted the first of these standards in 1922, and the U.S. Secretary of Education subsequently recognized the Council of the ABA's Section of Legal Education and Admissions to the Bar as the official credentialing organization for law schools.[48] Because all but a few states require graduation from an accredited law school as a condition of practice, the Council significantly influences the structure of legal education. Although there is a strong justification for some form of oversight of American law schools, the review process is flawed in several important respects.

The rationale for a system of accreditation is that a totally free market would not provide sufficient quality control. Students, the most direct beneficiaries of legal education, have limited information about the relative cost-effectiveness of particular schools, and limited capacity to assess the information that is available. Seldom do they have a basis for judging how characteristics like faculty/student ratios or reliance on adjuncts will affect their educational experience. Moreover, student interests are not necessarily consistent with those of the public. Education is one of the rare contexts in which buyers may feel that less is more. Many students would like to earn a degree with the least expense and effort necessary to pass a bar examination and land a job. In the absence of accreditation standards, law schools would need to compete for applicants who wanted the least demanding academic requirements. Similar attitudes are common among central university administrators. Without minimum requirements imposed by an accrediting body, more law schools might be forced to get by with fewer resources in order to subsidize less well-off academic departments. Finally, accreditation requirements can provide a useful catalyst for self-scrutiny and peer review.

Although these justifications support some form of oversight, the current process falls well short of protecting the public interest. A threshold problem lies in the composition of the Council. A majority of its members are lawyers and judges with little or no experience as legal educators.[49] Nor are they sufficiently independent of the profession, which has an obvious stake in preserving its social status and economic interests. However well intentioned, no occupational group is well positioned to make disinterested judgments on matters where its own livelihood is so directly implicated.

A related problem is that the system substitutes detailed regulation of educational inputs for more direct measures of educational outputs. It uses observable measures such as facilities, resources, and faculty/student ratios as highly imperfect predictors of the quality of teaching and research. Moreover, unlike the systems of accreditation for higher education generally, law school standards do not seek to enhance cost-effectiveness or to permit diversity in light of schools' potentially varying missions.[50] Rather, accreditors impose a one-size-fits-all structure that stifles innovation and leaves many students both underprepared and overprepared to meet societal needs.[51] Graduates are overqualified to offer many forms of routine assistance at affordable costs, but are often underqualified in practical and interdisciplinary skills. Accreditation structures have failed to recognize in form what is true in fact. Legal practice is becoming increasingly specialized, and it makes little sense to require the same training for a Wall Street securities lawyer and a small-town family practitioner. Three years in law school and passage of a bar exam are neither necessary nor sufficient to guarantee proficiency in many areas where needs are greatest, such as uncontested divorces, landlord–tenant matters, immigration, or bankruptcy.[52] Other countries allow nonlawyer experts to provide such services without demonstrable adverse affects.[53] The diversity in America's legal demands argues for corresponding diversity in legal education.

Curricula

Vanderbilt law professor Edward Rubin puts it bluntly: "Here we are at the beginning of the twenty-first century, using a model of legal education that was developed in the later part of the nineteenth." Although "the nature of legal practice has changed, and the theory of education has changed," many faculty are "still doing the same basic thing we were doing one hundred and thirty years ago."[54] Part of the problem is that we do little to educate educators about the art of teaching. Many, like me, are thrown into classrooms without experience or training. We then do unto others what was done to us, without much reflection or exposure to adult learning strategies.

The dominant approach has been a combination of lecture and Socratic dialogue that focuses on doctrinal analysis. From a pedagogic standpoint, this approach leaves much to be desired. The heavy emphasis on judicial decisions, which often neglects the role of clients and context, is like "geology without the rocks."[55] The hierarchical and competitive classroom climate also discourages participation by many students, particularly women, and fails to supply enough opportunities for interactive learning, teamwork, and feedback.[56] All too often, the search for knowledge becomes a scramble for status, with students vying to impress rather than inform.

Faculty commonly claim that our method of legal education teaches students to "think like lawyers." In fact, it teaches them to think like law professors. We lack empirical studies validating its effectiveness for performance in practice.[57] As commentators have long noted, law schools focus too little attention on practical skills.[58] Ninety percent of lawyers say that law school does not adequately prepare graduates to undertake legal work.[59] The deficiency has grown more acute as private employers have cut back on training.[60]

Although most law schools have responded to this longstanding criticism with expanded clinical offerings and related initiatives, these remain at the margins of the curricula.[61] Only 3 percent of schools require clinical training, and a majority of students graduate without it.[62] Law is the only profession that sends its students into practice without intensive clinical experience, and many educators believe that they suffer as a consequence.[63] As U.C. Irvine Dean Erwin Chemerinsky puts it, "There is no way to learn to be a lawyer except by doing it . . . It is unthinkable that medical schools could graduate doctors who had never seen patients or that they would declare that they just wanted to teach students to think like doctors."[64] In a joint study by the National Association of Law Placement and the American Bar Foundation, new lawyers rated clinical courses as the most helpful experiences, after legal employment, in making the transition to practice.[65] Students who lack such courses are also missing opportunities to develop cross-cultural competence and an understanding of how law functions, or fails to function, for the have-nots.

Schools are similarly weak in nonclinical courses that integrate experiential approaches and address practice-oriented topics, such as problem solving, marketing, practice and project management, interpersonal dynamics, and information technology.[66] In one survey, close to two-thirds of students and 90 percent of lawyers reported that law school does not teach the practical skills necessary to succeed in today's economy.[67]

Too many schools also lack sequenced interdisciplinary programs that would better prepare students in areas including finance, intellectual property, organizational behavior, public interest, and environmental law. Another gap involves preparation for leadership. Although no occupation produces such a large proportion of leaders as law, and leadership development is now a $45 billion industry, legal education has lagged behind.[68] Many law schools' mission statements include fostering leadership, but only two of these schools actually offer a leadership course.[69]

Although administrators often acknowledge these gaps, they view correctives as luxuries that students can ill afford. The expense of skills education makes it a tough sell in the current economic climate. Yet not all experiential, practice-oriented initiatives require additional investments in costly clinical courses. Much can be accomplished with existing resources through case histories, problems, simulations, cooperative projects with practitioners, and interdisciplinary collaboration.[70] The problem is less that these approaches are unaffordable than that they are unrewarded. Curricular improvements are not well reflected in rankings, and legal employers have not made practical training a priority in hiring.[71] As Harvard professor David Wilkins notes, "There's a lot of pious rhetoric coming out of law schools and the profession about what people want. They say they want this or that, but who do they ultimately hire? The kid on the law review."[72] So, too, faculty have not seen excellence and innovation in teaching as the path to greatest recognition.[73] Significant progress is likely to require a substantial change in academic reward structures.

Values

Another difficulty with legal education involves the values that it fosters, or fails to foster, concerning professional responsibility and professional identity. A prominent Carnegie Foundation report brought renewed attention to longstanding concerns about the marginalization of legal ethics.[74] Most schools relegate the subject to a single required course, which typically focuses on the rules of professional conduct that are tested on the bar's multiple-choice exam.[75] The result is legal ethics without the ethics.[76] A rules-oriented course also leaves out inadequacies in regulatory structures, access to justice, and the conditions of legal practice. In one survey, a majority of professors reported spending no time or less than two hours on the structure of the profession, including issues of discrimination and the realities of practice; 90 percent spent no time or less than two hours on pro bono service.[77]

Such oversights reflect deep-seated skepticism about the importance of professional ethics in professional education. Many law faculty believe that values are beyond the competence of law schools to teach.[78] Although most students report that their school emphasizes ethics, only half of students feel that law school has prepared them well to deal with ethical dilemmas in practice, and even fewer feel that they have had help in developing "a personal code of values and ethics."[79]

The dominant rule-bound approach to professional responsibility underestimates the role that broader coverage can play in developing ethical judgment. Law schools cannot be value-neutral on questions of values. Their curriculum and culture inevitably influence the formation of professional identity and the ethical norms underpinning it.[80] Given that reality, law professors need to be more intentional about the messages that they inevitably communicate. If, as the preamble to the ABA Model Rules of Professional Conduct maintains, a lawyer is a "public citizen having a special responsibility for the quality of justice," this responsibility should be reflected and reinforced throughout the law school experience.[81]

A substantial body of evidence indicates that significant changes occur during early adulthood in individuals' basic strategies for dealing with moral issues.[82] Through interactive education, such as problem solving and role playing, students can enhance their skills in moral analysis and gain awareness of the situational pressures, psychological dynamics, and regulatory failures that underpin misconduct. Failure to integrate professional responsibility issues throughout the curriculum undermines their significance. A minimalist attitude toward ethics marginalizes its importance. What the curriculum leaves unsaid sends a powerful message. Faculty cannot afford to treat professional responsibility as someone else's responsibility.

The same is true of access to justice and pro bono service. As Chapter 3 noted, issues concerning the distribution of legal services are missing or marginal in the core curriculum. Even texts for legal profession courses often fail to discuss access to justice.[83] Although the vast majority of schools have pro bono programs, only a minority of students participate.[84] Only about 10 percent of schools require service, and fewer still impose demands on faculty. Moreover, the amounts required are sometimes quite minimal; half the schools mandate only ten to twenty hours from students.[85] The quality of some programs is also open to question. Many students lack on-site supervision or a classroom opportunity to discuss their work or pro bono issues generally. My own national survey found that only 1 percent of attorneys reported that pro bono received coverage in their law school orientation programs or professional responsibility courses; only 3 percent observed visible faculty support for pro bono work.[86] An American Bar Foundation survey of recent law graduates ranked pro bono last on a list of educational experiences that practitioners felt had assisted them significantly in practice.[87] In the words of a Commission of the Association of American Law Schools on pro bono opportunities, "Law schools should do more."[88] Part of the professional responsibility of professional schools is to build cultures of commitment to public service.

Law schools should also do more to address issues of diversity and of biases based on race, gender, ethnicity, disability, class, and sexual orientation.[89] Minorities make up 37 percent of the population but only a quarter of law school classes.[90] To address that disparity, schools should reconsider the heavy emphasis on law school grades and LSAT scores, which penalize applicants of color and are not accurate predictors of performance in practice.[91] Schools should also focus on issues of climate. Women students, particularly women of color, report fewer opportunities for faculty mentoring, are less likely to speak in class, and experience higher levels of dissatisfaction, disengagement, and self-doubt than men.[92] In the only recent study of student perceptions of diversity and law school climate, half of students of color felt that the environment is sometimes or never welcoming to students regardless of race. Three-quarters agreed that nonwhite students face challenges that similarly situated white students do not face. Almost half reported experiencing an incident in which another student's behavior made them feel unwelcome or disrespected because of their race. Two-thirds of women agreed that female students faced challenges that similarly situated male students do not face.[93] Technology also has created new online opportunities for sexual harassment and widened its audience. One well-publicized case involved the posting of lewd and defamatory statements about female students on AutoAdmit, a law school message board.[94] So, too, women and minorities continue to be underrepresented among full professors and deans, and in other positions of greatest status and reward.[95] If, as bar leaders repeatedly insist, the profession is truly committed to values of diversity and inclusion, that commitment should be better reflected in legal education.[96]

A final problem with law school culture is its tendency to reinforce narrow views of professional fulfillment and to privilege objective measures of achievement at the expense of intrinsic measures of self-worth.[97] This highly competitive climate contributes to a decline in student mental health and disproportionate levels of substance abuse, stress, depression, and other disorders.[98] Estimates suggest that as many as 40 percent of law students experience significant levels of psychological distress and have rates of dysfunction much higher than medical and graduate students.[99] Entering law students have a psychological profile similar to that of the general public but leave with a greater incidence of psychological dysfunction.[100] Yet only one school has developed a comprehensive preventive approach to such problems, and many other schools have neglected the need for student support programs.[101] They have also failed to address the conditions of practice and to enrich students' understandings of the strategies for professional fulfillment. Anxieties associated with rising levels of debt and unemployment are bringing additional urgency to these concerns. As one third-year student put it, "I don't know anybody who is not nervous. Frankly, if you're not nervous, you haven't been paying attention."[102]

Law Reviews

As legal realist Fred Rodell famously observed three-quarters of a century ago, "There are only two things wrong with almost all legal writing. One is its style. The other is its content."[103] Student-run law journals are partly to blame. *New York Times* columnist Adam Liptak put it bluntly: "Law reviews are such a target-rich environment for ridicule that it is barely sporting to make fun of them."[104] Nonetheless, even the Chief Justice of the Supreme Court has taken a potshot:

> Pick up a copy of any law review that you see, and the first article is likely to be, you know, the influence of Immanuel Kant on evidentiary approaches in 18th-century Bulgaria, or something, which I'm sure was of great interest to the academic that wrote it, but isn't of much help to the bar.[105]

A large part of what appears in law reviews isn't even of use to other academics. In the most recent study on point, 43 percent of articles had never been cited.[106] Much of what claims to be cutting-edge scholarship is all dressed up with nowhere to go; its finery borrowed from other disciplines is off- putting to nonspecialists and of little relevance to practitioners. Few judges, policymakers, and practicing lawyers consult academic law reviews with any frequency; many do not look at them at all.[107]

A central problem lies in the editorial structure of law reviews. Unlike other disciplines, which rely exclusively on peer-reviewed journals, law leaves the selection and editing of articles largely up to students. These editors often lack the knowledge, training, expertise, and time to perform adequately in this role.[108] Because law journals are heavily subsidized by their schools, they lack any market discipline and many lack meaningful accountability for the quality of their work.

Editors who are poorly equipped to assess the value of submissions often use imperfect proxies, such as the reputation of the author's school or the extent of documentation. Footnotes have become prime sites for status displays. A single note can meander along for over five pages.[109] Erudition in excess is common. One can find an article of 490 pages and 4800 footnotes devoted to a single section of a single securities statute.[110] Yet such ostentatious displays are an unreliable measure of rigor. There is no guarantee that the author has actually read the sources cited or that they represent the best thinking in the field. And the convention of excessive documentation discourages original insights, which by definition cannot be attributed to someone else. Although surveys of faculty, judges, and practitioners consistently find consensus that articles are too long and too heavily footnoted, those views have done relatively little to curb the practice.[111]

A more fundamental question is whether the pressure to publish makes sense for all faculty. Not every gifted teacher is a gifted scholar. Most research shows no correlation between law professors' teaching effectiveness and scholarly influence.[112] Much of the effort that now goes into publishing articles of little interest to anyone beyond the author's family or tenure committee might be better focused on more teaching or on publications aimed at practitioners or the general public.

Strategies

> Nothing short of everything will really do.
> —Aldous Huxley[113]

Almost thirty years ago, the *New York Times* ran a Sunday magazine feature titled, "The Trouble with America's Law Schools."[114] The piece highlighted many of the curricular concerns common today, particularly the lack of practical training, the inattention to issues of professional responsibility, and the disengagement of upper-level law students. Underlying these concerns was a sense of inertia and complacency among the faculty. As one Stanford professor put it, "The present structure is very congenial to us. . . . We're not indifferent to the fact that our students are bored, but that to one side, law school works pretty well for us."[115]

Such attitudes remain common, and with reason. For most faculty, the pay, hours, and job security of their positions are enviable.[116] In one survey, 93 percent of legal academics reported being satisfied or very satisfied, the highest percentage of satisfaction among any of the reported legal fields.[117] A fundamental problem in American legal education is a lack of consensus among faculty that there *is* a fundamental problem, or one that they have a responsibility to address. Law schools have a long and unbecoming history of resistance to reform.[118] That is likely to change only if external pressure from students, accrediting authorities, donors, and courts demands it.

Finances

From the perspective of many faculty and students, the financial difficulties of law graduates call for redistributive solutions. Examples include expanding loan forgiveness, increasing public subsidies, and liberalizing bankruptcy rules to allow discharge of student debts. But the obstacles to those responses are substantial. Lawyers are not a group much beloved by American taxpayers, and their elected representatives are likely to resist having government take on additional burdens to aid the profession. In any event, given the current oversupply of lawyers and excessive hikes in law school tuitions, it may make more sense to curtail than to enhance the availability of easy credit.[119]

Less controversial reforms, such as increasing disclosure about job placement and salaries, are already under way. However, more needs to be done. David Stern, executive director of Equal Justice Works, proposes that every school offer students individualized financial counseling as well as a webpage with a breakdown of costs to attend, job placement, salary information, and loan burdens.[120] As he notes, students now encounter unnecessary difficulties in cobbling together this information and applying it to a complex federal student loan system.

Schools also need to look for more ways to cut costs and to diversify their revenue streams. More programs for nonlawyers, undergraduates, practicing attorneys, and foreign graduate students are obvious options.[121] Debt burdens for students could also be reduced by allowing them to attend after three years of college, as a few law schools now do.[122]

Structure

A further way of reducing the cost of at least some law schools would be for state supreme courts to eliminate the requirement that only graduates from ABA-accredited law schools may sit for the bar exam. In a Montana Supreme Court decision denying the request of a graduate of an unaccredited California law school to take the bar exam, two dissenting justices pointed out that "[n]o empirical data has been offered to suggest that the ABA standards correlate in any way to a quality legal education. What is evident is that the monopoly given to this private trade association to set standards for law schools increases the cost of legal education, [and] burdens new members with debt that limits their options for professional and public service. . . ."[123] As Brian Tamanaha argues, if a substantial number of states eliminated the requirement of an ABA-accredited legal education, the result would likely be to force greater price competition between lower-ranked schools and unaccredited institutions that are now one-third the cost.[124] Although graduates of unaccredited schools have much lower bar exam pass rates than graduates of accredited schools, it is hard to know how much of the difference is due to the caliber of the students and how much to the quality of educational preparation. In any event, a significant percentage of graduates of institutions that lack ABA accreditation do ultimately pass the bar, and this method of qualification is one way of making legal education affordable for those of limited means.[125]

Reducing the price of legal education more generally would become far easier if the influence of the *U.S. News and World Report* ranking system were challenged and if accreditation requirements were significantly curtailed. Law schools could work together with bar organizations to create an evaluation structure that did not use expenditures and vague reputational surveys as a proxy for quality. Instead of imposing the same requirements on all schools, accreditation authorities could take account of different institutional missions and priorities. As an ABA Task Force on the Future of Legal Education noted,

> The system of legal education would be better with more room for different models. Variety and a culture encouraging variety could facilitate innovation in programs and services; increase educational choices for students; lessen status competition; and aid the adaptation of schools to changing market and other external conditions.[126]

Just as higher education offers a range of choices, from community colleges to elite Ivy League institutions, legal education should provide greater diversity. To that end, accrediting authorities could eliminate uniform standards for matters such as facilities, adjunct teaching, distance learning, and faculty research support.[127] Institutions could vary in the specialties they offered, in their reliance on lower-cost adjuncts and online courses, and in the relative importance they attached to practical skills and legal scholarship. Giving students more options might reduce the regressive aspects of the current structure, which imposes crushing debts to subsidize the research and light teaching loads of relatively well-off faculty.

Schools could also offer a variety of degree options based on one-, two-, and three-year degree programs. States could license graduates of one-year programs to offer routine legal services. The ABA Task Force took a step in that direction by recommending that state authorities develop licensing systems for limited law-related services, and that accrediting authorities develop standards for programs preparing limited-service providers.[128] States could also license lawyers after two years to practice in a particular specialty, such as tax, family, or criminal law. In effect, the bar could move closer to other professions, such as medicine, which certify practitioners based on their extent of training.[129]

Proposals for more diversity in legal education are nothing new. A prominent 1921 report for the Carnegie Foundation by Alfred Reed recommended adoption of a two-tiered system. Full-time programs would train highly qualified lawyers to serve corporate and governmental clients; part-time programs and night schools would prepare general practitioners to meet routine legal needs.[130] By institutionalizing this division, the profession could accommodate concerns of both accessibility and quality. Again in 1972, the Carnegie Foundation produced another report, modeled on Paul Carrington's recommendations to the Association of American Law Schools. It proposed a two-year standard curriculum available to students after three years of college. It would provide graduates with a grounding in core subjects and opportunities for intensive instruction in professional skills. An advanced curriculum would be available to students who wanted a third year, and that year could also be completed in noncontinuous units after leaving law school.[131] The ABA flatly rejected both the Reed and Carrington proposals.[132] The only way that accredited schools can now offer a two-year program is to compress three years of credit-hours into two. Schools that do so charge the same tuition as three-year institutions, which significantly reduces the cost savings that a shorter program is designed to offer.

Proposals for a two-year degree have recently resurfaced, most prominently by President Obama. In a town hall meeting discussing how to make education more affordable, Obama said that "law schools would probably be wise to think about being two years instead of three. . . . The third year [students] would be better off clerking or practicing in a firm even if they weren't getting paid that much, but that step alone would reduce the costs for the student." While acknowledging that eliminating a third year could hurt a school's finances, the President added, "Now the question is can law schools maintain quality and keep good professors and sustain themselves without that third year? My suspicion is, that if they thought creatively about it, they probably could."[133] That proposal resonated with a growing number of commentators who have recommended letting students sit for the bar after two years of school, or replacing the third year with apprenticeships or externships at a nonprofit organization or governmental agency.[134]

Such proposals set off a firestorm of protest. Georgetown law professor Philip Schrag worried that "new lawyers would be exposed only to basic survey courses and would receive little of the specialized training that their future clients will need."[135] U.C. Irvine Dean Erwin Chemerinsky predicted, "If law school were two years, the first things to be cut would be clinical education and interdisciplinary courses, which are the best innovations since I went to law school in the mid-1970s."[136] Yale law professor Bruce Ackerman similarly claimed that shortening the degree requirements would

impoverish American public life. Once two-year graduates move into practice, they won't be able to deal adequately with bread-and-butter issues of antitrust, intellectual property, or corporate law, let alone with the challenges of civil rights or environmental law. It is frivolous to suppose that these lawyers would pick up the key skills on the job. Social science and statistics require systematic training, not a crash course in response to particular problems. . . . A two-year curriculum promises to lobotomize the profession by 2050.[137]

As columnist Paul Lippe responded,

I actually agree with the things Professor Ackerman says law schools should emphasize, but I saw nothing in his essay that suggested that they couldn't be addressed in a two-year curriculum, or that debt-strapped law students should continue to cross-subsidize his scholarship to a level that compromises their long-term financial solvency, or that the Yale model should be mandatory for all schools, which would be a pretty command-and-control way of looking at what could be a market choice.[138]

The fundamental issue is not whether there are benefits from a third year of training. It is whether the benefits are so critical that *all* students should be required to bear the costs. According to two-thirds of recent graduates, the traditional three-year law school education can be condensed into two years without negatively affecting the practice-readiness of new attorneys.[139] If bar exams were correspondingly condensed to test fewer doctrinal subjects, the task of paring down the law school experience would be easier.[140] Even as things stand, one- or two-year programs could well be sufficient to train graduates in areas where unmet legal needs are now greatest. In other nations, many of those needs are effectively met by specialists with less legal training than lawyers.[141]

Moreover, as federal judge and law professor Richard Posner argues, opening the legal academy to greater innovation and competition among different models is likely to produce a better educational experience.[142] Law schools would face greater pressure to demonstrate, not simply assert, the cost-effectiveness of their particular approach. If employers perceive a difference in quality among the graduates of two- and three-year programs, or in the schools that produce them, students will respond accordingly.

Curricula

Fundamental changes in the structure of law schools could prompt similarly fundamental changes in their curricula. Rather than taking the existing core courses for granted, educators should consider what competencies are necessary for legal practice and then adjust requirements accordingly. Such an approach would argue for greater focus on practical skills.[143] At a minimum, as the Clinical Legal Education Association has recommended, all students should be required to complete at least one clinical course or externship before they graduate.[144] If schools decline to impose such requirements, state supreme courts could do it for them.[145]

Models for more practice-oriented initiatives are readily available.[146] Northwestern Law School undertook its own analysis of "foundational core competencies" that legal employers desired, and developed a two-year program that stresses skills in project management, teamwork, communication, leadership, and quantitative analysis.[147] New Hampshire has begun granting licenses to students who are certified "client ready" after taking a two-year practice-oriented program at the state's only law school.[148] Participants take courses in negotiation, counseling, and trial and pretrial advocacy, along with a clinic or externship and electives in areas such as evidence, tax, and business associations.[149] Other schools have implemented changes in the third year that seek to reverse the decline in preparation and attendance that occurs during that year.[150] Reforms include subject-matter concentrations, experiential curricula, and capstone courses that aim to bridge the transition into practice.[151] More schools are sharing courses through local partnerships or online collaborations, and more are integrating interdisciplinary materials.[152] Yet despite the enormous effort that has gone into designing these initiatives, systematic evaluations of their effectiveness are unavailable. Such assessment should be a priority for any institution committed to curricular innovation.

Values

There is, however, a considerable body of research on teaching ethical analysis that can guide reform. It points up the value of experiential, interactive, and problem-oriented approaches.[153] Clinics are an especially effective way of teaching legal ethics; engagement tends to be greatest when students are dealing with real people facing real problems.[154] Ethical judgment in such settings demands more than knowledge of relevant rules and principles; it also demands a capacity to understand how those rules apply and which principles are most important in concrete settings.[155] When clinics involve clients from disadvantaged backgrounds, students can gain cross-cultural competence and an understanding of what passes for justice among the have-nots.[156] Although clinical courses necessarily address ethical issues that arise during the semester, not all clinicians have the time, interest, or expertise to provide comprehensive coverage of professional responsibility. Building in additional hours or linking a separate course to clinics may be necessary to ensure such coverage. Regardless of the approach chosen for the core professional responsibility course, it should not be the only site for sustained ethical analysis. Students are much more likely to take professional obligations seriously if the entire faculty does so as well. Every law school should provide incentives and accountability for the integration of ethical issues across the curriculum.

Schools should assume similar responsibility for supporting access to justice and pro bono service. Attention to these issues should be part of the core curriculum. Well-supported extracurricular programs concerning pro bono service can offer a wide range of practical skills as well as exposure to the urgency of unmet legal needs. For these reasons, the Association of American Law Schools Commission appropriately recommended that schools make available for every law student at least one well-supervised pro bono opportunity and either require student participation or find ways of encouraging the great majority of students to volunteer.[157] Schools should also do more to provide adequate support for student placements and to encourage and showcase public service by faculty.[158] As research on altruism makes clear, individuals learn more by example than by exhortation.[159] If law schools want to inspire a commitment to pro bono work among future practitioners, then professors need to lead the way, and legal academia needs to reward them for doing so. And if schools fail to take the initiative, courts can assume that role. New York has set an example by requiring applicants to the bar to complete 50 hours of service as a condition of admission, and California is poised to follow suit.[160]

Schools also need to do more to create cultures in which inclusiveness is valued in practice as well as principle. Every law school should have a formal structure that assigns responsibility for diversity issues. That responsibility should include gathering information about the experience of students and faculty and the diversity-related policies that affect them.[161] Workshops or teaching initiatives that assist faculty in creating more inclusive classroom climates should be priorities.

All of these curricular reform efforts need to include incentives for change. They should reward faculty who integrate ethical issues, supply sufficient student feedback, and use teaching methods that have been shown to be most effective.[162] Annual reports, peer assessments, and student evaluations could be used to hold faculty accountable for the quality of the educational experience, which too often now is valued more in theory than in practice.

Law schools would also benefit from strategies designed to help students cope with the stress and competition of legal education and legal practice. Efforts along these lines are beginning at a number of institutions.[163] More innovation and evaluation is needed. Given that a third of lawyers suffer from mental health or substance abuse problems, legal educators can ill afford to ignore the dysfunctions that begin in law school.[164]

Law Reviews

An obvious response to frustrations with student-run journals is to encourage more peer-reviewed substitutes. That, however, seems unlikely, given the economic challenges of academic publishing and schools' interest in subsidizing journals of pedagogic value to their students. Assuming the current model remains dominant, a recent empirical study of law professors, student editors, attorneys, and judges identified ways to improve the editorial process. One is for student editors to rely on blind reviews and to consult with faculty in selecting articles to publish.[165] Another is more training for student editors concerning selection and editing. Such training could help reduce the excessive length and references that have made articles so off-putting to nonacademic audiences.

This is not a modest agenda. Nor is this a context in which anything "short of everything will really do."[166] The cost, design, and reward structure of contemporary legal education work reasonably well for faculty, but fall seriously short in meeting the needs of students and society. The recent chorus of "crisis" rhetoric should remind us of our obligation to do better.

7

Conclusion

MY INTEREST IN ISSUES of professional regulation and access to justice spans four decades. As a Yale law student in the mid-1970s, I became enmeshed in a controversy over unauthorized practice of law. I was an intern in a legal aid office that was overwhelmed with routine divorce cases. The office's strategy was to accept new cases only one day a month, leaving the vast majority of poor people with no lawyer and no decent alternative. For a standard uncontested divorce case, attorneys in private practice charged what would now be $2000 to $3000 for completing three forms and attending a hearing that lasted an average of four minutes.[1] There were no kits for litigants trying to represent themselves until the legal aid office prepared one. In response, local bar association officials threatened to file charges of unauthorized practice of law. Under existing precedents, they had a good chance of winning. That ended that, as far as the legal aid office was concerned. I was outraged, and began work on an empirical study that challenged the bar's justifications for banning do-it-yourself assistance. I have returned to the subject with regularity over the succeeding decades.[2] Much has changed, but too much has remained the same. Kits and form-processing services are now readily available. Yet prevailing doctrine still bans personalized advice, including even the correction of obvious errors and omissions.[3] And millions of Americans remain priced out of legal services for routine but pressing needs.

No one proposing fundamental reforms in how the legal profession addresses such issues should be naïve about all that stands in the way. The bar is a conservative entity, with substantial control over its own regulation. Although lawyers are paid to solve problems for clients, they have been oddly passive when confronting problems in their own profession. And their independence from public involvement and accountability has shielded them from competition and innovation. The central premise of this book is that the profession can no longer afford such an insular perspective and that the public can no longer afford to leave issues of lawyer regulation solely in the hands of the organized bar.

The reforms necessary to meet contemporary challenges fall into two main categories. One involves priorities. Money needs to play a less prominent role in shaping the conditions of practice and access to justice. As Chapter 2 indicated, many lawyers overvalue the importance of financial success in determining personal satisfaction. This may be a tough message to sell in a culture as materialistic as that of the United States. But the bar's preoccupation with profit has taken a substantial toll on quality of life, and the key to greater fulfillment lies in revaluing professional reward structures. Diversity, work/family balance, and opportunities for pro bono service all should assume higher priority. Most of all, the profession needs to become more informed and reflective about the conditions that make for professional satisfaction, and less willing to settle for workplaces that fall short.

Money also needs to figure more substantially in debates over access to justice. The current plight of indigent criminal and civil litigants is an embarrassment to any civilized nation, let alone one that considers itself a world leader on the rule of law. There is no substitute for a greater societal and professional commitment to funding criminal defense and civil legal aid. Nor is there any excuse for the bar's inadequate levels of pro bono service, particularly at the nation's leading law firms. At a minimum, every lawyer should meet the ABA's modest standard of an hour a week or the financial equivalent. Courts should recognize a right to civil counsel in cases involving basic human needs, and ensure that funding is available to support it. Forty-nine countries recognize such a right, so models for workable standards are not in short supply.

A second cluster of reforms involves changes in the bar's regulatory structure. We need both less and more oversight. Fewer restrictions are in order on matters such as nonlawyer providers, multijurisdictional and multidisciplinary practice, nonlawyer investment, and law school accreditation. Although all of these issues call for some regulation, greater latitude should be available for market competition. Nonlawyer providers should be subject to licensing provisions that ensure basic competence and compliance with ethical rules. Lawyers with cross-jurisdictional practices should be subject to governance by their home state, but protectionist prohibitions on activities in other states should be replaced by an open-borders policy. Multidisciplinary practice and nonlawyer investment in law firms should be permitted, subject to reasonable conditions. On all of these issues, the bar should learn from the experience of other countries that have successfully implemented such reforms.

Legal education would also benefit from more innovation and competition. The current one-size-fits-all model of accreditation is ill suited to the realities of contemporary practice. The diversity in lawyers' work should be matched by diversity in their educational preparation. One-year, two-year, and three-year programs should be permitted, and schools should be allowed to vary in their priorities and in the balance that they strike between teaching and scholarship.

By contrast, more rigorous regulation is necessary regarding bar discipline and continuing legal education. Bar oversight should be strengthened for common client complaints, and lawyers should be required to carry malpractice insurance. The disciplinary system should be more proactive, and more focused on the causes of misconduct, not simply the symptoms. Continuing legal education should be taken more seriously. A mandatory CLE program for new lawyers and lawyers guilty of professional misconduct should be combined with a more demanding voluntary certification system for other lawyers.

This is not a modest agenda, and substantial obstacles stand in its way. State supreme courts' assertion of inherent authority to regulate the practice of law and their deference to professional interests remain major impediments to reform. But recent changes in the legal market and increasing challenges for law schools make this a particularly opportune time to rethink current norms. Given the levels of lawyer dissatisfaction and dysfunction, the declining enrollments and rising costs of legal education, and the cottage industry of criticism from within and outside the bar, change is clearly in order. And lawyers are capable of rising to the occasion. They have been at the forefront of every major movement for social justice in this nation's history. The time has come for them to turn more energy inward. They must demand a profession more capable of satisfying their highest aspirations to personal fulfillment and public service.

NOTES

Chapter 1

1. Steven J. Harper, *The Lawyer Bubble* (2013); Michael Trotter, *Declining Prospects* (2012); James E. Moliterno, *The American Legal Profession in Crisis: Resistance and Responses to Change* (2012); Richard Susskind, *The End of Lawyers* (2010); Thomas Morgan, *The Vanishing American Lawyer* (2010); Douglas Litowitz, *The Destruction of Young Lawyers: Beyond One L* (2006); Sol M. Linowitz with Martin Mayer, *The Betrayed Profession: Lawyering at the End of the Twentieth Century* (1994); Anthony Kronman, *The Lost Lawyer: Failing Ideals of the Legal Profession* (1993).

2. Gallup opinion poll, Honesty/Ethics in Professions, Nov. 26–29, 2012.

3. Sheldon Kranz, *The Legal Profession: What Is Wrong and How to Fix It* 1 (2013).

4. Samantha Melamed, For College Grads, Nannying Is Not Such a Bad Deal, Philly.com, Apr. 24, 2014, available at http://articles.philly.com/2014-04-24/entertainment/49351220_1_college-grads-labor-market-rough-job-market.

5. Ethan Bronner, Right to Lawyer Can Be Empty Promise for Poor, *N.Y. Times*, Mar. 16, 2013, available at http://www.nytimes.com/2013/03/16/us/16gideon.html?pagewanted=all&_r=0. Presley eventually found a lawyer from the Southern Center for Human Rights who provided such assistance.

6. Ellie Mystal, Departure Memo of the Day: Parenting Gets the Best of One Big Law Associate, Above the Law, Nov. 8, 2012, available at http://abovethelaw.com/2012/11/departure-memo-of-the-day-parenting-gets-the-best-of-one-big-law-associate/.

Chapter 2

1. *The Economist*, May 7, 2011, at 73.

2. For an exploration of these themes, see Anthony Kronman, *The Lost Lawyer: Failing Ideals of the Legal Profession* (1992).

3. In one American Bar Association study, 69 percent of lawyers saw declining civility and 90 percent of lawyers in large firms found competition between firms increasing. Stephanie Francis Ward, Pulse of the Legal Profession, *ABA J.*, Oct. 2007, at 31–32. See also Jeffrey A. Parness, Civility Initiatives: The 2009 Allerton House Conference, *96 Ill. B. J.* 636, 637 (Dec. 2008) (judges and lawyers agreed that there has been a significance increase in instances of incivility in civil litigation in the last decade).

4. NLJ 350: Our Annual Survey of the Nation's Largest Law Firms, *Nat'l L. J.*, Jun. 10, 2013 (which gives a figure of 4036). See Steven J. Harper, *The Lawyer Bubble* 69 (2013) (over 4200 in 2012).

5. William Henderson, From Big Law to Lean Law, *3 Int'l Rev. L. & Econ.* 1 (2013).

6. Thomas Morgan, *The Vanishing American Lawyer* 81 (2010). In 1950, there was one lawyer for every 687 Americans; today there is one for every 254. Benjamin Barton, *Glass Half Full: America's Lawyer Crisis and Its Upside* (forthcoming, 2015).

7. See Chapter 6.

8. Paul Campos, *Don't Go to Law School (Unless)* 5–6 (2013).

9. Norm Scheiber, The Last Days of Big Law, *New Republic*, Jul. 21, 2013.

10. *Bates v. Arizona State Bar*, 433 U.S. 350 (1977); *Zauderer v. Office of Disciplinary Counsel*, 471 U.S. 626 (1985); *Shapiro v. Kentucky Bar Association*, 486 U.S. 466 (1988).

11. Richard Susskind, *The End of Lawyers* (2010); Henderson, From Big Law to Lean Law.

12. Richard Susskind, *Tomorrow's Lawyers: An Introduction to Your Future* 3 (2013); Susskind, *The End of Lawyers*.

13. Rachel M. Zahorsky & William D. Henderson, Who's Eating Law Firms' Lunch? *ABA J.*, Oct. 2013, at 34.

14. Kim Isaac Eisler, *Shark Tank: Greed, Politics, and the Collapse of Finley Kumble, One of America's Largest Law Firms* 84 (1990).

15. Chris Klein, Big Firm Partners: Profession Sinking, *Nat'l L. J.*, May 26, 1997.

16. René Reich-Graefe, Keep Calm and Carry On, *27 Geo. J. Legal Ethics* 55, 63–66 (2014). For claims that the death of big law has been overstated for decades, see Mark Obbie, The Fascinating Vampire Squids of Law, *Slate*, Jul. 24, 2013, http://www.slate.com/articles/news_and_politics/jurisprudence/2013/07/death_of_big_law_new_republic_s_claim_is_grossly_exaggerated.html.

17. LexisNexis, *State of the Legal Industry Survey: Complete Survey Findings* 10 (2009).

18. Larry E. Ribstein, The Death of Big Law, 2010 *Wisc. L. Rev.* 749, 775.

19. William D. Henderson, More Complex than Greed, *Am. Law. Daily*, May 29, 2012.

20. Ribstein, The Death of Big Law, at 755–756; Barton, *Glass Half Full*; William D. Henderson & Leonard Beirman, An Empirical Analysis of Lateral Lawyer Trends from 2000 to 2007: The Emerging Equilibrium for Corporate Law Firms, *22 Geo. J. Legal Ethics* 1395 (2009); Harper, *The Lawyer Bubble*, at 70; Ben W. Heineman, Jr., William F. Lee, & David B. Wilkins, Lawyers as Professionals and Citizens: Key Roles and Responsibilities in the 21st Century 35 (2014).

21. Deborah L. Rhode, *In the Interests of Justice: Reforming the Legal Profession* 35 (2000); Ashby Jones, Law-Firm Life Doesn't Suit Some Associates, *Wall St. J.*, May 23, 2006, at B6.

22. Marie Beaudette, Associates Leave Firm in Droves, *Nat'l L. J.*, Oct. 6, 2003, at A1 (quoting Mark Plotkin).

23. Patrick J. Schlitz, On Being a Happy, Healthy, and Ethical Member of an Unhappy, Unhealthy, and Unethical Profession, *52 Vand. L. Rev.* 871 (1999).

24. Nancy Levit & Douglas O. Linder, *The Happy Lawyer: Making a Good Life in the Law* 54 (2010); Harper, *The Lawyer Bubble*, at 78.

25. Harper, *The Lawyer Bubble*, at 97.

26. Jonathan Foreman, My Life as an Associate, *City J.*, Winter 1997.

27. Marc S. Galanter & William D. Henderson, The Change Agenda: Tournament Without End, *Am. Law.*, Dec. 2008 (quoting Kramer).

28. David L. Chambers, Overstating the Satisfaction of Lawyers, *39 Law & Soc. Inq.* 1, 18 (2013).

29. Jerome M. Organ, *What Do We Know About the Satisfaction/ Dissatisfaction of Lawyers? A Meta-Analysis of Research on Lawyer Satis*faction and Well-Being, *8 U. St. Thomas L. J.* 225, 262 (2011).

30. Bryant Garth & Ronit Dinovitzer, Satisfaction, in *After the JD III* 50 (Gabriele Plickert, ed., 2014); Ronit Dinovitzer et al., *After the JD II: Second Results From a National Study of Legal Careers* (2009).

31. National Opinion Research Center, Job Satisfaction in the United States (2007).

32. Alan B. Krueger, Job Satisfaction Is Not Just a Matter of Dollars, *N.Y. Times*, Dec. 8, 2005, at C3.

33. Debra Cassnes Weiss, "Lawyer" Ranks 51st in US News List of Best Jobs in America, Down from 35th, *ABA J.*, Jan. 27, 2014.

34. On the Job, *Time*, Oct. 30, 2006.

35. Stephanie Ward, The Pulse of the Profession, at 34 (finding that 80 percent are proud, but only 44 percent would make the recommendation).

36. For surveys, see Levit & Linder, *The Happy Lawyer*, at 4; Becky Beaupre Gillespie & Hollee Schwartz Temple, Hunting Happy, *ABA J.*, Feb. 2011, at 41.

37. Chambers, Overstating the Satisfaction of Lawyers, at 7.

38. National Association for Law Placement (NALP), Update on Associate Attrition 11 (2006). See Kristin K. Stark & Blane Prescott, Why Associates Leave, *Legal Times,* May 7, 2007; National Association for Law Placement (NALP), Toward Effective Management of Associate Mobility 26 (2005) (40 percent leave within three years; 78 percent within five years).

39. See studies reviewed in Levit & Linder, *The Happy Lawyer,* at 6; Fred C. Zacharias, A Word of Caution for Lawyer Assistance Programs, *18 Geo. J. Legal Ethics* 237, 237 n1, 241 n15 (2004) (reviewing studies); Sue Shellenbarger, Even Lawyers Get the Blues: Opening Up About Depression, *Wall St. J.,* Dec. 13, 2007, at D1 (noting that about 19 percent of lawyers suffer from depression compared with 7 percent of the population, and 20 percent suffer from alcohol abuse, compared with 10 percent of the population). See Debra Cassins Weiss, Lawyer Depression Comes Out of the Closet, *ABA J.,* Dec. 2007; Jean Guiccione, Attorneys Find Defense Against Dependence, *L.A. Times,* Aug. 30, 2002, at B2.

40. Mark B. Schenker et al., Self-Reported Stress and Reproductive Health of Female Lawyers, *39 J. Occup. & Envt'l Med.* 556 (1997); Susan Saab Fortney, The Billable Hours Derby: Empirical Data on the Problems and Pressure Points, *33 Fordham Urb. L. J.* 171, 183 (2005).

41. See Deborah L. Rhode, *Balanced Lives: Changing the Culture of Workplace Practices* 20 (2002).

42. Rhode, *Balanced Lives,* at 21; Patti Giglio, Rethinking the Hours, *Legal Times,* Nov. 8, 2004, at 33; Stark & Prescott, Why Associates Leave, at 45; Cynthia Thomas Calvert, Linda Bray Chanow, & Linda Marks, Reduced Hours, Full Success: Part-Time Partners in U.S. Law Firms, *21 Hastings Women's L. J.* 223, 225 (2010).

43. Ronit Dinovitzer & Bryant Garth, Lawyer Satisfaction in the Process of Structuring Legal Careers, *41 Law & Soc'y Rev.* 1 (2007).

44. Zacharias, A Word of Caution, at 241 n15; Nick Badgerow, Apocalypse at Law: The Four Horsemen of the Modern Bar—Drugs, Alcohol, Gambling, and Depression, *18 Prof. Law.* 1 (2007).

45. Martin Moore-Ede, *The Twenty-Four-Hour Society: Understanding Human Limits in a World That Never Stops* 133 (1993); Yvonne Harrison & James Horne, The Impact of Sleep Deprivation on Decision Making: A Review, *6 J. Exp. Psych. Applied* 236 (2000); Susan Saab Fortney, Soul for Sale: An Empirical Study of Associate Satisfaction, Law Firm Culture, and the Effects of Billable Hour Requirements *58 UMKCI* 238, 273 (2000) (two-thirds of respondents agreed that working long hours adversely affects their ability to think critically and creatively).

46. Ward, The Pulse of the Legal Profession; Organ, What Do We Know About the Satisfaction/Dissatisfaction of Lawyers, at 265; Garth & Dinovitzer, Satisfaction.

47. Dinovitzer & Garth, *After the JD.*

48. Organ, What Do We Know About the Satisfaction/Dissatisfaction of Lawyers, at 265–266.

49. Ronit Dinovitzer et al., *After the JD: First Results of a National Study of Legal Careers* 64 (2004).

50. Dinovitzer et al., *After the JD,* at 58; ABA Commission on Women in the Profession, A Current Glance at Women in the Law 2 (2006); studies cited in Theresa Beiner, Not All Lawyers Are Equal: Difficulties That Plague Women and Women of Color, *58 Syr. L. Rev.* 317, 321 n21 (2008).

51. Vivia Chen, He Said, She Said, *Am. Law.,* Sept. 2013, at 44.

52. If their average ratings "were expressed as grades, . . . women of color would have given their [career] a B- or C plus; white men would have given their experience an A, and white women and men of color would have given theirs a B." Beiner, Not All Lawyers Are Equal, at 329. See also ABA Commission on Women in the Profession, Invisible Visibility: Women of Color in Law Firms and Minority Experience Study, discussed in D. M. Osborne, The Woman Question, *Am. Law.,* Nov. 2007, at 106 (noting that minority women gave firms lower ratings in quality of work, satisfaction with work, and professional growth).

53. Dinovitzer & Garth, Lawyer Satisfaction, at 8.

54. Organ, What Do We Know About the Satisfaction/Dissatisfaction of Lawyers, at 264.

55. David T. Lykken & Auke Tellegen, Happiness Is a Stochastic Phenomenon, *7 Psych. Sci.* 186 (1996); Edward Diener et al., Subjective Well-Being: Three Decades of Progress, *125 Psych. Bull.* 276 (1999); Kennon M. Sheldon & Sonja Lyubomirsky, Achieving Sustainable Gains in Happiness: Change Your Actions, Not Your Circumstances, *7 J. Happiness Stud.* 55, 56 (2006); Levit & Linder, *The Happy Lawyer,* at 42.

56. Martin E. P. Seligman, Why Lawyers Are Unhappy, *23 Cardozo L. Rev.* 1, 34 (2001); Levit & Linder, *The Happy Lawyer,* at 75. For an overview of lawyers' personality types, see Susan Daicoff, *Lawyer, Know Thyself: A Psychological Analysis of Personality Strengths and Weaknesses* (2004); Susan Daicoff, Lawyer, Know Thyself: A Review of Empirical Research on Attorney Attributes Bearing on Professionalism, *46 Am. U. L. Rev.* 1337 (1997). For the importance of optimism, see Edward Diener et al. Subjective Well Being: Three Decades of Progress, *125 Psych. Bull.* 276 (1999).

57. David T. Lykken, *Happiness: The Nature and Nurture of Joy and Contentment* 60 (2000); Sheldon & Lyubomirsky, Achieving Sustainable Gains in Happiness 55, 57–58, 60 (2006).

58. Levit & Linder, *The Happy Lawyer*, at 44; William C. Compton, *Introduction to Positive Psychology* 48–49, 53–54 (2004); Kennon M. Sheldon, What Is Satisfying About Satisfying Events? Testing 10 Candidate Psychological Needs, *80 J. Personality & Soc. Psych.* 325, 325–327 (2001); Diener et al., Subjective Well-Being, at 276.

59. David G. Myers, *The Pursuit of Happiness* 32–38 (1992); David G. Myers & Edward Diener, Who is Happy? *6 Psych. Sci.* 13 (1995); surveys reviewed in Deborah L. Rhode, *In the Interests of Justice* 26 (1999). For discussion of strengths and virtues, see Compton, *Introduction to Positive Psychology*, at 170–172; C. Peterson & Martin P. Seligman, *Character Strengths and Virtues: A Handbook and Classification* (2004).

60. Laura Nash & Howard Stevenson, Success That Lasts, *Harv. Bus. Rev. Rev.*, Feb. 2004, at 104. See also Laura Nash & Howard Stevenson, *Just Enough: Tools for Creating Success in Your Work and Life* (2004).

61. Nash & Stevenson, *Just Enough*.

62. See research summarized in Alan Luks with Peggy Payne, *The Healing Power of Doing Good* xi–xii, 17–18, 45–54, 60 (2d ed., 2001); John Wilson & Marc Musick, The Effects of Volunteering, *62 Law & Contemp. Probs.* 141, 142–143 (1999); Marc A. Musick, A. Regula Herzog, & James S. House, Volunteering and Mortality Among Older Adults: Findings From a National Sample, *548 J. Gerontol.* S173, S178 (1999); John M. Darley, Altruism and Prosocial Behavior Research: Reflections and Prospects, in *Prosocial Behavior* 312–327 (Margaret S. Clark, ed., 1991).

63. Deborah L. Rhode, *Pro Bono in Principle and in Practice* 29–30 (2005); Deborah L. Rhode, Profits and Professionalism, *33 Fordham Urb. L. J.* 49, 58 (2005).

64. Allen K. Roston, Lawyers, Law and the Movies: The Hitchock Cases, *86 Cal. L. Rev.* 211, 214 (1998).

65. Dinovitzer & Garth, Lawyer Satisfaction; see also K. Charles Cannon, *The Ultimate Guide to Your Legal Career* 4, 9 (2007) (noting the disillusionment of associates trapped in tedious document review who feel "this is not what they went to Harvard Law School for").

66. Seligman, Why Lawyers Are Unhappy, at 47–48 (discussing adversarial nature of practice); Ward, Pulse of the Profession, at 31 (noting that 69 percent of lawyers believe that the profession has become less civil); Walt Bachman, *Law vs. Life: What Lawyers Are Afraid to Say About the Legal Profession* 117 (1995) (describing acrimony).

67. Douglas O. Linder & Nancy Levit, *The Good Lawyer: Seeking Quality in the Practice of Law*, 108 (2014).

68. Levit & Linder, *The Happy Lawyer*, at 65.

69. National Association for Law Placement [NALP], Toward Effective Management of Associate Mobility: A Status Report on Attrition 35–36, 39, 42(2005); NALP, Update on Associate Attrition 25 (2006).

70. Ward, The Pulse of the Profession, at 32.

71. ABA Young Lawyers Division, Career Satisfaction Survey 20 (2000); ABA Young Lawyers Division, Career Satisfaction Survey 11 (1995).

72. ABA Young Lawyers Division, Career Satisfaction Survey 17 (2000).

73. Cannon, *The Ultimate Guide*, at 13.

74. Richard Delgado & Jean Stefancic, *How Lawyers Lose Their Way* 15 (2005).

75. Dinovitzer et al., *After the JD*, at 49.

76. Rhode, *Pro Bono*, at 147–148.

77. Rhode, *Pro Bono*, at 20, 148; ABA Standing Committee on Pro Bono and Public Service, Supporting Justice II: A Report on the Pro Bono Work of America's Lawyers (2013). The ABA study used an extremely broad definition of pro bono, based on Model Rule 6.1, which included participation in bar association activities.

78. Rhode, *Pro Bono*, at 138–140.

79. Lee Collum, *The New Yorker*, Oct. 30, 1998, available at http://www.Cartoonbank.com.

80. Joan Williams, *Unbending Gender* 71–73 (2000); Boston Bar Association Task Force on Work-Family Challenges, Facing the Grail: Confronting the Course of Work Family Imbalance 39 (1999); Catalyst, A New Approach to Flexibility: Managing the Work Time Equation 20–21 (1997). They spend over twice as much time on care of children as men, and over three times as much time on household tasks as men. U.S. Department of Labor, Bureau of Labor Statistics, American Time Use Survey, 2012; Ruth Davis Konigsberg, Chore Wars, *Time*, Aug. 8, 2011, at 47.

81. Jean E. Wallace, Juggling It All: Exploring Lawyers' Work, Home, and Family Demands and Coping Strategies 15 (Law School Admission Council Research Report, RR-00–02, Sept. 2002).

82. Sylvia Ann Hewlett & Carolyn Buck Luce, Off Ramps and On Ramps: Keeping Talented Women on the Road to Success, *Harv. Bus. Rev.*, Mar. 2005, at 43, 45 (of surveyed professional women who had opted out, a quarter failed to find acceptable jobs, and half failed to find full-time positions).

83. ABA Young Lawyers Division Survey, Career Satisfaction, Table 20 (2000).

84. Gregory J. Mazores, Association Retention for Law Firms: What Are Your Lawyers Saying About You? *29 Cap. U. L. Rev.* 903, 904 (2002) (finding that only a third of associates believe that lawyers at their firms are encouraged to create a balance between work and life outside it); Martha Neil, Lawyers Shun Firms' Offers of Part-Time Work, *Chi. L. Bull.,* Dec. 18, 2000, at 1 (suggesting that about half of surveyed practitioners doubt that their employers truly support flexible workplace arrangements).

85. Noam Scheiber, The Last Days of Big Law, *New Republic,* Jul. 21, 2013.

86. Almost half of women lawyers, and almost two-thirds of those working more than 45 hours a week, report such stress levels have adverse effects on reproductive health. Schenker et al., Self-Reported Stress and Reproductive Health of Female Lawyers. See also Mary Beth Grover, Daddy Stress, *Forbes,* Sept. 6, 1999, at 202 (noting problems for men). Stress levels also adversely affect happiness. Gregg Easterbrook, *The Progress Paradox: How Life Gets Better While People Feel Worse* 191 (2003). For general discussion of the costs of excessive workloads, see Sylvia Ann Hewlett & Carolyn Buck Luce, Extreme Jobs: The Dangerous Allure of the 70-Hour Workweek, *Harv. Bus. Rev.,* Dec. 2006; Jill Andresky Fraser, *White-Collar Sweatshop* 36–37 (2001); Families and Work Institute, Feeling Overworked: When Work Becomes Too Much 5–8 (2001).

87. Daniel Kahneman et al., Would You Be Happier if You Were Richer? A Focusing Illusion, *312 Science* 1908 (2006); Christopher K. Hsee & Reid Hastie, Decision and Experience: Why Don't We Choose What Makes Us Happy, *10 Trends Cogn. Sci.* 31 (2006).

88. Seligman, *Authentic Happiness,* 49; Edward Diener, Richard E. Lucas, & Christie Napa Scollon, Beyond the Hedonic Treadmill: Revising the Adaptation Theory of Well-Being, *61 Am. Psych.* 305 (2006); Kennon M. Sheldon & Sonia Lyubomirsky, Achieving Sustainable Gains in Happiness: Change Your Actions, Not Your Circumstances, *7 J. Happiness Stud.* 55, 60 (2006); Edward Diener & Robert Biswas-Diener, Will Money Increase Subjective Well Being? A Literature Review and Guide to Needed Research, *57 Soc. Ind. Res.* 119 (2002).

89. Myers, *Pursuit of Happiness,* at 63.

90. Myers, *Pursuit of Happiness,* at 39.

91. Sonja Lyubomirsky, *The How of Happiness; A New Approach to Getting the Life You Want* 44 (2007); Eric Weiner, *The Geography of Bliss* 310 (2008).

92. David G. Myers & Ed Diener, Who Is Happy? *6 Psych. Sci.* 12, 13 (1995); Juliet B. Schur, *The Overspent American* 7 (1998); Robert F. Frank, *Luxury Fever* 72, 112–113 (1999); Rhode, *In the Interests of*

Justice, at 26; Levit & Linder, *The Happy Lawyer*, at 38–39; Matthew Herper, Money Won't Buy You Happiness, *Forbes*, Sept. 21, 2004, http://www.forbes.com/2004/09/21/cx_mh_0921happiness.html; Eric Quinones, Link Between Income and Happiness Is Mainly an Illusion, Jun. 29, 2006, http://www.princeton.edu/main/news/archive/S15/15/09S18/index.xml.

93. Frank, *Luxury Fever*, at 183; Robert E. Lane, Does Money Buy Happiness, *113 Pub. Int.* 56, 61, 63 (1993). See Daniel Gilbert, *Stumbling on Happiness* 217 (2006) (noting that people who earn $5 million are not much happier than those who earn $100,000).

94. Dinovitzer, *After the JD*, at 8, 10; Kenneth G. Dau-Schmidt & Kaushik Mukhopadhaya, The Fruits of Our Labors: An Empirical Study of the Distribution of Income and Job Satisfaction Across the Legal Profession, *49 J. Legal Educ.* 342, 346–347 (1999); Marc Galanter, Old and in the Way: The Coming Demographic Transformation of the Legal Profession and Its Implications for the Provision of Legal Services, 1999 *Wisc. L. Rev.* 1081, 1105–1106.

95. Lyubomirsky, *The How of Happiness*, at 17 (quoting Daniel Gilbert).

96. Seligman, *Authentic Happiness*, at xiii (arguing that pleasure is less related to enduring happiness than engagement in relationships and a sense of meaning, which involves using personal capacities to make a broader societal contribution); Herper, Money Won't Buy You Happiness; Jonathan Haidt, *The Happiness Hypothesis: Finding Modern Truth in Ancient Wisdom* 83 (2006) (noting how adaptation to improved material circumstances erodes their value).

97. Kahneman et al., Would You Be Happier, at 1910. See also Myers, *Pursuit of Happiness*, at 39 (noting that satisfaction is a function more of perceived than actual wealth); Compton, *Introduction to Positive Psychology*, at 62 (discussing perception of comparative well-being).

98. Robert H. Frank, How Not to Buy Happiness, *Daedelus*, Spring 2004, at 69–79. See also Compton, *Introduction to Positive Psychology*, at 62 (discussing social comparisons).

99. Levit & Linder, *The Happy Lawyer*, at 87.

100. Steven Brill, "Ruining" the Profession, *Am. Law.*, Jul./Aug. 1996, at 5.

101. Robert H. Frank & Philip J. Cook, *The Winner Take All Society: How More and More Americans Compete For Ever Fewer and Bigger Prizes, Encouraging Economic Waste, Income Inequality, and an Impoverished Cultural Life* 41, 66 (1995); O'Neil, *The Paradox of Success* 29–30 (1994); William R. Keates, *Proceed With Caution: A Diary of the First Year at One of America's Largest, Most Prestigious Law Firms* 144 (1997); Juliet B. Schor, *The Overspent American: Upscaling, Downshifting, and the New Consumer* 5–12 (1998); Mike Papantonio, Legal Egos on the Loose, *ABA J.*, Sept. 1999, at 108.

102. Vivia Chen, Rich Lawyer, Poor Lawyer, *Am. Law.*, Dec. 2007, at 15 (noting that lawyers in the "uberprivileged enclaves of New York and Silicon Valley" live in the shadow of financial investors who skew wealth comparisons upward).

103. For a discussion of the need to impress, see Richard Conniff, *The Natural History of the Rich: A Field Guide* 145 (2002).

104. Patrick J. Schlitz, On Being a Happy, Healthy, and Ethical Member of an Unhappy, Unhealthy, and Unethical Profession, *52 Vand. L. Rev.* 871, 903 (1999).

105. Michel Janati, A Nation Overworked: Abandoning Happiness and Health for Paychecks, *Wash. Times,* Apr. 22, 2012; Stark & Prescott, Why Associates Leave, at 45.

106. Sonja Lyubomirsky et al., The Benefits of Frequent Positive Affect: Does Happiness Lead to Success? *131 Psych. Bull.* 803, 822 (2005); Lyubomirsky, *The How of Happiness*, at 25; Peter Huang & Rick Swedloff, Authentic Happiness and Meaning at Law Firms, *58 Syr. L. Rev.* 335, 337 (2008) (citing studies); John M. Zelensky, Steven A. Murphy, & David A. Jenkins, The Happy-Productive Worker Thesis Revisited, *9 J. Happiness Stud.* 517, 533 (2008).

107. Nathan A. Bowling, Kevin J. Eschleman, & Qiang Wang, A Meta-Analytic Examination of the Relationship Between Job Satisfaction and Subjective Well-Being, *83 J. Occup. & Org. Psych.* 915 (2010).

108. Richard Ellsberry, The Family Friendly Office, *Off. Sys.,* Mar. 1, 1999, at 42; Mackenzie Carpenter, A Few Ounces of Prevention, *Pittsburgh Post Gazette*, Jun. 5, 1998, at A1; Keith Cunningham, Note, Father Time: Flexible Work Arrangements and Law Firms' Failure of the Family, *53 Stan. L. Rev.* 967, 1004 (2001).

109. Joan Williams, *Unbending Gender,* 112 (2001); Joan Williams, Canaries in the Mine: Work/Family Conflicts and the Legal Profession, *70 Fordham L. Rev.* 221, 227 (2007); Boston Bar Association Task Force on Work Family Challenges, Facing the Grail: Confronting the Causes of Work-Family Imbalance 25 (1999); Lotte Bailyn, *Breaking the Mold: Men, Women, and Time in the New Corporate World* 80–84 (1993); Linda Bray Chanow, Report for the Women's Bar Association of D.C., Lawyers, Work, and Family: A Study of Alternative Schedules at Law Firms in the District of Columbia 8 (2000); M. Diane Vogt and Lori-Ann Rickard, *Keeping Good Lawyers: Best Practices to Create Career Satisfaction,* 55 (2000).

110. John B. Heinz & Paul S. Schnorr, with Edward O. Laumann & Robert L. Nelson, Lawyers' Roles in Voluntary Associations: Declining Social Capital? *26 Law & Soc. Inq.* 597, 599 (2001); Jill Schachner Chanen, Pro Bono's Pros—and Cons: Rewards Are Great but It Takes a Deft Balance of Time and Effort, *ABA J.,* May 1998,

at 80; Donald W. Hoagland, Community Service Makes Better Lawyers, in *The Law Firm and the Public Good* 104, 109 (1995); Jack W. Londen, The Impact of Pro Bono Work on Law Firm Economics, *9 Geo. J. Legal Ethics* 925 (1996); Thomas J. Brannan, Pro Bono: By Choice or By Chance, *Ill. B. J.*, 481 (Sept. 1996); Ronald J. Tabak, Integration of Pro Bono into Law Firm Practice, *9 Geo. J. Legal Ethics* 931, 932 (1996).

111. Talcott J. Franklin, Practical Pro Bono: How Public Service Can Enhance Your Practice, *S.C. L.*, Feb. 1999, at 14, 19–20.

112. Peter D. Hart Research Associates, *A Survey of Attitudes Nationwide Toward Lawyers and the Legal System* 18 (1993).

113. For the decline in status, see Williams, *Unbending Gender*, at 1, 8–9; Debra Cassans Weiss, Legal Careers Lose Their Allure, Drop to Dentistry Status, *ABA J.-L. News,* Jan. 11, 2008, available at http://www.abajournal.com/news/legal_careers_lose_their_allure_drop_to_dentistry_status/. For the decline in applications, see Chapter 6.

114. Harry Frankfurt, The Importance of What We Care About, *53 Synthesis* 257 (1982).

115. Levit & Linder, *The Happy Lawyer*, at 105. For similar suggestions, see Martin E. P. Seligman, *Authentic Happiness: Using the New Positive Psychology to Realize Your Potential for Lasting Fulfillment* (2002); Huang & Swedloff, Authentic Happiness; Seligman & Steen, Positive Psychology Programs, *60 Am. Psych.* 410 (2005); Sheldon & Lyubormirsky, Achieving Sustainable Gains, at 82.

116. The student-run Building a Better Legal Profession considers diversity, billable hours, and pro bono activities. See Peter Schmidt, Advocates of Diversity Grasp for Ways to Drive Change in the Legal Profession, *Chronicle of Higher Education,* Nov. 27, 2007; G. M. Filisko, Students Aim for BigLaw Change, *ABA J.,* Dec. 2007, at 28. The *American Lawyer* A-List considers profitability, associate satisfaction, diversity, and pro bono work. See The A-List, *Am. Law.,* Jul. 2007, at 80.

117. Linda Babcock & Sara Laschever, *Women Don't Ask* 1–11 (2003). For other research on the forces that socialize women to avoid seeming pushy or aggressive, see Sheryl Sandberg, *Lean In: Women, Work, and the Will to Lead* (2013); Deborah L. Rhode & Barbara Kellerman, Women and Leadership: The State of Play, in *Women and Leadership: The State of Play and Strategies for Change* 7, 101 (Barbara Kellerman & Deborah L. Rhode, eds., 2007); Alice Eagly & Steven Karau, Role Congruity Theory of Prejudice toward Female Leaders, *109 Psych. Rev.* 573 (2002); Todd L. Pittinsky, Laura M. Bacon, & Brian Welle, The Great Women Theory of Leadership: Perils of Positive Stereotypes and Precarious Pedestals, in Kellerman & Rhode, *Women and Leadership*, at 101.

118. Kimberly A. Eddleston, David C. Baldridge, & John F. Veiga, Toward Modeling the Predictors of Managerial Career Success: Does Gender Matter? *19 Manage. Psychol.* 360 (2004).

119. Examples include women's networks within law firms, and bar association task forces that enlist legal employers to commit to hiring and advancement goals and timetables. See Rhode & Kellerman, *Women and Leadership,* at 1, 30, 34.

120. Levit & Linder, *The Happy Lawyer,* at 110.

121. For problems with diversity policies, see Kimberly Krawiec, Cosmetic Compliance and the Failure of Negotiated Governance, *81 Wash. L. Q.* 487 (2005). For the inadequacies in mentoring policies, see Katherine Giscombe & M. G. Mattis, Leveling the Playing Field for Women of Color in Corporate Management: Is the Business Case Enough? *37 J. Bus. Ethics* 103 (2002).

122. Rhode, *Pro Bono in Principle,* at 138–140. For the ABA's rule, see ABA Model Rules of Professional Conduct, Rule 6.1.

123. For examples of innovative arrangements see Natasha Sarkisian, Who Says Being a Lawyer Has to Suck?, *San Francisco Mag.,* Oct. 2007; Lisa Belkin, Who's Cuddly Now? Law Firms, *N.Y. Times,* Jan. 24, 2008, at G1, G8.

124. Leigh Jones, The Rise of the New Model Firm, *Nat'l L. J.,* May 21, 2007.

125. See http:www//.axiom.legal.com.

126. ABA Commission on Billable Hours, Report to the House of Delegates (2002).

127. Stark & Prescott, Why Associates Leave; NALP Foundation for Research and Education: Keeping the Keepers: Strategies for Associate Retention in a Time of Attrition 14 (1998).

128. Susan Saab Fortney, Soul for Sale, at 283; American Bar Association Commission on Women in the Profession, Visible Invisibility 18–19 (2012).

129. ABA Commission on Billable Hours Report 48 (2002).

130. For the importance of training and evaluating those in supervisory positions, see Stark & Prescott, Why Associates Leave; NALP, Effective Management, at 58–59.

131. For the value of 360-degree performance evaluations, see Elizabeth Goldberg, Playing Nice, *Am. Law.,* Aug. 2007, at 100.

132. Sheila M. Gutterman, *Collaborative Law: A New Model for Dispute Resolution* (2004); Sherrie R. Abney, *Avoiding Litigation: A Guide to Civil Collaborative Law* (2006); Pauline H. Tessler, *Collaborative Law: Achieving Effective Resolution in Divorce Without Litigation* (2001); Principles and Guidelines for the Practice of Collaborative Law, available at http://www.mediate.com/articles/coallabpg.cfm.

133. For clients' diversity efforts, see Deborah L. Rhode & Lucy Ricca, Diversity in the Legal Profession: Perspectives from Managing Partners and General Counsel, *Fordham L. Rev.* (forthcoming, 2015); Karen Donovan, Pushed By Clients, Law Firms Step Up Diversity Efforts, *N.Y. Times,* Jul. 21, 2006, at C1; Diversity Calls, *Cal. Law.,* Nov. 2005.

134. See Rhode, *Pro Bono*, at 168.

135. Laura Stiller Rickleen, *Ending the Gauntlet: Removing the Barriers to Women's Success in Law* 372–374 (2006) (discussing the San Francisco Glass Ceiling Initiative and the Chicago Bar Alliance for Women Call to Action); Rhode & Kellerman, *Women and Leadership*, at 34.

136. Nine states require reporting. See Chapter 3. For the value of such rules see Rhode, *Pro Bono*, at 167–169. For bar initiatives, see ABA Commission on the Renaissance of Idealism in the Legal Profession, Final Report (Aug. 2006).

137. See Kenneth G. Dau-Schmidt & Kaushik Mukhopadhaya, The Fruits of Our Labors: An Empirical Study of the Distribution of Income and Job Satisfaction Across the Legal Profession, *49 J. Legal Educ.* 342 (1999).

138. Robert P. Schwerk, The Law Professor as Fiduciary: What Duties Do We Owe to Our Students, *45 S. Tex. L. Rev.* 753, 764–766 (2004) (noting that most law professors are unfamiliar with the psychological dysfunction of their students or attribute the causes to factors outside law school control); Accord, Lawrence S. Krieger, Institutional Denial About the Dark Side of Law School and Fresh Empirical Guidance for Constructively Breaking the Silence, *52 J. Legal Educ.* 112 (2002). For the general problem, see Thomas Adcock, Despite '93 Report, Substance Abuse Persists at Law Schools, *N.Y.L.J.*, Jun. 30, 2003; Kenneth M. Sheldon & Lawrence S. Krieger, Understanding the Negative Effects of Legal Education on Law Students: A Longitudinal Test of Self-Determination Theory, *33 Personality & Soc. Psych.* 853 (2007).

139. Levit & Linder, *The Happy Lawyers*, at 123.

140. Law School Survey of Student Engagement, Student Engagement in Law School: Enhancing Student Learning 7 (2009).

141. Law School Survey of Student Engagement, Student Engagement, at 8.

142. William Sullivan et al., *Educating Lawyers* 187 (2007); Rhode, *Pro Bono*, at 162.

143. Harlan F. Stone, The Public Influence of the Bar, *48 Harv. L. Rev.* 1, 11 (1934).

144. Stone, The Public Influence, at 11.

145. David B. Wilkins, The Professional Responsibility of Professional Schools to Study and Teach About the Profession, *49 J. Legal Educ.* 76 (1999).

Chapter 3

1. This chapter draws on Deborah L. Rhode, Access to Justice: A Roadmap for Reform, *41 Fordham Urb. L. J.* 1227 (2014). For research suggesting that the United States ranks first or second among countries with advanced economies see Charles Keckler, Lawyered Up: A Book Review Essay, *27 T.M. Cooley L. Rev.* 57 (2010); America Lawyers: Guilty as Charged, *The Economist,* Feb. 2, 2013.
2. World Justice Project Rule of Law Index 175 (2013).
3. For a discussion of legal needs among low-income individuals, see Legal Services Corporation, Documenting the Justice Gap in America: The Current Unmet Civil Needs of Low-Income Americans 1–13 (2009), available at http://www.lsc.gov/pdfs/dcoumenting_the_justice_gap_in_america_2009.pdf. Surveys find that between two-fifths and three-quarters of the needs of middle-income individuals are unaddressed, with most finding at least half. See Deborah L. Rhode, Access to Justice 3, 79 (2004); Luz E. Herrera, Rethinking Private Attorney Involvement in the Delivery of Civil Legal Services for Low- and Moderate-Income Clients, *42 Loy. L. Rev.* 1 (2009).
4. *Gideon v. Wainwright,* 372 U.S. 335 (1963).
5. Debra Cassens Weiss, Would Decriminalizing Minor Offenses Help Indigent Defense Crisis? ABA Committee Weighs In, *ABA J.,* Jan. 8, 2013, http://www.abajournal.com/news/article/decriminalizing_minor_offenses_could_help_indigent_defense_crisis_aba_commi/.
6. No Fair Trial unless You Can Buy One, *Atlanta J.-Const.,* Sept. 9, 2001, at 8D (quoting Paula McMichen).
7. Stephen Bright, Counsel for the Poor: The Death Sentence Not for the Worst Crime but for the Worst Lawyer, *103 Yale L. J.* 1835, 1850–1854 (1994).
8. David Cole, *No Equal Justice: Race and Class in the American Criminal Justice System* 64, 84 (1999); Douglas McCollum, The Ghost of *Gideon, Am. Law.,* Mar. 2003, at 63, 67.
9. Rhode, Access to Justice, at 140.
10. For the constitutional guarantee, see *Strickland v. Washington,* 466 U.S. 668 (1984). Recent decisions have shown somewhat less tolerance for ineffective performance. See cases reviewed in Deborah L. Rhode, David Luban, & Scott Cummings, *Legal Ethics* 211–212 (6th ed., 2013).
11. Rhode, Access to Justice, at 122; Laurence Hurley, Second Guesses, *Cal. Law.,* Jan. 2012, at 29, 31 (describing the barriers to remedies for ineffective assistance).
12. Michelle Alexander, *The New Jim Crow: Mass Incarceration in the Age of Color Blindness* 6–9 (2010); William Stuntz, *The Collapse of American Criminal Justice* 247 (2011).

13. Roger A. Fairfax, Jr., Searching for Solutions to the Indigent Defense Crisis in the Broader Criminal Justice Reform Agenda, *122 Yale L. J.* 2316, 2319, 2321 (2013); Joe Davidson, Budget Cuts "Threaten" Justice for the Poor; Defenders Furloughed but not Prosecutors, *Wash. Post,* Aug. 20, 2013; ABA Standing Committee on Legal Aid and Indigent Defendants, *Gideon's* Broken Promise: America's Continuing Quest for Equal Justice 7–14 (2004).

14. Accessing Counsel and Courts, *Liman Cent. Newslet.,* Fall 2003, at 19 (quoting Brandon Buskey, ACLU Criminal Justice Reform Project).

15. For the number of plea bargains, see George Fisher, *Plea Bargaining's Triumph: A History of Plea Bargains in the United States* 134, 222, 223 (2003).

16. Ron Nixon, Public Defenders Are Tightening Belts Because of Steep Federal Budget Cuts, *N.Y. Times,* Aug. 24, 2013, at A14; Karen Houppert, *Chasing* Gideon: *The Elusive Quest for Poor People's Justice* 154 (2013).

17. See James C. McKinley, Jr., Cuomo Pledges More Aid for Indigents in Court, *N.Y. Times,* Oct. 22, 2014, at A22; Robert C. Boruchowitz et al., Minor Crimes, Massive Waste: The Terrible Toll of America's Broken Misdemeanor Courts 22–27 (2009) (providing data on average misdemeanor caseloads in major metropolitan areas such as Chicago, Atlanta, and Miami), available at http://www.nacdl.org/WorkArea/DownloadAsset.aspx?id=20808.

18. David Rudovsky, *Gideon* and the Effective Assistance of Counsel: The Rhetoric and the Reality, *32 J. L. & Inequality* 372, 379 n43 (2014).

19. Jenna Greene, A Muted Trumpet, *Nat'l L. J.,* Mar. 18, 2013, at A4; Eve Brensike Primus, Not Much to Celebrate, *Nat'l L. J.,* Mar. 18, 2013, at 26; Rudofsky, *Gideon,* 379; Carol S. Steiker, *Gideon's* Problematic Promises, *Daedalus,* Summer 2014, at 53.

20. Federal Oversight on Public Defense, *N.Y. Times,* Sept. 8, 2013, at SR10; Matt Apuzzo, Holder Backing New York Suit Over Legal Service for the Poor, *N.Y. Times,* Sept. 25, 2014, at A24.

21. Amy Bach, Justice on the Cheap, *The Nation,* May 21, 2001, at 25; Contract Lawyer Can't Get the Job Done, *Atlanta J.-Const.,* May 5, 2001, at F10; Martin Lasden, For a Fistful of Dollars, *Cal. Law.,* Nov. 2001, at 28.

22. National Association of Criminal Defense Lawyers, Rationing Justice: The Underfunding of Assigned Counsel Systems 8 (2013); Greene, A Muted Trumpet.

23. Alan Berlow, Requiem for a Public Defender, *Am. Prospect,* Jun. 5, 2000, at 28; ABA, *Gideon's* Broken Promise, at 16.

24. Benjamin H. Barton, Against Civil *Gideon* (and for Pro Se Court Reform), *62 Fla. L. Rev.* 1227, 1253 (2010); Rhode, Access to Justice, at 124.

25. Adam Liptak, County Says It's Too Poor to Defend the Poor, *N.Y. Times,* Apr. 15, 2003, at A1, A13 (quoting Thomas Pearson).

26. Jonathan Oosting, NPR: Want to Know What's Wrong with the Nation's Public Defender System? Just Look at Detroit, MLive, Aug. 18, 2009, available at http://www.mlive.com/news/detroit/index.ssf/2009/08/npr_want_to_know_whats_wrong_w.html (quoting Bob Slameka).

27. Primus, Not Much to Celebrate, at 26.

28. Primus, Not Much to Celebrate, at 26. For other cases of delay, see Houppert, *Chasing* Gideon, at 153 (describing 16-month wait).

29. Mary Sue Backus & Paul Marcus, The Right to Counsel in Criminal Cases, A National Crisis, *57 Hastings L. J.* 1031, 1032 (2006); Stephen Bright, Fifty Years of Defiance and Resistance After *Gideon v. Wainwright, Liman Cent. Newslet.,* Fall 2003, at 3.

30. Rhode, Access to Justice, at 129.

31. Texas Defender Service, *Lethal Indifference* (2002), available at http://www.texasdefender.org.

32. No Fair Trial Unless You Can Buy One.

33. For reversible error, see James S. Liebman, Jeffrey Fagan, & Valerie West, *A Broken System: Error Rates in Capital Cases, 1973–1995* (2000) (finding counsel who conduct no investigation, make no objections, and waive cross-examination or closing arguments); Death Penalty Information Center, Innocence and the Crisis in the American Death Penalty (2004), available at http://www.deathpenaltyinfo.org/innocence-and-crisis-american-death-penalty (noting that inadequate representation is a cause of wrongful convictions).

34. See Backus & Marcus, The Right to Counsel, at 1083i; Dennis E. Curtis & Judith Resnik, Grieving Criminal Defense Lawyers, *70 Fordham L. Rev.* 1615, 1617–1621 (2002).

35. See Meredith J. Duncan, The (So-Called) Liability of Criminal Defense Attorneys: A System in Need of Reform, *Brigham Young U. L. Rev.* 1, 30–43 (2002); John Leubsdorf, Legal Malpractice and Professional Responsibility, *48 Rut. L. Rev.* 101, 111–119 (1995); Backus & Marcus, The Right to Counsel, at 1084.

36. *Strickland v. Washington,* 466 U.S. 668 (1984).

37. Cole, *No Equal Justice,* 80; Victor E. Flango & Patricia McKenna, Federal Habeas Corpus Review of State Court Convictions, *31 Cal. W. L. Rev.* 237, 259–260 (1995).

38. Stephen B. Bright & Sia M. Sanneh, *Gideon v. Wainwright,* Fifty Years Later, *The Nation,* Mar. 20, 2013; Rhode, Access to Justice, 136; Stephen B. Bright, Sleeping on the Job, *Nat'l L. J.,* Dec. 4, 2000, at A26.

39. See Stephen B. Bright, Keep the Dream of Equal Justice Alive, Address at Yale Law School, May 24, 1999. http://www.schr.org/files/resources/commence.pdf.

40. *Tippins v. Walker,* 77 F. 2d 682 (2d Cir. 1996); *Burdine v. Texas,* 66 F. Supp. 2d 854 (S.D, Tex. 1999), aff'd sub nom. *Burdine v. Johnson,* 362 F. 2d 386 (5th Cir.) cert. den. sub nom;. *Cockrell v. Burdine,* 535 U.S. 1120 (2002); *McFarland v. State,* 928 S.W. 2d 482, 506 (1996).

41. Bruce Shapiro, Sleeping Lawyer Syndrome, *The Nation,* Apr. 7, 1997, at 29 (quoting Judge Doug Shaver).

42. Bright & Sanneh, *Gideon v. Wainwright.*

43. Texas Defender Service, *Lethal Indifference,* at xii.

44. ABA, Perceptions of the U.S. Justice System 59 (2000).

45. For the capacities and limitations of such lawsuits, see Cara H. Drinan, Getting Real about *Gideon*: The Next Fifty Years of Enforcing the Right to Counsel, *70 Wash. & Lee L. Rev.* 1309, 1331 (2013); Backus & Marcus, The Right to Counsel, at 1116–1117.

46. *State ex. rel. Missouri Public Defender Commission v. Waters,* 370 S.W. 3d 592 (2012); *Public Defender, Eleventh Judicial Circuit of Florida v. State of Florida,* discussed in Richard Bust, When the Defenders Are the Plaintiffs, *ABA J.,* Oct. 2013, at 14–15.

47. Donald A. Dripps, Why *Gideon* Failed; Politics and Feedback Loops in the Reform of Criminal Justice, *70 Wash. & Lee L. Rev.* 883, 903 (2013).

48. Joel M. Schumm, Standing Committee on Legal Aid and Indigent Defendants, National Indigent Defense Reform, The Solution Is Multifaceted 37 (2012), available at http://www.nacdl.org/reports/indigentdefensereform/; Fairfax, Searching for Solutions, at 2331.

49. Debra Cassens Weiss, Would Decriminalizing Minor Offenses Help Indigent Defense Crisis? ABA Committee Weighs In, *ABA J.,* Jan. 2013.

50. Greg Berman & John Feinblatt, Problem Solving Courts: A Brief Primer (2001); Julia Weber, Domestic Violence Courts, *2 J. Cent. Fam. Children & Cts.* 23 (2000); Anthony C. Thomson, Courting Disorder: Some Thoughts on Community Courts, *10 Wash. U. J. L. & Pol'y* 63(2002).

51. Fairfax, Searching For Solutions, at 2332; Backus & Marcus, The Right to Counsel, at 1125–1126; Peter Joy, Rationing Justice by Rationing Lawyers, *37 Wash. U. J. L. & Pol'y* 205 (2011); Norman Lefstein, ABA Standing Committee on Legal Aid & Indigent

Defendants, *Securing Reasonable Caseloads: Ethics and Law in Public Defense* 19–24 (2011).

52. Drinan, Getting Real about *Gideon*, at 1330.
53. Schumm, National Indigent Defense Reform, at 10.
54. See *ABA Standards for Criminal Justice: Providing Defense Services Standard* 44–45 (3d ed., 1992).
55. Adam Liptak, Need-Blind Justice, *N.Y. Times,* Jan. 5, 2014, at wk. 4 (describing Seattle court ruling).
56. Drinan, Getting Real about *Gideon*, at 1343.
57. Paul D. Butler, Poor People Lose: *Gideon* and the Critique of Rights, *122 Yale L. J.* 2176 (2013).
58. Legal Services Corporation, Documenting the Justice Gap in America 19 (2009).
59. Rhode, Access to Justice, at 14.
60. The 2013 federal allocation for legal aid was $340.8 million. See Legal Services Corporation, http://www.lsc.gov/congress/lsc-funding.
61. For expenditures, see Gillian K. Hadfield, Higher Demand, Lower Supply? A Comparative Assessment of the Legal Resource Landscape for Ordinary Americans, *37 Fordham Urb. L. J.* 129, 139 (2010); Earl Johnson, Jr., Justice for America's Poor in the Year 2020: Some Possibilities Based on Experiences Here and Abroad, *58 DePaul L. Rev.* 393, 397–398 (2009); Raven Lidman, Civil *Gideon* as a Human Right: Is the U.S. Going to Join Step with the Rest of the Developed World? *15 Temp. Pol. & Civ. Rts. L. Rev.* 769, 780 (2006). For intermediary institutions, see Rebecca Sandefur, The Fulcrum Point of Access to Justice: Legal and Nonlegal Institutions of Remedy, *42 Loy. L. A. L. Rev.* 949, 957–962 (2009).
62. Hadfield, Higher Demand, at 139.
63. Rebecca L. Sandefur, The Impact of Counsel: An Analysis of Empirical Evidence, *9 Seattle J. Soc. Just.* 56, 60 (2010).
64. Robert J. Derocher, The IOLTA Crash: Fallout for Foundations, *B. Leader,* Sept./Oct. 2012 (reporting declines in IOLTA [Interest on Lawyers Trust Fund Accounts] funding); Lonnie A. Powers, As Fiftieth Anniversary Approaches, Public Funding of Civil Legal Aid Remains Vital to Justice, Huffington Post, Dec. 19, 2013 (noting that 2014 IOLTA funds would be 85 percent less than what they were five years ago); Emily Savner, Expand Legal Services Now, *Nat'l L. J.,* Jun. 28, 2010 (reporting increases in demand and 75 percent drop in IOLTA funds between 2007 and 2009); Need a Lawyer, Good Luck, *N.Y. Times,* Oct. 14, 2010; Karen Sloan, Perfect Storm Hits Legal Aid, *Nat'l L. J.,* Jan. 2011, at 1, 4 (noting decline in funds from government IOLTA, and tight private fundraising climate, together with increased demand for services); Erik Eckholm, Interest Rate Drop Has Dire Results for Legal Aid Groups, *N.Y. Times,* Jan. 19,

2009, at A12 (reporting a 30 percent increase in requests for legal aid); Richard Zorza, Access to Justice: Economic Crisis Challenges, Impacts, and Responses 8–9 (Self-Represented Network, 2009), available at http://www.Selfhelpsupport.org (finding that a majority of judges reported increase in pro se caseloads, but that 39 percent also reported cuts in self-help services budget).

65. See Legal Services Corporation, Temporary Operating Budget and Special Circumstance Operating Authority for Fiscal Year 2014; Erik Eckholm & Ian Lovett, A Push for Legal Aid in Civil Cases Finds Its Advocates, *N.Y. Times*, Nov. 22, 2014. For foundation cutbacks, see Sara K. Gould, Foundation Center, *Diminishing Dollars: The Impact of the 2008 Financial Crisis on the Field of Social Justice Philanthropy* (2011).

66. Rebecca Sandefur & Aaron C. Smyth, Access Across America: First Report of the Civil Justice Infrastructure Mapping Project, American Bar. Foundation at v (Oct. 7, 2011).

67. Ethan Bronner, Right to Lawyer Can Be Empty Promise for Poor, *N.Y. Times,* Mar. 16, 2013, at A1, A6.

68. Bronner, Right to Lawyer, at A6.

69. Sandefur & Smyth, Access Across America.

70. Jeanne Charn, Celebrating the "Null" Finding: Evidence-Based Strategies for Improving Access to Justice, *122 Yale L. J.* 2206, 2216 (2013).

71. Charn, Celebrating the "Null" Finding, at 2212.

72. American Bar Association Resolution 112A(2006), available at http:// www.americanbar.org/content/dam/aba/administrative/legal_aid_ indigent_defendants/ls_sclaid_06A112A.authcheckdam.pdf.

73. These are collected at the website of the Coalition for a Civil Right to Counsel, at http://civilrighttocounsel.org/.

74. For historical examples of opposition, see Deborah L. Rhode, Professionalism in Perspective: Alternative Approaches to Nonlawyer Practice, *22 N.Y. U. Rev. L. & Soc. Change* 701, 705 (1996). For the bar's current opposition and enforcement efforts, see Richard Zorza & David Udell, New Roles for Non-Lawyers to Increase Access to Justice, *41 Fordham Urb. L. J.* 1259, 1278 (2014); Deborah L. Rhode & Lucy Ricca, Unauthorized Practice Enforcement: Protection of the Public or the Profession, *82 Fordham L. Rev.* 2588, 2588 (2014).

75. Steven Gillers, A Profession, If You Can Keep It, *63 Hastings L. J.* 953, 979 (2012).

76. See, e.g., Russell Engler, Connecting Self-Representation to Civil *Gideon*: What Existing Data Reveal About When Counsel Is Most Needed, *37 Fordham Urb. L. J.* 37, 41–43 (2010) (summarizing reports on representation rates in housing, small claims, and family law cases).

77. Alan W. Houseman, Civil Legal Aid in the United States: An Update for 2007 20–21 (2007), available at http://www.clasp.org/publications/civil_legal_aid_2007.pdf.

78. The problem is long-standing. See Jona Goldschmidt, How Are Courts Handling Pro Se Litigants? *82 Judicature* 13, 20–22 (1998) (describing services available).

79. Charn, Celebrating the "Null" Finding, at 2225, 2226.

80. See the website for Citizens Advice Bureaus, at http://www.citizensadvice.org.uk/index/aboutus/ourhistory.htm.

81. Gillian K. Hadfield & Jamie Heine, Life in the Law-Thick World: The Legal Resource Landscape for Ordinary Americans, in *Beyond Elite Law: Access to Civil Justice for Americans of Average Means* (Samuel Estreicher & Joy Radice, eds., forthcoming).

82. ABA Consortium on Legal Services and the Public, Legal Needs and Civil Justice: A Survey of Americans; Major Findings from the Comprehensive Legal Needs Study 7–19 (1994).

83. Amanda Ripley, Who Needs Lawyers? *Time* Jun. 12, 2000, at 62.

84. Marsha Kline Pruett & Tamara D. Jackson, The Lawyer's Role During the Divorce Process: Perceptions of Parents, Their Young Children, and Their Attorneys, *33 Fam. L. Q.* 283, 298 (1999).

85. Pruett & Jackson, The Lawyer's Role, at 298.

86. See research summarized in Rebecca Aviel, Why Civil *Gideon* Won't Fix Family Law, *122 Yale L. J.* 2106, 2117–2118 (2013).

87. For examples, see Deborah L. Rhode, Policing the Professional Monopoly: A Constitutional and Empirical Analysis of Unauthorized Practice Prohibitions, *34 Stan. L. Rev.* 1, 45, n135 (1981). For state courts' reluctance to offer a definition, see cases cited in Susan D. Hoppock, Enforcing Unauthorized Practice of law Prohibitions: The Emergence of the Private Cause of Action and its Impact on Effective Enforcement, *20 Geo. J. Legal Ethics* 719,722 n35 (2007).

88. Rhode, Policing, at n136.

89. Rhode, Policing, at n140–n142; Ga. Code Ann. Section 9–401.

90. *Fifteenth Judicial District Unified Bar Association v. Glasgow,* 1999 WL 1128847 (Tennessee Appellate 1999); *Florida Bar v. Brumbaugh,* 355 So. 2d 1186 (Fla. 1978).

91. *In re Reynoso,* 477 F.3d 1117 (9th Cir. 2007); *Committee v. Parsons Technology,* 179 F. 3d 956 (5th Cir. 1999); *Janson v. LegalZoom,* 802 F. Supp. 1053 (W.D. Mo. 2011). A Texas ruling was overturned by a legislative exemption and the Missouri case was subsequently settled without banning the services altogether. See Tom McNichol, Is LegalZoom's Gain Your Loss? *Cal. Law.,* Sept. 2010, at 20. In 2014, LegalZoom was battling lawsuits in four states. See also Susan Beck, The Future of Law, *Am. Law.,* Aug. 2014, at 36.

92. John M. Greacen, No Legal Advice from Court Personnel: What Does That Mean? *10 Judges J.* 10, 10–12 (Winter 1995).

93. Rhode, Access to Justice, at 83.

94. Rhode, Access to Justice, at 83.

95. *Kentucky Bar Ass'n v. Tarpinian,* 337 S.W.3d 627 (Ky. S.Ct. 2011) (adopting Special Commissioner's report); *Louisiana State Bar Ass'n v. Carr and Assocs., Inc.,* 15 So.3d 158, 167 (Louisiana Ct. App. 2009).

96. Rhode & Ricca, Protecting the Public or the Profession, at 2604.

97. Rhode & Ricca, Protecting the Public or the Profession, at 2595.

98. Mathew Rotenberg, Stifled Justice: The Unauthorized Practice of Law and Internet Legal Resources, *97 Minn. L. Rev.* 709, 722 (2012).

99. Rhode, Access to Justice, at 89; Julian Lonbay, Assessing the European Market for Legal Services: Developments in the Free Movement of Lawyers in the European Union, *33 Fordham Int'l L. J.* 1629, 1636 (2010) (discussing Swedish legal advice providers); Herbert Kritzer, Rethinking Barriers to Legal Practice, *81 Judicature* 100, 101 (1997) (discussing Citizens Advice Bureaus in the United Kingdom with trained nonlawyer volunteers).

100. Richard Moorhead, Alan Paterson, & Avrom Sherr, Contesting Professionalism: Legal Aid and Nonlawyers in England and Wales, *37 Law & Soc. Rev.* 765, 785–787 (2003). For discussion, see Deborah J. Cantrell, The Obligation of Legal Aid Lawyers to Champion Practice by Nonlawyers, *73 Fordham L. Rev.* 883, 888–890 (2004).

101. Moorhead, Paterson, & Sherr, Contesting Professionalism, at 795.

102. David B. Morris, Report to the Attorney General of Ontario 12 (Nov. 2012).

103. Herbert Kritzer, *Legal Advocacy: Lawyers and Nonlawyers at Work* 76, 108, 148, 190, 201 (1998).

104. Kritzer, *Legal Advocacy.*

105. *Turner v. Rogers,* 131 S. Ct. 2507, 2517–2518 (2011) (quoting *Mathews v. Eldridge,* 424 U.S. 3.19, 335 (1976)).

106. *Turner v. Rogers,* at 2519.

107. *Turner v. Rogers,* at 2519.

108. Norman Reimer, *Turner v. Rogers:* The Right to Counsel Haunted by the Ghost of Gagnon, *Concurring Opinions,* Jun. 27, 2011. See also Peter B. Edelman, Does the Supreme Court Get It in *Turner? Concurring Opinions,* Jun. 27, 2011: Russell Engler, *Turner v. Rogers* and the Essential Role of the Courts in Delivering Access to Justice, *7 Harv. Law & Pol'y Rev.* 31, 41 (2013).

109. Mark Walsh, A Sour Note from Gideon's Trumpet: Playing the Blues for the Right of Counsel in Civil Cases, *ABA J.,* Sept. 2011, at 14 (quoting Peter Edelman).

110. Engler, *Turner v. Rogers,* at 56.

111. Walsh, A Sour Note (quoting Russell Engler).

112. Judith Resnik, Comment, Fairness in Numbers: A Comment on *AT&T v. Concepcion, Wal-Mart v. Dukes,* and *Turner v. Rogers, 125 Harv. L. Rev.* 78, 158 (2012).

113. Resnik, Comment, at 158.

114. Resnik, Comment, at 160.

115. Resnik, Comment, at 160.

116. Houseman, Civil Legal Aid in the United States, at 16. The litigation history of Civil *Gideon* is collected on the website of the Coalition for a Civil Right to Counsel, http://www.civilrightocounsel.org/advances/litigation/.

117. Clare Pastore, Life After *Lassiter*: An Overview of State-Court Right to Counsel Decisions, *40 Clearinghouse Rev.* 186, 189–191 (2006); Laura K. Abel & Max Rettig, State Statutes Providing for a Right to Counsel in Civil Cases, *40 Clearinghouse Rev.* 245 (2006).

118. Houseman, Civil Legal Aid in the United States, at 16.

119. Abel & Rettig, State Statutes, at 246–247.

120. Abel & Rettig, State Statutes, at 248.

121. Robert A. Katzman, The Legal Profession and the Unmet Needs of the Immigrant Poor, *21 Geo. J. Legal Ethics* 3, 7–8 (2008). More than 40 percent of noncitizens in deportation hearings lack counsel. Robert A. Katzmann, When Legal Representation Is Deficient: The Challenge of Immigration Cases for the Courts, *Daedalus,* Summer 2014, at 37.

122. 45 C.F.R. Section 1626 (2009).

123. See *Aguilera-Enriquez v. INS,* 516 F. 2d 565, 568 (6th Cir. 1075); Thomas Alexander Alienikoff, David A. Martin, & Hiroshi Motomura, *Immigration and Citizenship* 645 (5th ed., 2003).

124. For lawyers' advantages over consumers in lobbying over matters such as anticompetitive licensing restrictions, see Larry E. Ribstein, Lawyers as Lawmakers: A Theory of Lawyer Licensing, *69 Mo. L. Rev.,* 299, 314 (2004).

125. In a survey commissioned by the American Bar Association, 55 percent strongly agreed that it was essential that legal services be available; 33 percent somewhat agreed. ABA Survey Summary, Economic Downturn and Access to Legal Resources (Apr. 2009), available at http://www.abanow.org/wordpress/wp-content/files/flutter 1268261059_20_7_upload_file.pdf. For the public's belief about the right to counsel, see Johnson, Justice For America's Poor, at 393; ABA, Perceptions of the U.S. Justice System 63 (1999) available at http://www.abanet.org/media/perceptions/pdf.

126. ABA, Perceptions of the U.S. Justice System.

127. Barbara Curran & F. Spaulding, *The Legal Needs of the Public* 231 (1977). The bar has not recently asked that question.

128. See Beck, Future of Law; Benjamin H. Barton, The Lawyer's Monopoly—What Goes and What Stays, *82 Fordham L. Rev.* 3067–3090 (2014); Deborah L. Rhode, Professionalism in Perspective, at 701, 705. For the Texas bar effort to ban a self-help computer software program that was overturned by the Texas legislature, see *Unauthorized Practice of Law Committee v. Parsons Technology*, 1999 WL 47235 (N.D. Tex), vacated and remanded 179 F. 3d 956 (1999); Randall Samborn, So What Is a Lawyer Anyway? *Nat'l L. J.,* Jun. 21, 1993, at 1, 12. For bar suits against LegalZoom despite high rates of customer satisfaction, see Rhode & Ricca, Protecting the Profession or the Public, at 2605; Terry Carter, LegalZoom Hits a Legal Hurdle in North Carolina, *ABA J.,* May 2013, http://www.abajournal.com/news/article/legalzoom_hits_a_hurdle_in_north_Carolina.

129. Rhode, Access to Justice, at 88; ABA Select Committee Report on the 2000 Midyear Meeting, available at http://www.abanet.org/leadership/2000house.html; James Podgers, Legal Profession Faces Rising Tide of Nonlawyer Practice, *ABA J.,* Dec. 1993, at 51, 56.

130. Benjamin H. Barton & Stephanos Bibas, Triaging Appointed-Counsel Funding and Pro Se Access to Justice, *160 U. Pa. L. Rev.* 967, 994 (2012).

131. Benjamin Barton, *The Lawyer-Judge Bias in the American Legal Profession* (2011); Benjamin Barton, Do Judges Systematically Favor the Interests of the Legal Profession?, 59 Ala. L. Rev. 453 (2007).

132. Bar ethical codes and efforts to require pro bono service are chronicled in Deborah L. Rhode, *Pro Bono in Principle and in Practice* 15–17 (2005). One state, New York, requires 50 hours of unpaid work as a condition of admission but does not impose requirements on already licensed lawyers. Mosi Secret, Judge Details a Rule Requiring Pro Bono Work by Aspiring Lawyers, *N.Y. Times*, Sept. 19, 2012, at A25.

133. ABA Standing Committee on Pro Bono and Public Service, Supporting Justice II: A Report on the Pro Bono Work of America's Lawyers vi (2009); Model Rules of Professional Conduct, Rule 6.1.

134. Only 44 percent performed at least 20 hours of service. Where the Recession Lingers, *Am. Law.*, Jun. 2013, at 47.

135. ABA State by State Pro Bono Service Rules, available at http://apps.americanbar.org/legalservices/probono/pbreporting.html.

136. See Rhode, *Pro Bono in Principle*, at 13–14.

137. Russell Engler, *Turner v. Rogers* and the Essential Role of the Courts in Delivering Access to Justice, *7 Harv. Law & Pol'y Rev.* 31, 45 (2013).

138. For access to justice commissions, see Richard Zorza, *Turner v. Rogers*: The Implications for Access to Justice Strategies, *95 Judicature* 255, 264 (2012). For the consortium, see Deborah L. Rhode, Access to Justice: An Agenda for Legal Education and Research, *62 J. Legal Educ.* 531 (2013).

139. Elizabeth Chambliss, Law School Training for Licensed "Legal Technicians"? Implications for the Consumer Market, *65 S.C. L. Rev.* 579 (2014); Don J. DeBenedictis, State Bar to Weigh Licensing Nonlawyers, *San Francisco Daily J.*, Apr. 11, 2013, at 1; Joyce E. Cutler, California State Bar Group Approves Report to Spur Support for Nonlawyer Practitioners, *29 ABA/BNA Law. Man. Prof. Conduct*, Jul. 3, 2013, at 416; Jonathan Lippman, The State of the Judiciary 2014 8 (2014).

140. Barton, The Lawyer's Monopoly, at 3067–3090.

141. See Rhode, Access to Justice, at 88.

142. Sargent Shriver Civil Counsel Act, A.B. 590 (Cal. 2009); Engler, *Turner v. Rogers*, at 49 (describing Massachusetts proposals).

143. Eckholm & Lovett, A Push for Legal Aid.

144. American Bar Association Task Force on the Future of Legal Education, Report and Recommendations (2014), available at http://www.americanbar.org/content/dam/aba/administrative/professional_responsibility/report_and_recommendations_of_aba_task_force.authcheckdam.pdf.

145. James R. Silkenat, Connecting Supply and Demand, *ABA J.*, Oct. 2013, at 8; Sarah Parvini, ABA Seeks Match of Lawyers, People Needing Services, *San Francisco Daily J.*, Apr. 11, 2004, at 4.

146. Charn, Celebrating the "Null Finding," at 2232.

147. See Barton & Bibas, Triaging Appointed-Counsel, at 987–990.

148. Russell Engler, Connecting Self-Representation to Civil *Gideon*: What Existing Data Reveal About When Counsel Is Most Needed, *27 Fordham Urb. L. J.* 37, 79 (2010).

149. Richard Zorza, National Center for State Courts, *The Self-Help Friendly Court: Designed From the Ground Up to Work for People Without Lawyers* (2002).

150. Engler, *Turner v. Rogers*, at 58.

151. Cynthia Gray, American Judicature Society and State Justice Institute, *Reaching Out or Overreaching: Judicial Ethics and Self-Represented Litigants* 51–57 (2005).

152. The Self-Represented Litigation Network, Core Materials on Self-Represented Litigation Innovation (2006).

153. For the New York magistrate court, see Lois Bloom & Helen Hershkoff, Federal Courts, Magistrate Judges and the Pro Se Plaintiff,

16 Notre Dame J. L. Ethics & Pub. Pol'y 475, 493–497 (2002). For the San Antonio staff attorney program, see Anita Davis, A Pro Se Program That Is Also "Pro" Judges, Lawyers, and the Public, *63 Tex. B. J.* 896 (2000).

154. Engler, *Turner v. Rogers*, at 42. See also Sheldon Krantz, *The Legal Profession: What Is Wrong and How to Fix It* 97–98 (2013).

155. Jona Goldschmidt, The Pro Se Litigant's Struggle for Access to Justice: Meeting the Challenge of Bench and Bar Resistance, *40 Fam. Ct. Rev.* 6, 40 (2002). For negative perceptions about pro se litigants and the burdens they create, see Stephen Landsman, The Growing Challenge of Pro Se Litigation, *13 Lewis & Clark L. Rev.* 439, 449 (2009).

156. See Julia Cheever, Deep Cuts to Court Funding Make CA Chief Justice "Afraid to See the Future," *SF Appeal,* Aug. 9, 2013, available at http://sfappeal.com/2013/08/deep-cuts-to-court-funding-make-ca-chief-justice-afraid-to-see-the-future/; Sheri Qualters, No Respite: State Courts Face Another Year of Lean Budgets and Tough Cuts, *Nat'l L. J.,* Feb. 20, 2012, at 1.

157. Christine Parker, *Just Lawyers: Regulation and Access to Justice* 184–189 (1990). For preferences, see Michael Zander, *The State of Justice* 29–32 (2000); and Hazel G. Genn, *Paths to Justice: What People Do and Think about Going to Law* 217–218 (1999). For online dispute resolution, see Ross Todd, Look Ma, No Judge, *Am. Law.,* Aug. 2014, at 34.

158. See Miles B. Farmer, Mandatory and Fair? A Better System of Mandatory Arbitration, *121 Yale L. J.* 2346, 2355–2360 (2012); Katherine V. W. Stone, Rustic Justice: Community and Coercion under the Federal Arbitration Act, *77 North Car. L. Rev.* 931, 1015–1017 (1999).

159. *Supreme Court of Colorado v. Employers Unity* 716 P.2d 460, 463 (Col. 1986).

160. *Culum v. Heritage House Realtors*, 694 P. 2d 630 (Wash. 1985).

161. Steven Gillers, How to Make Rules for Lawyers, *40 Pepp. L. Rev.* 365, 417 (2013): Richard Zorza & David Udell, New Roles for Non-Lawyers to Increase Access to Justice, *41 Fordham Urb. L. J.* 1259, 1304–1315 (2014).

162. Kritzer, Rethinking Barriers, at 101; Emily A. Unger, Solving Immigration Consultant Fraud through Expanded Federal Accreditation, *29 Law & Ineq.* 425, 448 (2011). See also Zachery C. Zurek, The Limited Power of the Bar to Protect Its Monopoly, *3 St. Mary's J. Legal Malpractice & Ethics* 242, 265 (2013) (discussing requirements for nonlawyer patent specialists).

163. For fraud, see Unger, Solving Immigration Consultant Fraud; Careen Shannon, Regulating Immigration Legal Service Providers: Inadequate Representation and Notario Fraud, *78 Fordham L. Rev.*

577, 589 (2009); Jessica Wesberg & Bridget O'Shea, Fake Lawyers and Notaries Prey on Immigrants, *N.Y. Times*, Oct. 23, 2011, at A25. For unmet need, see Erin B. Corcoran, Bypassing Civil *Gideon*: A Legislative Proposal to Address the Rising Costs and Unmet Legal Needs of Unrepresented Immigrants, *115 W. Va. L. Rev.* 643, 654–655 (2012).

164. Ann E. Langford, What's in a Name? Notarios in the United States and the Exploitation of a Vulnerable Latino Immigrant Population, *7 Harv. Latino L. Rev.* 115, 119–120 (2004).

165. For the role of registered migration agents in Australia, see Information for Consumers, Australian Government Office of the Migration Agents Registration Authority, https://www.mara.gov. au/Consumer-Information/Information-for-Consumers/default. aspx. For the role of authorized immigration consultants in Canada, see Citizenship and Immigration Canada, Use an Authorized Immigration Representative, available at http://www.cic.gc.ca/english/ information/representative/rep-who.asp. For the role of regulated immigration advisors in the United Kingdom, see Office of The Immigration Services Commissioner, The Code of Standards: The Commissioner's Rules, available at http://oisc.homeoffice.gov.uk/ servefile.aspx?docid=6.

166. See 8 C. F. R. Section 1292.1 (2012); Shannon, Regulating Immigrant Legal Service Providers, at 602–603.

167. See Unger, Solving Immigration Consultant Fraud, at 443–449; Careen Shannon, To License or Not to License? A Look at Differing Approaches to Policing the Activities of Nonlawyer Immigration Service Providers, *33 Cardozo L. Rev.* 437 (2001).

168. For the need for such a matching system, see Johnson, Justice for America's Poor, at 420–421; Charn, Celebrating the "Null" Finding.

169. For alternative doctrinal standards, see Engler, Self-Representation and Civil *Gideon*, at 81, 85.

170. ABA Report of the House of Delegates 13 (2006).

171. *Powell v. Alabama*, 285 U.S. 45, 68–69 (1932).

172. Raven Lidman, Civil *Gideon* as a Human Right: Is the U.S. Going to Join Step with the Rest of the Developed World? *15 Temp. Pol. & Civ. Rights L. Rev.* 769, 771 (2006).

173. See ABA Standing Committee on Legal Aid and Indigent Defendants, *Gideon's* Broken Promise: America's Continuing Quest for Equal Justice (2004); Barton & Bibas, Triaging Appointed-Counsel, at 967, 973–977.

174. Rebecca May & Marguerite Roulet, Center For Family Policy and Practice, A Look at Arrests of Low-Income Fathers For Child Support Nonpayment: Enforcement, Court and Program Practices 45 (2005), available at http://www.cpr-mn.org/Documents/noncompliance.pdf.

175. Barton & Bibas, Triaging Appointed-Counsel, at 993–994.

176. Access to Justice Working Group, And Justice For All: Report to the State Bar of California 49–50, 58–60 (1996); Talbot "Sandy" D'Alembert, Tributaries of Justice: The Search for Full Access, *25 Fl. St. L. Review* 631 (1998).

177. See Mark Richardson & Steven Reynolds, The Shrinking Public Purse: Civil Legal Aid in New South Wales, Australia, *5 Md. J. Contemp. L. Issue* 349, 360 (2004); Jeremy Cooper, English Legal Services: A Tale of Diminishing Returns, *5 Md. J. Contemp. L. Issue* 247, 253 (2004); Sarah Conn Martin, Appointed Counsel in Civil Cases: How California's Pilot Project Compares to Access to Counsel in Other Developed Countries, *37 J. Legal Prof.* 281, 290 (2013); *Quail v. Municipal Court,* 171 Cal App. 3d 572, 590 n13 (1985).

178. California's pilot Civil *Gideon* program is funded through fees associated with nonessential court services. Access to Justice—Civil Right to Counsel—California Establishes Pilot Program to Expand Access to Counsel for Low-Income Persons, *123 Harv. L. Rev.* 1532, 1536 (2010).

179. Jeffrey D. Koelemay, Public Interest: Individual Pro Bono Not Enough, Judges Say: Pro Se Problem Needs Coordinated Attention, *15 ABA/BNA Law. Man. Prof. Conduct* 32 (2014).

180. Omnibus Consolidated Rescissions and Appropriations Act of 1996, 110 Stat. 1321; 45 Code of Federal Regulations pt. 1610–1642. See Alan Houseman & Linda E. Perle, What Can and Cannot Be Done: Representation of Clients by LSC-Funded Programs (2001).

181. Tigran W. Elred & Thomas Schoenherr, The Lawyer's Duty of Public Service: More than Charity? *96 W. Va. L. Rev.* 367, 391 n.97 (1993–1994); Michael J. Mazzone, Mandatory Pro Bono: Slavery in Disguise, *Tex. L.,* Oct. 22, 1990, at 22.

182. See Rhode, *Pro Bono in Principle*, at 28.

183. Rhode, *Pro Bono in Principle,* at 29; Robert A. Stein, Champions of Pro Bono, *ABA J.,* Aug. 1997, at 100.

184. Rhode, *Pro Bono in Principle,* at 30.

185. Rhode, *Pro Bono in Principle,* at 138–145.

186. ABA Young Lawyers Division, Career Satisfaction Survey 19–20 (2000).

187. Cal. Bus. & Prof. Code § 6072 (West 2013).

188. Rhode, Access to Justice, at 180–181.

189. See Deborah L. Rhode, Senior Lawyers Serving Public Interests; Pro Bono and Second Stage Careers, *21 Prof. Law.* 1 (2011).

190. See Forrest S. Mosten, Unbundling Legal Services: Servicing Clients within Their Ability to Pay, *Judges J.,* Winter 2001, at 15; Forrest S. Mosten, Unbundled Legal Services Today—and Predictions for the Future, *35 Fam. Advoc.* 14 (2012); ABA Modest Means Task Force,

Handbook on Limited Scope Legal Assistance (2003), available at http://www.abamet/prg/litigation/taskforces/modest/report.pdf.

191. Will Hornsby, Unbundling and the Lawyer's Duty of Care, *35 Fam. Advoc.* 27 (2012).

192. See Model Rules of Professional Conduct, Rule 1.2 (2002) (providing for limited representation); Mosten, Unbundled Legal Services, at 18 (proposing civil immunity for lawyers); Margaret Graham Tebo, Loosening Ties: Unbundling of Legal Services Can Open Door to New Clients, *ABA J.,* Aug. 2003, at 35 (noting state rules).

193. Carol J. Williams, Aid Expands for the Middle Class, *L.A. Times,* Mar. 10, 2009, at 6; Kevin Lee, Company Bets on First Retail Legal Store, *San Francisco Daily J.,* Feb. 8, 2013, at 1.

194. Kathryn Alfisi, Low Bono Widens Path to Access to Justice, *Wash. Law.,* Sept. 2013, at 24; Deborah L. Rhode, Whatever Happened to Access to Justice, *42 Loy. L.A. L. Rev.* 868, 898–899 (2009).

195. Barton & Bibas, Triaging Appointed-Counsel, at 991 (noting scarcity of credible data and conflicting findings); research discussed in Laura K. Abel, Evidence-Based Access to Justice, *13 U. Pa. J. L. & Soc. Change* 295 (2010) (describing conflicting outcomes); Rhode, Access to Justice: An Agenda, at 538–539 (discussing scarcity of data and conflicting results); Gillian K. Hadfield, Higher Demand, at 129 (noting "slim empirical basis" for evaluating lawyers' performance); Charn, Celebrating the "Null" Finding, at 2222 (noting that we lack "empirical evidence that would support confident advice to claimants about what assistance would best meet their needs"); Resnik, Fairness in Numbers, at 158 (noting that neither judges nor litigants have the basis for knowing "whether adding lawyers would enhance accuracy"); Engler, Self-Representation and Civil *Gideon*, at 69–73 (noting lack of evaluation of pro se assistance on case outcomes and problems in using satisfaction as a measure of success for hotlines and self-help programs); D. James Greiner & Cassandra Wolos Pattanayak, Randomized Evaluation in Legal Assistance: What Difference Does Representation (Offer and Actual Use) Make, *121 Yale L. J.* 2118 (2012) (discussing methodological weaknesses of many studies and conflicting results); Engler, *Turner v. Rogers*, at 53 (quoting Laura Abel, noting the "shortage of solid, reliable data concerning which types of legal assistance various types of litigants need to obtain meaningful access").

196. Compare D. James Greiner & Cassandra Wolos Pattanayak, Randomized Evaluation in Legal Assistance: What Difference Does Representation (Offer and Actual Use) Make? *121 Yale L. J.* 2118 (2012) (finding that access to representation did not correlate with favorable outcomes), with Caroll Seron, Martin Frankel, Gregg Van Syzin, & Jean Kovath, The Impact of Legal Counsel on Outcomes

for Poor Tenants in New York City's Housing Court: Results of a Randomized Experiment, *35 Law & Soc'y Rev.* 419 (2001) (tenants with lawyer assistance did better than those without). See also D. James Greiner, Cassandra Wolos Pattanayak, & Jonathan P. Hennessy, The Limits of Unbundled Legal Assistance: A Randomized Study in a Massachusetts District Court and Prospects for the Future, *126 Harv. L. Rev.* 901 (2013) (finding tenants with access to lawyers fared better than those who were randomly assigned to information and self-help).

197. See Laura K. Abel & Susan Vignola, Economic and Other Benefits Associated with the Provision of Civil Legal Aid, *9 Seattle J. Soc. Just.* 139, 148–150 (2010) (describing studies attempting to quantify long-term consequences); Gary Blasi, Framing Access to Justice: Beyond Perceived Justice for Individuals, *42 Loy. L.A. L. Rev.* 913, 920–923, 936–939 (2009); Gary Blasi, How Much Access? How Much Justice? *73 Fordham L. Rev.* 865, 871 (2004) (discussing a case in which a slum landlord declined to make necessary improvements despite a series of litigation losses).

198. Molly M. Jennings & D. James Greiner, The Evolution of Unbundling in Litigation: Three Case Studies and a Literature Review, *89 Den. U. L. Rev.* 825, 827–828 (2012). For the only randomized study on point, see Greiner, Pattanayak, & Hennessy, The Limits of Unbundled Legal Assistance.

199. See sources cited in Rhode, Access to Justice, at 121, 228 n.38; and Milan Markovic, LegalZoom Redux, *Legal Ethics F.*, May 5, 2014, http://www.legalethicsforum.com/blog/.

200. For fuller elaboration of this problem, see Deborah L. Rhode, Rethinking the Public in Lawyers' Public Service: Pro Bono, Strategic Philanthropy, and the Bottom Line, *77 Fordham L. Rev.* 1435, 1452 (2008).

201. Scott Cummings & Deborah L. Rhode, Managing Pro Bono: Doing Well by Doing Better, *78 Fordham L. Rev.* 2357, 2401–2403 (2010).

202. Rhode, Rethinking the Public, at 1446.

203. Deborah L. Rhode, Public Interest Law: The Movement at Midlife, *60 Stanford L. Rev.* 2027, 2071 (2008).

204. Scott L. Cummings & Rebecca L. Sandefur, Beyond the Numbers: What We Know—and Should Know—About American Pro Bono, *7 Harv. L. & Pol'y Rev.* 83, 105(2013).

205. For the marginalization of substantive issues generally, see William M. Sullivan et al., *Educating Lawyers: Preparation for the Practice of Law* 141, 187 (2007).

206. For discussion of "legal ethics without the ethics," see Deborah L. Rhode, *In the Interests of Justice: Reforming the Legal Profession* 200 (2003); Sullivan et al, *Educating Lawyers,* at 149.

207. Rhode, *Pro Bono in Principle,* at 162.

208. Association of American Law Schools, Commission on Pro Bono and Public Service Opportunities in Law Schools, Learning to Serve: A Summary of the Findings and Recommendations of the AALS Commission on Pro Bono and Public Service in Law Schools 2 (1999).

209. Thirty-nine schools require students to provide service as a condition of graduation. See http://apps.americanbar.org/legalservices/probono/lawschools/pb_programs_chart.html. In many of these schools, the number of hours is fewer than ten a year. ABA Standing Committee on Professionalism, Report of Survey on Law School Professionalism Programs 46–47 (2006).

210. Law School Survey on Student Engagement, Student Engagement in Law School: Enhancing Student Learning 8 (2009).

211. Laurie Barron et al., Don't Do It Alone: A Community-Based Collaborative Approach to Pro Bono, *23 Geo. J. Legal Ethics* 323 (2010).

212. American Bar Association, Standards for Approval of Law Schools 302(b)(2), http://www.americanbar.org/groups/legal_education/resources/standards.html.

213. The ABA already requires that schools provide instruction in the rules and responsibilities of the legal profession and its members. ABA Standards and Rules of Procedure for Approval of Law Schools, Standard 302 (a)(5). Rule 6.1 of the ABA Model Rules of Professional Conduct recognizes enhancing access to justice as such a responsibility. ABA Model Rules of Professional Conduct, Rule 6.1 Comment ("Every lawyer . . . has a responsibility to provide legal services to those unable to pay . . .").

214. David G. Savage, The Race to the White House: A Trial Lawyer on Ticket Has Corporate U.S. Seeing Red, *L.A. Times,* Sept. 13, 2004, at 1 (noting that 80 percent of Americans believe that there is too much litigation).

215. James Carter, Remarks at the 100th Anniversary Luncheon of the Los Angeles County Bar Association, May 4, 1978), printed in *64 ABA J.* 840, 842 (1978).

Chapter 4

1. This article draws on Deborah L. Rhode, *Lawyers as Leaders* 129–153 (2013), and Deborah L. Rhode, From Platitudes to Priorities: Diversity and Gender Equity in Law Firms, *21 Geo. J. Legal Ethics* 1041 (2011).

2. Elizabeth Chambliss, *Miles to Go: Progress of Minorities in the Legal Profession* ix (2000). For example, minorities account for about 25 percent of doctors and 21 percent of accountants, but only 11 percent of lawyers. Sara Eckel, Seed Money, *Am. Law.,* Sept. 1, 2008, at 20;

ABA Legal Profession Statistics, available at http://www.americanbar.
org/resources_for_lawyers/profession_statistics.html.

3. Deborah L. Rhode, Perspectives on Professional Women, *40 Stan.*
   L. Rev. 1163 (1988).

4. For new entrants, see Andrew Buck & Andrew Cantor, Supply,
   Demand, and the Changing Economics of Large Firms, *60 Stan*
   L. Rev. 2087, 2103 (2008); Margaret Rivera, A New Business and
   Cultural Paradigm for the Legal Profession, *ACC Docket,* Oct.
   2008, at 66, 68. For specialties, see Fiona Kay & Elizabeth Gorman,
   Women and the Legal Profession, *4 Ann. Rev. Law & Soc. Sci.* 299,
   303 (2008).

5. See Chapter 2; Kay & Gorman, Women in the Legal Profession, at
   316 (summarizing studies); John P. Heinz et al., *Urban Lawyers: The*
   New Social Structure of the Bar 260 (2006).

6. ABA Commission on Women in the Profession, A Current Glance
   at Women in Law, 2013, available at http://www.americanbar.
   org/content/dam/aba/uncategorized/2011/cwp_current_glance_
   statistics_2011. Minority Corporate Counsel Association, MCCA
   Survey: Women General Counsel at Fortune 500 Companies Reaches
   New High, Aug. 8, 2012, at 1; Catalyst, Women in Law in the United
   States: Quick Take, Mar. 11, 2013.

7. Theresa Beiner, Not All Lawyers Are Equal: Difficulties that Plague
   Women and Women of Color, *58 Syracuse L. Rev.* 317, 328 (2008);
   Mary C. Noonan, Mary E. Corcoran, & Paul N. Courant, Is the
   Partnership Gap Closing for Women? Cohort Differences in the Sex
   Gap in Partnership Chances, *37 Soc. Sci. Res.* 156, 174–175 (2008).

8. A study of young lawyers by the American Bar Foundation (ABF)
   found that women attained equity partner status at about half the
   rate of men. See Ronit Dinovitzer et al., National Association for Law
   Placement [NALP] Foundation for Career Research and Education
   and the American Bar Foundation, *After the JD II: Second Results from*
   a National Study of Legal Careers, 63 (2009), available at http://law.
   du.edu/documents/directory/publications/sterling/AJD2.pdf. See also
   Joyce Sterling, Rebecca Sandefur, & Gabriele Plickert, Gender, in
   After the JD III: Third Results from a National Study of Legal Careers
   66 (Gabriele Plickert, ed., 2014). A study by the Federal Equal
   Employment Opportunity Commission found that male lawyers were
   five times as likely to become partners as their female counterparts.
   See Equal Employment Opportunity Commission, Diversity in Law
   Firms 9 (2003), available at http://www.eeoc.gov/eeoc/statistics/
   reports/index.cfm.

9. Mary C. Noonan & Mary Corcoran, The Mommy Track and
   Partnership: Temporary Delay or Dead End? *596 Annals Am. Acad.*

Pol. & Soc. Sci. 130, 142 (2004); Kenneth Gleen Dau-Schmidt, Marc Galanter, Kaushik Mukhopadhaya, & Kathleen E. Hull, Men and Women of the Bar: The Impact of Gender on Legal Careers, *16 Mich. J. Gender & L.* 49, 96–97, 100–102, 107, 111–112 (2009).

10. National Association of Women Lawyers and the NALP Foundation, Report of the Eighth Annual NAWL National Survey on Retention and Promotion of Women in Law Firms (Feb. 2014). See Vivia Chen, The Careerist: Female Equity Partnership Rate Is Up! (Just Kidding), *Am. Law.,* Feb. 25, 2014.

11. Jake Simpson, Firms Eyeing Gender Equality Should Adopt a Corporate Culture, *Law 360,* Apr. 22, 2014; Nancy Reichman & Joyce Sterling, Parenthood Status and Compensation in Law Practice, *20 Ind. J. Global Legal Stud.* 1203, 1221 (2013); Catalyst, Women in Law; Maria Pabon Lopez, The Future of Women in the Legal Profession: Recognizing the Challenges Ahead by Reviewing Current Trends, *19 Hastings Women's L. J.* 53, 71 (2008); Joan C. Williams & Veta T. Richardson, New Millennium, Same Glass Ceiling? The Impact of Law Firm Compensation Systems on Women, *The Project for Attorney Retention and Minority Corporate Counsel Association* 14 (2010).

12. Kathleen J. Wu, "Bossy" Is "Bitch" on Training Wheels, *Tex. Law.,* Apr. 29, 2014 (referring to *Law 360* survey).

13. Sterling, Sandefur, & Plickert, Gender, at 66 (pay gap between men and women after 12 years in practice is 20 percent); Zach Warren, Average Partner Compensation Growing, Gender Pay Gap Remains Wide, Inside Counsel, Sept. 17, 2014 (citing survey by Major, Lindsey & Africa finding that the average woman partner made $248,000 less than the average male partner, $531,000 vs. $779,000). Women also have lower billing rates. Jennifer Smith, Legal Fees and Gender Gap, *Wall St. J.,* May 5, 2014, at B4.

14. Marina Angel et al., Statistical Evidence on the Gender Gap in Law Firm Partner Compensation, *Temp. U. Legal Studies, Research Paper No. 2010–24* (2010); Ronit Dinovitzer, Nancy Reichman, & Joyce Sterling, Differential Valuation of Women's Work: A New Look at the Gender Gap in Lawyer's Incomes, *88 Soc. Forces* 819, 835–847 (2009).

15. Ronit Dinovitzer et al., *After the JD: First Results of a National Study of Legal Careers* 58 (2004); Lopez, The Future of Women, at 69; Nancy J. Reichman & Joyce S. Sterling, Sticky Floors, Broken Steps, and Concrete Ceilings in Legal Careers, *14 Tex. J. Women & L.* 27, 47 (2004).

16. Kay & Gorman, Women in the Legal Profession, 317–318.

17. David Chambers, Accommodation and Satisfaction: Women and Men Lawyers and the Balance of Work and Family, *14 Law & Soc. Inq.* 251, 280 (1989).

18. Marc Galanter & Thomas Palay, *Tournament of Lawyers: The Transformation of the Big Law Firm* 39 (1991).

19. National Association for Legal Career Professionals [NALP], Women and Minorities in Law Firms by Race and Ethnicity—An Update. *NALP Bulletin*, Apr. 2013; Minority Corporate Counsel Association, *Diversity and the Bar*, Sept./Oct. 2012, at 30.

20. Julie Treadman, Profession Backsliding on Diversity, *Nat'l L. J.*, Jun. 2, 2014, at 1.

21. Levit & Linder, *The Happy Lawyer*, at 250 n55.

22. Deepali Bagati, Women of Color in U. S. Law Firms 1–2 (2009).

23. American Bar Association Commission on Women in the Profession, Visible Invisibility 28 (2006).

24. Veronica Root, Retaining Color, *47 U. Mich. J. L. Reform* 575, 633 (2014).

25. Dinovitzer et al., *After the JD II*, at 64.

26. Levit & Linder, *The Happy Lawyer*, at 14.

27. John M. Conley, Tales of Diversity: Lawyers' Narratives of Racial Equity in Private Firms, *31 Law & Soc. Inq.* 831, 841–842, 851–852 (2006).

28. Richard Sander, The Racial Paradox of the Corporate Law Firm, *84 N.C. L. Rev.* 1755, 1775–1776 (2006); T. T. Clyesdale, A Forked River Runs Through Law School: Toward Understanding Race, Gender, Age, and Related Gaps in Law School Performance and Bar Passage, *29 Law & Soc. Inq.* 711, 740 (2004).

29. Around 80 percent of male partners and around 70 percent of female partners hold these views. Minority Corporate Counsel Association, Sustaining Pathways to Diversity: The Next Steps in Understanding and Increasing Diversity and Inclusion in Large Law Firms 16 (2009).

30. Conley, Tales of Diversity, at 841.

31. Conley, Tales of Diversity, at 844.

32. Conley, Tales of Diversity, at 850.

33. Deborah L. Rhode & Lucy Buford Ricca, Diversity in the Legal Profession: Perspectives from Managing Partners and General Counsel, *Fordham L. Rev.* (forthcoming, 2015).

34. Rhode & Ricca, Diversity in the Legal Profession.

35. Lopez, The Future of Women, at 65.

36. Bagati, Women of Color 37 (2009); Tiffani Darden, The Law Firm Caste System: Constructing a Bridge Between Workplace Equity Theory and the Institutional Analyses of Bias in Corporate Law Firms *30 Berkeley J. Emp. & Lab. L.* 85, 125 (2009); Lopez, The Future of Women, at 73.

37. Bagati, Women of Color, at 13.

38. David B. Wilkins & G. Mitu Gulati, Why Are There So Few Black Lawyers in Corporate Law Firms? An Institutional Analysis, *84 Cal.*

L. Rev. 493, 526–527 (1996); James B. Rebitzer & Lowell J. Taylor, Efficiency Wages and Employment Rents: The Employer-Size Wage Effect in the Job Market for Lawyers, *13 J. Lab. Econ.* 678, 690 (1995).

39. Simpson, Firms Eyeing Gender Equality.

40. Root, Retaining Color, at 612; Maria Chávez, *Everyday Injustice* 72 (2011); Jill L. Cruz & Melinda S. Molina, Hispanic National Bar Association National Study on the Status of Latinas in the Legal Profession, Few and Far Between: The Reality of Latina Lawyers, *37 Pepp. L. Rev.* 971, 1010 (2010); Garner K. Weng, Racial Bias in Law Practice, *Cal. Mag.,* Jan. 2003, at 37–38; Lu-in Wang, Race as Proxy: Situational Racism and Self-Fulfilling Stereotypes, *53 DePaul L. Rev.* 1013, 1014 (2004).

41. ABA Commission, Visible Invisibility, at 25; Weng, Racial Bias, at 37–38.

42. Institute for Inclusion in the Legal Profession, The State of Diversity, at 76; LeeAnn O'Neill, Hitting the Legal Diversity Market Home: Minority Women Strike Out, *The Modern American*, Spring 2007, at 7, 9; Bagati, Women of Color, at 37; ABA Commission, Visible Invisibility, at 25; Sonia M. Ospina & Erica G. Foldy, A Critical Review of Race and Ethnicity in the Leadership Literature: Surfacing Context, Power, and the Collective Dimensions of Leadership, *20 Leadership Q.* 876, 880 (2009).

43. ABA Commission, Visible Invisibility, at 18; Cruz & Molina, Few and Far Between, at 1010; O'Neill, Hitting the Legal Diversity Market, at 8; Gladys Garcia-López, "Nunca Te Toman En Cuenta [They Never Take You into Account]": The Challenges of Inclusion and Strategies for Success of Chicana Attorneys, *22 Gender & Soc'y* 590, 601–603(2008).

44. David A. Thomas, The Truth about Mentoring Minorities: Race Matters, *Harv. Bus. Rev.,* Apr. 2001, at 99, 104.

45. Arin N. Reeves, Written in Black & White: Exploring Confirmation Bias in Racialized Perceptions of Writing Skills 3 (2014), available at http://www.nextions.com/wp-content/files_mf/1413987796_magicfields__attach_1_1.pdf; Debra Cassens Weiss, Partners in Study Gave Legal Memo a Lower Rating When Told Author Wasn't White, *ABA J.,* Apr. 21, 2014.

46. Ella L. J. Edmondson Bell & Stella M. Nkomo, *Our Separate Ways: Black and White Women and the Struggle for Professional Identity* 145 (2001).

47. Lynette Clemetson, The Racial Politics of Speaking Well, *N.Y. Times,* Feb. 4, 2007, Sec. 4, at 1.

48. For competence, see Eli Wald, Glass Ceilings and Dead Ends: Professional Ideologies, Gender Stereotypes and the Future of Women Lawyers at Large Law Firms, *78 Fordham L. Rev.* 2245, 2256 (2010);

Cecilia L. Ridgeway & Paula England, Sociological Approaches to Sex Discrimination, in *Sex Discrimination in the Workplace* 189, 195 (Faye J. Crosby, Margaret S. Stockdale, & S. Ann Rupp, eds., 2007). For women's need to work harder, see Lopez, Future of Women, at 73. Even in experimental situations where male and female performance is objectively equal, women are held to higher standards, and their competence is rated lower. Martha Foschi, Double Standards in the Evaluation of Men and Women, *59 Soc. Psychol. Q.* 237 (1996). For the special pressures faced by women of color, see Garcia-López, They Never Take You into Account, at 598, 603–604.

49. Deborah L. Rhode & Joan Williams, Legal Perspectives on Employment Discrimination, in *Sex Discrimination in the Workplace*, at 235, 245; Minority Corporate Counsel Association, Sustaining Pathways, at 32.

50. Monica Beirnat, M. J. Tocci, & Joan C. Williams, The Language of Performance Evaluations: Gender-Based Shifts in Content and Consistency of Judgment, *3 Soc. Psych. & Pers. Sci.* 186 (2011).

51. Janet K. Swim & Lawrence J. Sanna, He's Skilled, She's Lucky: A Meta-Analysis of Observers' Attributions for Women's and Men's Successes and Failures, *22 Pers. & Soc. Psychol. Bull.* 507 (1996); Jeffrey H. Greenhaus & Saoj Parasuraman, Job Performance Attributions and Career Advancement Prospects: An Examination of Gender and Race Effects, *55 Org. Behav. & Hum. Decision Processes* 273, 276, 290 (1993).

52. Amy J. C. Cuddy, Susan T. Riske, & Peter Glick, When Professionals Become Mothers, Warmth Doesn't Cut the Ice, *60 J. Soc. Issues* 701, 709 (2004); Kathleen Fuegen, Monica Biernat, Elizabeth Haines, & Kay Deaux, Mothers and Fathers in the Workplace: How Gender and Parental Status Influence Judgments of Job-Related Competence, *60 J. Soc. Issues* 737, 745 (2004).

53. ABA Commission, Visible Invisibility, at 83. For other research, see Reichman & Sterling, Sticky Floors, at 63–64.

54. Sylvia A. Hewlett et al., The Sponsor Effect: Breaking Through the Last Glass Ceiling, *Harv. Bus. Rev.*, Jan. 2011, at 24; Michele Mayes & Kora Sophia Baysinger, *Courageous Counsel* 129 (2011) (quoting Dana Mayer).

55. Deborah L. Rhode & Barbara Kellerman, Women and Leadership: The State of Play, in *Women and Leadership: The State of Play and Strategies for Change* 7 (Barbara Kellerman & Deborah L. Rhode, eds., 2007); Catalyst, Women Take Care, Men Take Charge: Stereotyping of Business Leaders (2005); Linda L. Carli & Alice H. Eagly, Overcoming Resistance to Women Leaders: The Importance of Leadership Styles, in *Women and Leadership*, at 127–129; Wald, Glass Ceilings, at 2256.

56. Alice Eagly, Female Leadership Advantage and Disadvantage: Resolving the Contradictions, *31 Psych. Women Q.* 1, 5, 9 (2007); Carli & Eagly, Overcoming Resistance, at 128–129; Laurie A. Rudman & Stephen E. Kilianski, Implicit and Explicit Attitudes toward Female Authority, *26 Pers. & Soc. Psych. Bull.* 1315 (2000).

57. D. Anthony Butterfield & James P. Grinnell, Reviewing Gender, Leadership, and Managerial Behavior: Do The Decades of Research Tell Us Anything? in *Handbook of Gender and Work* 223, 235 (Gary N. Powell, ed., 1998); Jeanette N. Cleveland, Margaret Stockdale, & Kevin R. Murphy, *Women and Men in Organizations: Sex and Gender Issues at Work* 106–107 (2000).

58. Alice Eagly & Steven Karau, Role Congruity Theory of Prejudice toward Female Leaders, *109 Psych. Rev.* 574 (2002); Alice H. Eagly, Achieving Relational Authenticity in Leadership, *16 Leadership Q.* 470 (2005); Catalyst, The Double Bind Dilemma for Women in Leadership: Damned if You Do, Doomed if You Don't (2007); Linda Babcock & Sara Laschever, *Women Don't Ask: The High Cost of Avoiding Negotiation—and Positive Strategies for Change* 87–89 (2007); Mayes & Baysinger, *Courageous Counsel*, at 131.

59. Carli & Eagly, Overcoming Resistance, at 130; Williams & Richardson, New Millennium, at 48; Laurie A. Rudman, To Be or Not to Be (Self-Promoting): The Consequences of Counterstereotypical Impression Management, in *Power and Influence in Organizations* 290 (Roderick M. Kramer & Margaret A. Neale, eds., 1998).

60. Francis Flynn, Cameron Anderson, & Sebastien Brion, Too Tough Too Soon, Familiarity and the Backlash Effect (2011) (Stanford Business School, unpublished paper).

61. Rick Schmidt, Prophet and Loss, *Stan. Mag.*, Mar./Apr. 2009 (quoting Arthur Levitt), available at https://alumni.stanford.edu/get/page/magazine/article/?article_id=30885; Michael Hirsh, *Capitol Offense: How Washington's Wise Men Turned America's Future Over to Wall Street* 12, 1 (2010) (quoting Robert Rubin and unnamed staffer).

62. Schmidt, Prophet and Loss (quoting Michael Greenberger).

63. Katha Pollitt, Hillary Rotten, in *Thirty Ways of Looking at Hillary: Reflections by Women Writers* 16–18 (Susan Morrison, ed., 2008).

64. Marie Cocco, Misogyny I Won't Miss, *Wash. Post,* May 15, 2008, at A14; Kathleen Deveny, Just Leave Your Mother out of It, *Newsweek,* Mar. 17, 2008, at 32.

65. David L. Hamilton & Jim W. Sherman, Stereotypes, in *Handbook of Social Cognition* 1–68 (Robert S. Wyler & Thomas K. Scrull, eds., 1994); for confirmation bias generally, see Paul Brest & Linda Krieger, *Problem Solving, Decision Making and Professional Judgment* 277–289 (2010).

66. Robin Ely, Herminia Ibarra, & Deborah M. Kolb, Taking Gender into Account: Theory and Design for Women's Leadership Development Programs, *10 Acad. Mgmt. Learning & Educ.* 474, 477 (2010); Martha Foschi, Double Standards in the Evaluation of Men and Women, at 237; ABA Commission, Visible Invisibility, at 27.

67. Linda Hamilton Krieger, The Content of Our Categories: A Cognitive Bias Approach to Discrimination and Equal Employment Opportunity, *47 Stan. L. Rev.* 1161, 1234 (1995).

68. Williams & Richardson, New Millennium, at 49–50; Ridgeway & England, Sociological Approaches, at 197; Marilyn B. Brewer & Rupert J. Brown, Intergroup Relations, in *The Handbook of Social Psychology* 554–594 (Daniel T. Gilbert, Susan T. Fiske, & Gardner Lindzey, eds., 1998); Susan T. Fiske, Stereotyping, Prejudice and Discrimination, in *The Handbook of Social Psychology*, at 357–414.

69. The term comes from Pierre Bourdieu, The Forms of Capital, in *Handbook of Theory and Research for the Sociology of Education* 241, 248 (John G. Richardson, ed., 1986). For discussion in the legal context, see ABA Commission, Visible Invisibility, at ix; Cindy A. Schipani, Terry M. Dworkin, Angel Kwolek-Folland, & Virgina G. Maurer, Pathways for Women to Obtain Positions of Organizational Leadership: The Significance of Mentoring and Networking, *16 Duke J. Gender L. & Pol'y* 89 (2009); Fiona Kay & Jean E. Wallace, Mentors as Social Capital: Gender, Mentors, and Career Rewards in Legal Practice, *79 Soc. Inq.* 418 (2009).

70. For minorities, see ABA Commission, Visible Invisibility, at 18; Wilkins & Gulati, Why Are There So Few Black Lawyers in Corporate Law Firms? at 493. For women, see Reichman & Sterling, Sticky Floors, at 65; Timothy O'Brien, Up the Down Staircase, *N.Y. Times,* Mar. 19, 2006, at A4; Williams & Richardson, New Millennium, at 16–17.

71. ABA Commission, Visible Invisibility, at 35; Jill Schachner Chanen, Early Exits, *ABA J.,* Aug. 2006, at 36.

72. Sarah Dinolfo, Christine Silva, & Nancy M. Carter, High Potentials in the Pipeline: Leaders Pay It Forward 7 (2012), available at http://www.catalyst.org/knowledge/high-potentials-pipeline-leaders-pay-it-forward.

73. Dinolfo, Silva, & Carter, High Potentials, at 7.

74. David Hekman, Does Valuing Diversity Result in Worse Performance Ratings for Minority and Female Leaders? (paper presented at the Academy of Management 2014 meeting), discussed in Rachel Feintzeig, Women Penalized for Promoting Women, Study Finds, *Wall St. J.,* Jul. 24, 2014, at D3.

75. See studies cited in Rhode, From Platitudes, at 1071–1072.

76. ABA Commission, Visible Invisibility, at 14.

77. For the role of sexual concerns, see Hewlett et al., Sponsor Effect, at 35. For race-related barriers in mentoring, see Monique R. Payne-Pikus, John Hagan, & Robert L. Nelson, Experiencing Discrimination: Race and Retention in America's Largest Law Firms, *44 Law & Soc'y Rev.* 553, 561 (2010).

78. ABA Commission, Visible Invisibility, at 27. See also Thomas, The Truth about Mentoring Minorities, at 105; Julie Treadman, The Diversity Crisis: Big Firms' Continuing Failure, *Am. Law.,* May 2014.

79. ABA Commission, Visible Invisibility, at 15–16: Marc Galanter & William Henderson, The Elastic Tournament, *60 Stan. L. Rev.,* 1 (2008); Payne-Pikus, Hagan, & Nelson, Experiencing Discrimination, at 576.

80. Institute for Inclusion in the Legal Profession, The State of Diversity, 46.

81. Bagati, Women of Color, at 16; ABA Presidential Initiative Commission on Diversity, Diversity in the Legal Profession: The Next Steps 43 (2010).

82. ABA Commission, Visible Invisibility, at 21; Wilkins & Gulati, Why Are There So Few Black Lawyers in Corporate Law Firms? at 493, 565–571.

83. ABA Commission, Visible Invisibility, at 21.

84. Williams & Richardson, New Millennium, at 42.

85. ABA Commission, Visible Invisibility, at 21; O'Neill, Hitting the Legal Diversity Market, at 10.

86. Linda A. Mabry, The Token, *Cal. Law.,* Jul. 2006, at 76.

87. ABA Commission, Visible Invisibility, at 26; David Wilkins, From "Separate Is Inherently Unequal" to "Diversity Is Good for Business": The Rise of Market-Based Diversity Arguments and the Fate of the Black Corporate Bar, *117 Harv. L. Rev.* 1548–1595 (2004).

88. ABA Commission, Visible Invisibility, at 26.

89. National Association for Law Placement, Most Lawyers Working Part Time Are Women—Overall Number of Lawyers Working Part Time Remains Small (Dec. 17, 2009, news release).

90. Paula A. Patton, Women Lawyers: Their Status, Influence, and Retention in the Legal Profession, *William & Mary J. Women & L.* 173, 180 (2005). For lower partnership rates, see Beiner, Not All Lawyers Are Equal, at 326; Dau-Schmidt, Galanter, Mukhopadhaya, & Hull, Men and Women of the Bar, at 49; Mona Harrington & Helen Hsi, MIT Workplace Center, Women Lawyers and Obstacles to Leadership, 28–29 (2007), available at http://nysbar.com/blogs/generalpractice/2007/05/women_lawyers_and_obstacles_to.html.

91. David Leonhardt, Financial Careers Come at a Cost to Families, *N.Y. Times,* May 27, 2009, at B1; Dau-Schmidt, Galanter, Mukhopadhaya, & Hull, Men and Women of the Bar, at 95–96; Beiner, Not All Lawyers Are Equal, at 326.

92. Noonan & Corcoran, The Mommy Track, at 130, 146.

93. See Deborah L. Rhode, Balanced Lives for Lawyers, *70 Fordham L. Rev.* 2207, 2213 (2002); for stigma, see Holly English, *Gender on Trial* 212 (2003) (reporting perceptions about slackers); Lopez, Future of Women, at 95; Cynthia Thomas Calvert, Linda Bray Chanow, & Linda Marks, The Project for Attorney Retention, Reduced Hours, Full Success: Part-Time Partners in U.S. Law Firms (2009) (reporting that even among lawyers who had achieved partnership, about 40 percent feel stigma from taking part-time schedules), available at http://amlawdaily.typepad.com/files/part-timepartner.pdf.

94. Deborah L. Rhode, *What Women Want: An Agenda for the Women's Movement* 59–60 (2014); Bureau of Labor Statistics, American Time Use Survey 2010 (2011).

95. Nancy Gertner, *In Defense of Women: Memoirs of an Unrepentant Advocate* 246 (2011).

96. Dinovitzer et al., *After the JD II*, at 62.

97. Noonan & Corcoran, The Mommy Track, at 137.

98. Dau-Schmidt, Galanter, Mukhopadhaya, & Hull, Men and Women of the Bar, at 112–113; Levit & Linder, *Happy Lawyer*, at 12–13.

99. Marci Krufka, The Young & the Restless, *Law Prac.,* Jul./Aug. 2004, at 48; Galanter & Henderson, Elastic Tournament, at 1922–1923.

100. Sheryl Gay Stolberg, He Breaks for Band Recitals, *N.Y. Times,* Feb. 12, 2010.

101. Galanter & Henderson, Elastic Tournament, at 1921.

102. Rhode & Ricca, Diversity in the Legal Profession.

103. Calvert, Chanow, & Marks, Reduced Hours, at 13, 22.

104. Calvert, Chanow, & Marks, Reduced Hours, at 9, 13, 21.

105. Deloitte and Touche has been a leader. See Susan Sturm, Second Generation Employment Discrimination: A Structural Approach, *101 Colum. L. Rev.* 458, 493 (2001).

106. Levit & Linder, *Happy Lawyer*, at 170; Wal-Mart Legal News, Nov. 2009, at 1; Calvert, Chanow, & Marks, Reduced Hours, at 10–12.

107. Minority Corporate Counsel Association, Sustaining Pathways, at 16.

108. Minority Corporate Counsel Association, Sustaining Pathways, at 25.

109. Minority Corporate Counsel Association, Sustaining Pathways, at 15.

110. Ben Martin, Letter to the Editor, *Nat'l L. J.,* Nov. 6, 2006, at 23.

111. Walter La Grande, Getting There, *ABA J.,* Feb. 1999, at 54.

112. La Grande, Getting There, at 54.

113. Wilkins, From "Separate Is Inherently Unequal," at 1572–1573.

114. See Eyana J. Smith, Employment Discrimination in the Firm: Does the Legal System Provide Remedies for Women and Minority Members of the Bar? *6 U. Pa. J. Lab. & Emp. L.* 789 (2004).

115. Title VII of the federal Civil Rights Act prohibits employment discrimination based on race, color, religion, sex, or national origin.

42 US. Code Section 2000 (e)(2). For an overview, see Katherine T. Bartlett, Deborah L. Rhode, & Joanna Grossman, *Gender and Law: Theory, Doctrine, Commentary* 89 (6th ed., 2013).

116. Rhode & Williams, Legal Perspectives on Employment Discrimination, at 243; *Riordan v. Kaminers*, 831 F. 2d 690, 697 (7th Cir. 1987).

117. The problem is true of employment discrimination litigation generally. See Laura Beth Nielson & Robert L. Nelson, Rights Realized? An Empirical Analysis of Employment Discrimination Litigation as a Claiming System, *2005 Wis. L. Rev.* 663; Linda Hamilton Krieger, The Watched Variable Improves: On Eliminating Sex Discrimination in Employment, in *Sex Discrimination in the Workplace*, at 296, 309–310.

118. ABA Commission, Visible Invisibility, at 20 (aggressive, bitch); Williams & Richardson, New Millennium, at 38 (confrontational); Reichman & Sterling, Sticky Floors, at 65 (bitch); Marcia Coyle, Black Lawyer's Life, Suit Told by a White Author, *Nat'l L. J.*, Jan. 11, 1999, at A14 (quoting Mungen) (angry black).

119. For the advice, see Robert Kolker, The Gay Flannel Suit, *N.Y. Mag.*, Feb. 26, 2007, available at http://nymag.com/news/features/28515/; ABA Commission, Visible Invisibility, at 21. For negative consequences following complaints about compensation, see Williams & Richardson, New Millennium, at 38.

120. National Association for Law Placement Foundation, How Associate Evaluations Measure Up, A National Study of Associate Performance Assessments 74 (2006).

121. ABA Commission, Visible Invisibility, at 27.

122. Kolker, Gay Flannel Suit.

123. Deborah L. Rhode, What's Sex Got to Do with It: Diversity in the Legal Profession, in *Legal Ethics: Law Stories* 233, 246 (Deborah L. Rhode & David Luban, eds., 2005) (quoting Charles Kopp).

124. Rhode, What's Sex Got to Do with It, at 235.

125. *Ezold v. Wolf, Block, Schorr & Solis-Cohen*, 751 F. Supp. 1175, 1184–1186 (E.D. Pa.1990), reversed, 983 F.2d 509 (3d Cir. 1992), *cert. denied*, 510 U.S. 826 (1993).

126. *Ezold v. Wolf, Block, Schorr & Solis-Cohen*, 751 F. Supp.1175.

127. 983 F.2d 509 528 (3d Cir. 1992). See Rhode, What's Sex Got to Do with It, at 243.

128. Rhode, What's Sex Got To Do with It, at 245 (quoting Robert Segal).

129. *Equal Opportunity Commission v. Bloomberg*, 778 F. Supp. 2d 458, 485 (S.D.N.Y 2011).

130. Amelia J. Uelman, The Evils of Elasticity: Reflections on the Rhetoric of Professionalism and the Part-Time Paradox in Large Firm Practice, *33 Fordham Urb. L. J.* 81, 83 (2005).

131. *Fisher v. University of Texas*, 570 U.S. (2013).

132. Sturm, Second Generation, at 468, 470–41, 475–476.

133. Wilkins, From "Separate Is Inherently Unequal," at 1570 n1010 (quoting Scott Mitchell).

134. ABA Presidential Initiative Commission on Diversity, Diversity in the Legal Profession, at 9.

135. Rhode & Ricca, Diversity in the Legal Profession.

136. Center for Women in Law at the University of Texas School of Law, Austin, Manifesto on Women in Law, May 1, 2009.

137. Cedric Herring, Does Diversity Pay? Race, Gender and the Business Case for Diversity, *74 Am. Soc. Rev.* 208, 220 (2009); Elizabeth Mannix & Margaret A. Neale, What Differences Make a Difference? The Promise and Reality of Diverse Teams on Organizations, *6 Psychol. Sci. Pub. Int.* 31, 35 (2005); Douglas E. Brayley & Eric S. Nguyen, Good Business: A Market-Based Argument for Law Firm Diversity, *34 J. Legal Prof.* 1, 13 (2009).

138. See Brayley & Nguyen, Good Business, at 13–14; David A. Carter et al., Corporate Diversity and Firm Value, *38 Fin. Rev.* 33, 51 (2003). For a review of this evidence and its methodological limitations, see Deborah L. Rhode & Amanda K. Packel, Diversity on Corporate Boards: How Much Difference Does Difference Make? *39 Delaware J. Corp. L.* 377, 384–390 (2014).

139. Lissa Lamkin Broome & Kimberly Krawiec, Signaling through Board Diversity: Is Anyone Listening? *77 U. Cinn. L. Rev.* 431, 446–448 (2008).

140. See studies discussed in Rhode & Packel, Diversity on Corporate Boards, at 384–390.

141. See studies discussed in Brayley & Nguyen, Good Business; Frank Dobbin & Jiwook Jung, Corporate Board Diversity and Stock Performance: The Competence Gap or Institutional Investor Bias, *89 N. Carolina L. Rev.* 809 (2011); David L. Levine & Aparna Joshi, Do Birds of a Feather Shop Together? The Effects on Performance of Employees' Similarity with One Another and with Customers, *25 Org. Behav.* 731 (2004); Wilkins, From "Separate but Equal," at 1588–1590.

142. See studies discussed in Rhode & Packel, Diversity on Corporate Boards, at 387; Dobbin & Jung, Corporate Board Gender Diversity.

143. Brayley & Nyugen Good Business, at 34; Rhode & Packel, Diversity on Corporate Boards; Kathleen A. Farrell & Philip L. Hersch, Additions to Corporate Boards: The Effect of Gender, *11 J. Corp. Fin.* 85 (2005).

144. Minority Corporate Counsel Association, A Call to Action: Diversity in the Legal Profession Commitment Statement.

145. Neta Ziv & Christopher Whelan, Privatizing the Profession: Clients' Control of Lawyers' Ethics, *80 Fordham L. Rev.* 2577 (2012).

146. Ziv & Whelan, Privatizing the Profession, at 2597–2600; Claire Tower Putnam, Comment: When Can a Law Firm Discriminate among Its Own Employees to Meet a Client's Request? Reflections on the ACC's Call to Action, *9 U. Pa. J. Lab. & Emp. L.* 657, 660 (2007); Karen Donovan, Pushed by Clients, Law Firms Step Up Diversity Efforts, *N.Y. Times,* Jul. 21, 2006, at C6.

147. California Minority Counsel Program, Diversity Business Matters: Corporate Programs Supporting Business for Diverse Outside Counsel 18 (2011).

148. Melanie Lasoff Levs, Carrot Money to Diversity, *Diversity and the Bar*, Sept./Oct. 2008, at 59.

149. Rhode & Ricca, Diversity in the Legal Profession.

150. For a sampling of criticism, see Williams & Richardson, New Millennium, at 51–55.

151. Catalyst, Women in Corporate Leadership, 15, 21; Eleanor Clift & Tom Brazaitis, *Madame President* 321, 324 (2003).

152. Linda Babcock & Sara Laschever, *Ask for It* 252 (2008).

153. Babcock & Laschever, *Ask for It*, at 252–262.

154. Joan Biskupic, *Sandra Day O'Connor* 56 (2009) (quoting Benie Wynn).

155. Ely, Ibarra, & Kolb, Taking Gender into Account; Erin White, Female Training Classes Flourish, *Wall St. J.,* Sept. 25, 2006, at B3. The Leadership Council on Legal Diversity also offers a fellowship program for minorities on the leadership track.

156. Mayes & Baysinger, *Courageous Counsel* 82 (2011).

157. Mayes & Baysinger, *Courageous Counsel*, at 69.

158. Mayes & Baysinger, *Courageous Counsel*, at 75.

159. Linda Addison Delivers Advice to All with a "Lawyer's Dozen," *Forbes*, Apr. 25, 2014, available at http://www.forbes.com/sites/gaygaddis/2014/04/25/linda-addison-delivers-advice-to-all-with-a-lawyers-dozen (quoting Xerox CEO Ursula Burns).

160. Susan A. Berson, The Rules (for Women), *ABA J.*, Jan. 2012, at 28; Chanow & Rikleen, Power in Law, at 15.

161. Linda Addison Delivers Advice.

162. Frank Dobbin, Alexandra Kalev, & Erin Kelly, Diversity Management in Corporate America, *Context,* Fall 2007, at 21; Catalyst, Advancing Women in Business, at 6, 12–13; Catalyst, Women of Color in Corporate Management, at 69.

163. Frank Dobbin & Alexandra Kalev, The Architecture of Inclusion: Evidence from Corporate Diversity Programs, *30 Harv. J. L. & Gender* 279, 283 (2007); Jeanine Prime, Marissa Agin, & Heather Foust-Cummings, Strategy Matters: Evaluating Company Approaches

for Creating Inclusive Workplaces 6 (2010), available at http://www.catalyst.org/knowledge/strategy-matters-evaluating-company-approaches-creating-inclusive-workplaces; Beiner, Not All Lawyers, at 333.

164. ABA Presidential Initiative Commission on Diversity, Diversity in the Legal Profession, at 23.

165. Emilio J. Castilla, Gender, Race, and Meritocracy in Organizational Careers, *113 Am. J. Soc.* 1479, 1485 (2008); Stephen Benard, In Paik, & Shelley J. Correll, Cognitive Bias and the Motherhood Penalty, *59 Hastings L. Rev.* 1359, 1381 (2008).

166. Simpson, Firms Eyeing Gender Equality.

167. Bagati, Women of Color, 49; Rhode & Kellerman, Women and Leadership, at 27; Ridgeway & England, Sociological Approaches, at 202; Ely, Ibarra, & Kolb, Taking Gender into Account, at 481; Joanna Barsh & Lareina Lee, Unlocking the Full Potential of Women at Work 11 (2011), available at http://www.mckinsey.com/client_service/organization/latest_thinking/unlocking_the_full_potential.

168. Dobbin & Kalev, The Architecture of Inclusion, at 293–294; Dobbin, Kalev, & Kelly, Diversity Management, at 23–24.

169. See http://jezebel.com/is-this-the-most-offensively-misguided-office-memo-youv-1568180278.

170. Darden, The Law Firm Caste System, at 85–100. For the limited research and mixed or negative findings on effectiveness, see Deborah L. Rhode, Social Research and Social Change: Meeting the Challenge of Gender Inequality and Sexual Abuse, *30 Harv. J. L. & Gender* 11, 13–14 (2007); Elizabeth Levy Paluck, Diversity Training and Intergroup Contact: A Call to Action Research, *62 J. Soc. Issues* 577, 583, 591 (2006).

171. Dobbin & Kalev, The Architecture of Inclusion, at 293–295; Dobbin, Kalev, & Kelly, Diversity Management, at 23–25.

172. Darden, The Law Firm Caste System, at 117; Diane Vaughan, Rational Choice, Situated Action, and the Social Control of Organizations, *32 Law & Soc'y Rev.* 23, 34 (1998).

173. Rhode & Ricca, Diversity in the Legal Profession.

174. NALP National Survey on Retention and Promotion of Women in Law Firms, Nov. 2007, at 15.

175. Schipani et al., Pathways, at 131; Alexandra Kalev, Frank Dobbin, & Erin Kelly, Best Practices or Best Guesses: Assessing the Efficacy of Corporate Affirmative Action and Diversity Policies, *71 Am. Soc. Rev.* 589, 594 (2006); Rhode & Kellerman, Women and Leadership, at 30.

176. Bob Yates, Law Firms Address Retention of Women and Minorities, *Chi. Law.,* Mar. 2007.

177. Dobbin, Kalev, & Kelly, Diversity Management, at 25.

178. Kalev, Dobbin, & Kelly, Best Practices, at 594; Rhode & Kellerman, Women and Leadership at 30; Schipani et al., Pathways 89, 100–101 (2009); Abbott, *The Lawyer's Guide to Mentoring*, at 25, 32–33.
179. Minnesota State Bar Association, Diversity and Gender Equity in the Legal Profession, Best Practices Guide, available at http://msba.mnbar.org/.
180. Minnesota State Bar Association, Diversity and Gender Equity.
181. Minority Corporate Counsel Association, Mentoring Across Differences, available at http://www.mcca.com/_data/n_001/rsrources/live/GoldBookExecutiveSummary.pdf.; Leigh Jones, Mentoring Plans Failing Associates, *Nat'l L. J.*, Sept. 15, 2006, available at http://www.law.com/jsp/nlj/PubArticleNLJ.jsp?id=900005462642.
182. Catalyst, The Pipeline's Broken Promise 5 (2010).
183. American Bar Association, Search the Pipeline Diversity Directory, available at http://www.americanbar.org/groups/diversity/diversity_pipeline/resources/pipeline_diversity_directory.html. For discussion of such programs, see Jason P. Nance & Paul E. Madsen, An Empirical Analysis of Diversity in the Legal Profession (2014).
184. Sara Eckel, Seed Money, *Am. Law.*, Sept. 2008, at 20.
185. Eckel, Seed Money, at 20 (quoting Ruth Ashby).
186. Frederick A. Miller & Judith H. Katz, The Inclusion Breakthrough: Unleashing the Real Power of Diversity 37–38 (2002).

Chapter 5

1. ABA Commission on Ethics 20/20, Introduction and Overview (2012), available at http//www.americanbar.org/content/dam/aba.
2. James E. Moliterno, Crisis Regulation, *2012 Mich. St. L. Rev.* 307, 340–341 (2012).
3. David Maister, The Trouble with Lawyers, *Am. Law.*, Apr. 2008, at 33; Moliterno, Crisis Regulation, at 344. In one survey, fewer than a fifth of law firm leaders described their role as leading innovation and change. Leadership Partners or Managing Partners, *10 Law Off. Mgmt. & Ad.*, 1, 20 (Oct. 2010).
4. Benjamin Barton, In Defense of the Status Quo: A Critique of the ABA's Role in the Regulation of the American Legal Profession, *45 Suffolk U. L. Rev.* 1009, 1021–1022 (2012); Deborah L. Rhode, *In the Interests of Justice: Reforming the American Legal Profession* 16 (2000).
5. Jack A. Guttenberg, Practicing Law in the Twenty-First Century in a Twentieth (Nineteenth) Century Straitjacket: Something Has to Give, *2012 Mich. St. L. Rev.* 415, 491 (2012); James E. Moliterno, The Future of Legal Education Reform, *40 Pepp. L. Rev.* 423, 436 (2013); Moliterno, Crisis Regulation, at 341.

6. James Podgers, Clear Track Ethics 20/20 Commission Can Now Address Issues of Fee Splitting with Nonlawyers, *ABA J.*, Oct. 2012, at 20; Stephen Gillers, How to Make Rules for Lawyers: The Professional Responsibility of the Legal Profession, *40 Pepp. L. Rev.* 365, 399–402 (2013).

7. Laurel Rigertas, Stratification of the Legal Profession: A Debate in Need of a Public Forum, *2012 Prof. Law.* 79, 111 (2012). See generally Charles W. Wolfram, Lawyer Turf and Lawyer Regulation: The Role of the Inherent Powers Doctrine, *12 U. Ark. Little Rock L. J.* 1 (1989).

8. Rigertas, Stratification, at 112; Charles Wolfram, Barriers to Effective Public Participation in the Regulation of the Legal Profession, *62 Minn. L. Rev.* 619, 636–641 (1978).

9. For inaccessibility, see Benjamin H. Barton, An Institutional Analysis of Lawyer Regulation: Who Should Control Lawyer Regulation— Courts, Legislatures, or the Market? *37 Ga. L. Rev.* 1167, 1200 (2003). For the role of the bar, see Wolfram, Lawyer Turf and Lawyer Regulation, at 16.

10. Wolfram, Lawyer Turf and Lawyer Regulation, at 17.

11. Gillian K. Hadfield, Higher Demand, Lower Supply? A Comparative Assessment of the Legal Resource Landscape for Ordinary Americans, *37 Fordham Urb. L. J.* 129, 154 (2011).

12. Barton, An Institutional Analysis, at 1176; Benjamin H. Barton, Do Judges Systematically Favor the Interests of the Legal Profession?, *59 Ala. L. Rev.* 453, 456, 459 (2008); Benjamin H. Barton, *The Lawyer-Judge Bias in the American Legal System* (2010).

13. Barton, An Institutional Analysis, at 1187, 1195; Barton, Do Judges Systematically Favor the Interests of the Legal Profession?, at 458.

14. Kelly Armitage, Denial Ain't Just a River in Egypt: A Thorough Review of Judicial Elections, Merit Selection, and the Role of State Judges in Society, *29 Cap. U. L Rev.* 625, 656 (2002); Barton, An Institutional Analysis, at 1199.

15. Barton, *The Lawyer-Judge Bias,* at 133; Barton, Do Judges Systematically Favor the Interests of the Legal Profession?, at 458; Barton, An Institutional Analysis, at 1200.

16. Barton, An Institutional Analysis, at 1203.

17. HALT, http://www.halt.org/about_halt/.

18. The American Bar Association alone has nearly 400,000 members. See http://www.americanbar.org/membership.html.

19. Ted Schneyer, Thoughts on the Compatibility of Recent UK and Australian Reforms with U.S. Traditions in Regulating Law Practice, *2009 J. Prof. Law.*, 13, 25.

20. Gillers, How to Make Rules for Lawyers: The Professional Responsibility of the Legal Profession, at 365, 372.

21. Elizabeth J. Cohen, Modest Changes That Ethics 20/20 Urged Can be Seen as Positive, or Lost Opportunity, *29 ABA/BNA Law. Man. Prof. Conduct* 690, 691 (2013) (quoting George Jones).
22. ABA Model Rules of Professional Conduct, Rule 5.5.
23. *Leis v. Flynt,* 441 U.S. 956 (1979).
24. ABA Report of the Commission on Multijurisdictional Practice (Aug. 2002), available at http://www.abanet.org/cpr/mjp/final_mjp_rpt_5–13.pdf.
25. Bruce A. Green, Assisting Clients with Multi-State and Interstate Legal Problems: The Need to Bring the Professional Regulation of Lawyers into the 21st Century (2000), available at http://www.americanbar.org/groups/professional_responsibility/committees_commissions/commission_on_multijurisdictional_practice/mjp_bruce_green_report.html.
26. Stephen Gillers, A Profession, if You Can Keep It: How Information Technology and Fading Borders Are Reshaping the Law Marketplace and What We Should Do About It, *63 Hastings L. J.* 953, 976–978 (2012); Stephanie L. Kimbro, Regulatory Barriers to the Growth of Multijurisdictional Virtual Law Firms and Potential First Steps to Their Removal, *13 N.C. J. L. & Tech.* 165 (2012).
27. Gillers, A Profession, at 998, 996.
28. ABA Report of the Commission on Multijurisdictional Practice, 10–12 (2002).
29. ABA Model Rules of Professional Conduct, Rule 5.5 (c)(1).
30. Eli Wald, Federalizing Legal Ethics, Nationalizing Law Practice, and the Future of the American Legal Profession in a Global Age, *48 San Diego L. Rev.* 489, 506 (2011).
31. Wald, Federalizing Legal Ethics, at 528; Stephen Gillers, Protecting Their Own, *Am. Law.,* Nov. 1998, at 118.
32. Charles Wolfram, Sneaking Around in the Legal Profession: Interjurisdictional Unauthorized Practice by Transactional Lawyers, *36 S. Tex. L. Rev.* 665, 685 (1995); Christine R. Davis, Approaching Reform: The Future of Multijurisdictional Practice in Today's Legal Profession, *29 Fla. St. L. Rev.* 1339, 1344–1345 (2002); Wald, Federalizing Legal Ethics, at 501; James Moliterno, *The American Legal Profession in Crisis* 198 (2013).
33. Guttenberg, Practicing Law, at 415, 424.
34. Wolfram, Sneaking Around, at 706; Anthony E. Davis, Multijurisdictional Practice by Transactional Lawyers—Why the Sky Really Is Falling, *Prof. Law.,* Winter 2000, at 1359.
35. Murray Hawkins, Australian Legal Education and Bar Admissions, *B. Exam.,* Feb. 2008, at 18.

36. For similar open-border proposals, see Wald, Federalizing Legal Ethics, at 538–539; Davis, Multijurisdictional Practice, at 27; Gillers, Protecting Their Own, at 118.

37. Wald, Federalizing Legal Ethics, at 537; Davis, Multijurisdictional Practice, at 1359.

38. See James M. Moliterno & George C. Harris, *Global Issues in Legal Ethics* 7–22 (2007); Roger J. Goebal, The Liberalization of Interstate Legal Practice in the European Union: Lessons for the United States? *34 Int'l L.* 307 (2000).

39. See Geoffrey C. Hazard, Jr., The New Shape of Lawyering, *Nat'l L. J.*, Jul. 23, 2001, at A21.

40. Colorado Rules of Professional Conduct Rule 5.5 (2010). See Robert R. Keating et al., Colorado Adopts Rules Governing Out-of-State Attorneys, *Colo. Law.*, Feb. 2003, at 27.

41. Colorado Rules Civil Procedure, 220.

42. Joan C. Rogers, Ethics 20/20 Commission Gets Earful About Its Draft Proposals on Foreign Lawyers, MJP, *27 ABA/BNA Law. Man. Prof. Conduct* 669, 671 (2011) (quoting James Coyle).

43. Rodgers, Ethics 20/20 Commission, at 671 (paraphrasing Carolyn Lamm).

44. ABA Model Rules of Professional Conduct, Rule 5.4. This discussion of multidisciplinary practice draws on Deborah L. Rhode, David Luban, & Scott L. Cummings, *Legal Ethics* 776–779 (6th ed., 2013).

45. The CCBE Code does not mention multidisciplinary practice but provides simply that fee splitting with nonlawyers is prohibited except in jurisdictions where permitted by local law and ethical rules. For an overview of European practice, see Rees M. Hawkins, Not "If," but "When" and "How": A Look at Existing De Facto Multidisciplinary Practices and What They Can Teach Us about the Ongoing Debate, *83 N.C. L. Rev.* 481, 494–496 (2005).

46. Geoffrey Hazard, Accountants vs Lawyers: Let's Consider Facts, *Nat'l L. J.*, Nov. 9, 1998, at A24.

47. See sources cited in Hawkins, Not "If" but "When." The Brave New World of Multidisciplinary Practice, Future of the Profession: A Symposium on Multidisciplinary Practice, *84 Minn. L. Rev.* 1083 (2000). See also Mary C. Daly, Choosing Wise Men Wisely: The Risks and Rewards of Purchasing Legal Services from Lawyers in a Multidisciplinary Partnership, *13 Geo. J. Legal Ethics* 217 (2000).

48. For a sampling of these arguments, see New York State Bar Association, Special Committee on the Law Governing Firm Structure and Operation, Preserving the Core Values of the American

Legal Profession: The Place of Multidisciplinary Practice in the Law Governing Lawyers 324 (2000).

49. Steven C. Krane, Let Lawyers Practice Law, *Nat'l L. J.*, Jan. 28, 2002, at A16; Geanne Rosenberg, Scandal Seen as Blow to Outlook for MDP, *Nat'l. L. J.*, Jan. 21, 2002, at A1.

50. American Bar Association Commission on Multidisciplinary Practice, Report to the ABA House of Delegates, reprinted in *10 Prof. Law.* (1999).

51. Paul D. Paton, Multidisciplinary Practice Redux; Globalization, Core Values, and Reviving the MDP Debate in America, *78 Fordham L. Rev.* 2193, 2209 (2010). See also MDP Rides Again, *ABA J.*, Feb. 2000, at 96.

52. American Bar Association Center for Professional Responsibility Recommendation 10F, available at http://www.abanet.org/cpr/md;/mdprecom10f.html.

53. Robert R. Keating, Colorado and Denver in the House: MDP Declared Heresy by the ABA House of Delegates, *Colo. Law.*, Sept. 2000, at 48.

54. Commission on Multidisciplinary Practice, Report to the House of Delegates.

55. For discussion of these arguments, see David Luban, Asking the Right Questions, *72 Temp. L. Rev.* 839 (1999); Rhode, *In the Interests of Justice*, at 138.

56. New York State Bar Association Committee on Professional Ethics, Op. 765, Jul. 22, 2003 (approving nonexclusive reciprocal referral arrangements); see also Hawkins, Not "if" but "When," at 498.

57. See Hawkins, Not "if" but "When," at 511, 512 (describing Boston Legal Collaborative, which employs seven attorneys, a psychologist, a financial planner, and a work consultant in handling employment, family, and business matters).

58. This discussion of nonlawyer investment draws on Deborah L. Rhode, Reforming American Legal Practice and Legal Education: Rethinking Licensing Structures and the Role of Nonlawyers in Delivering and Financing Legal Services, *16 Legal Ethics* 243 (2013).

59. ABA Commission on Ethics 20/20, For Comment, Issues Paper Concerning Alternative Business Structures, Apr. 5, 2011, at 7–17.

60. ABA Commission on Ethics 20/20, at 7–19.

61. Katherine H. Reardon, It's Not Your Business! A Critique of the UK Legal Services Act of 2007 and Why Nonlawyers Should Not Own or Manage Law Firms in the United States, *40 Syracuse J. Intl L. & Com.* 155 (2012); New York State Bar Association, Report of the Task Force on Nonlawyer Ownership 73–74 (Nov. 17, 2012).

62. ABA Model Rules of Professional Conduct, Rule 5.4, Comment.

63. John Eligon, Selling Pieces of Law Firms, *N.Y. Times,* Oct. 29, 2011, at B1 (quoting Andrew Perlman, reporter for Ethics 20/20 Commission).

64. Jennifer Smith, Law Firms Split Over Nonlawyer Investors, *Wall St. J.,* Apr. 2, 2012, B1 (quoting David J. Carr).

65. Trio of Federal Suits Challenge Ethics Rule That Stops Private Equity Investment in Firms, *27 ABA/BNA Law. Man. Prof. Conduct* 382 (2011) (quoting Lawrence Fox).

66. Joanne Stagg-Taylor, Lawyers' Business: Conflicts of Duties Arising from Lawyers' Business Models, *14 Legal Ethics* 173, 183 (2011).

67. Stagg-Taylor, Lawyers' Business, at 185; Reardon, It's Not Your Business, at 179.

68. ABA Commission on Ethics 20/20, Discussion Paper on Alternative Practice Structures, Dec. 2, 2011, at 4.

69. ABA Commission on Ethics 20/20, Issues Paper Concerning Alternative Business Structures, Apr. 5, 2011, at 15.

70. ABA Ethics Commission on Ethics 20/20, Issues Paper, at 9, 115.

71. Andrew Grech & Kirsten Morrison, Slater & Gordon: The Listing Experience, *22 Geo. J. Legal Ethics* 535, 555 (2009).

72. Eligon, Selling Pieces of Law Firms (quoting Ken Fowlie).

73. Letter from Thomas M. Gordon to the ABA Commission on Ethics 20/20 Working Group on Alternative Business Structures, May 31, 2011.

74. Guttenberg, Something's Got to Give, at 473–474.

75. Joan C. Rogers, Speakers Debate Nonlawyers' Role in Firms at First Ethics 20/20 Commission Hearing, ABA/BNA Manual on Professional Conduct, *26 Law. Man. Prof. Conduct*, Feb. 17, 2010, at 110.

76. Milton C. Regan, Jr., Lawyers, Symbols and Money: Outside Investment in Law Firms, *27 Penn. St. Int'l L. Rev.* 407, 422 (2008).

77. See Tyler Cobb, Have Your Cake and Eat It Too: Appropriately Harnessing the Advantages of Nonlawyer Ownership, *54 Ariz. L. Rev.* 765, 777 (2012); Deborah L. Rhode, *Lawyers as Leaders* 167–172 (2013).

78. Mathew Rotenberg, Stifled Justice: The Unauthorized Practice of Law and Internet Legal Resources, *97 Minn. L. Rev.* 709, 729, 738–741 (2012).

79. Rachel M. Zahorsky & William D. Henderson, Who's Eating Law Firms' Lunch? *ABA J.*, Oct. 2013, at 37; Gilliam K. Hadfield, Innovating to Improve Access: Changing the Way Courts Regulate Legal Markets, *Daedalus*, Summer 2014, at 83.

80. Hadfield, Innovating to Improve Access.

81. William D. Henderson & Rachel M. Zahorsky, Paradigm Shift, 2011 *ABA J.* 40, 45–47.

82. Steven Johnson, *Where Good Ideas Come From: The Natural History of Innovation* 41, 58, 166, 246 (2010).

83. Richard Susskind, *The End of Lawyers? Rethinking the Nature of Legal Services* 254 (2008).

84. Thomas D. Morgan, *The Vanishing American Lawyer* 170 (2010).

85. Nick Robinson, When Lawyers Don't Get All the Profits: Non-Lawyer Ownership of Legal Services, Access and Professionalism (2014), available at http://papers.ssrn.com/sol3/papers.cfm?abstract_id=2487878.

86. Malcolm Mercer, Professionalism and the "Fear of Walmart": Would You Like Some Bananas With That Tort? *Slaw*, Apr. 25, 2014, available at http://www.slaw.ca/2014/04/25/professionalism-and-the-fear-of-walmart-would-you-like-some-banannas-with-that-tort/.

87. Renee Newman Knake, Democratizing the Delivery of Legal Services, *73 Ohio St. L. J.* 1, 7 (2012).

88. John Flood, Will There Be Fallout from Clementi? The Repercussions for the Legal Profession After the Legal Services Act 2007, *2012 Mich. St. L. Rev.* 537, 557 (2012).

89. Knake, Democratizing the Delivery of Legal Services. For a less optimistic assessment, see Robinson, When Lawyers Don't Get All the Profits.

90. *Jacoby & Meyers, LLP v. Presiding Justices of First, Second, Third & Fourth Departments, Appellate Div. of Supreme Court of New York*, 847 F. Supp. 2d 590, 593 (S.D.N.Y. 2012), vacated and remanded, 488 Fed. App'x 526 (2d Cir. 2012).

91. Gillers, How to Make Rules for Lawyers, at 365, 401.

92. For the need for more research and an overview of the evidence to date, see Robinson, When Lawyers Don't Get All the Profits.

93. This discussion of continuing legal education draws on Deborah L. Rhode & Lucy Ricca, Revisiting MCLE: Is Compulsory Passive Learning Building Better Lawyers? *22 Prof. Law.* 1 (2014).

94. American Bar Association, MCLE Information by State, available at http://www.americanbar.org/cle/mandatory_cle/mcle_states.html.

95. For examples see Carrie Dolan, California Lawyers, Required to Study, Study at Club Med, *Wall St. J.*, May 21, 1992, at A1; George M. Kraw, Classroom Capers, *S.F. Daily J.*, Jan. 7, 1997, at 4; Alan Ogden, Mandatory Continuing Legal Education: A Study of Its Effects, *13 Colo. Law.* 1789 (1984); Lisa A. Grigg, The Mandatory Continuing Legal Education (MCLE) Debate: Is It Improving Lawyer Competence or Just Busy Work? *12 B.Y. U. J. Pub. L.* 417, 429 (1988).

96. State Bar of California, MCLE Evaluation Commission Report 15 (2001); Rocio Aliaga, Framing the Debate on Mandatory

Continuing Legal Education (MCLE): The District of Columbia Bar's Consideration of MCLE, *8 Geo. J. Legal Ethics* 1145, 1153 (1995).

97. Stuart M. Israel, On Mandatory CLE, Tongue Piercing and Other Related Subjects, *Lab. & Emp. L. Notes*, Spring 1999, at 4 (quoting Thomas Lenga).

98. Paul W. Wolkin, On Improving the Quality of Lawyering, *50 St. John's L. Rev.* 523, 544 n82 (1976) (citing attendance rates ranging from 5 percent to 66 percent); Cheri A. Harris, MCLE: The Perils, Pitfalls, and Promise of Regulation, *40 Valp. L. Rev.* 359, 370 (2006) (less than half of Ohio and Colorado lawyers were regularly attending CLE before requirements were implemented); J. Thomas Lenga, Minimum Continuing Legal Education—Not Your Father's Oldsmobile, *Lab. & Emp. L. Notes*, Spring 1999, at 2 (citing research suggesting that 35 to 50 percent of Michigan lawyers do not take continuing legal education courses); Molly McDonough, Mandatory CLE Again Rears Its Pointy Little Head, *Chi. Daily L. Bull.*, May 15, 1988, at 1 (fewer than 30 percent of Illinois lawyers attend).

99. Janis E. Clark, Transition Education: One Step in a Lifetime of Learning for Lawyers, *40 Valp. U. L. Rev.* 427, 435 (2006).

100. Grigg, Mandatory Continuing Legal Education, at 427.

101. Ogden, Mandatory Continuing Legal Education, at 1789 (estimating that if the average cost of CLE were $20 a credit-hour, a dubious assumption if lawyers' time were also valued, the out-of-pocket cost passed on to the client would be 60 cents an hour). But see Paul-Noel Chretien, The Bar's Back-to-School Scam, *Wall St. J.*, Jan. 17, 1996, at A15 (estimating an annual cost to the public of a "staggering $350 million a year").

102. Aliaga, Framing the Debate, at 1160–1161; David Thomas, Why Mandatory CLE Is a Mistake, *6 Utah B. J.*, Jan. 1993, at 14 (describing report by Utah bar).

103. Ogden, Mandatory Continuing Legal Education, at 10.

104. Chretien, The Bar's Back-to-School Scam, at A15 (quoting D.C. bar report).

105. See Lenga, Minimum Continuing Legal Education, at 2 (referring to medicine and accounting).

106. State Bar of California, MCLE Evaluation Commission Report 10, 154, discussed in Jack W. Lawson, Mandatory Continuing Legal Education and the Indiana Practicing Attorney, *40 Val. U. L. Rev.* 401, 405 (2006).

107. Herschel H. Friday, Continuing Legal Education: Historical Background, Recent Developments, and the Future, *50 St. John's L. Rev.* 502, 508 (1975).

108. Wolkin, On Improving the Quality of Lawyering, at 523, 529 (1976).

109. Donald S. Murphy & Thomas Schwen, The Future: Transitioning from Training Lawyers to Improving Their Performance, *40 Val. L. Rev.* 521, 524 (2006); James C. Mitchell, MCLE—The Joke's on Us, *36 Ariz. Att'y*, Aug./Sept. 1999, at 27; Douglas Shaw Palmer, Why the CLE Board Should Allow Credit for Self-Study, *Wash. St. B. News*, Jun. 1985, at 17.

110. Plato, The Republic, Book VII, 423 (Classics Club ed., 1942).

111. Wolkin, On Improving the Quality of Lawyering, at 529.

112. Wolkin, On Improving the Quality of Lawyering, at 525.

113. William S. Stevens, Ethics and CLE, *Phil. Law.*, Winter 1993, at 27.

114. Wolkin, On Improving the Quality of Lawyering, at 530; David A. Garvin, *Learning in Action: A Guide to Putting the Learning Organization to Work* (2000); M. David Merrill, First Principles of Instruction, *50 Educ. Tech. Res. & Dev.* 43, 44–45 (2002); S. D. Brookfield, *Understanding and Facilitating Adult Learning: A Comprehensive Analysis of Principles and Effective Practices* (1986).

115. Dave Davis, Impact of Formal Continuing Medical Education, *282 JAMA*, Sept. 1, 1999, at 867, 870. See also D. E. Kanouse & I. Jacoby, When Does Information Change Practitioners' Behavior? *4 Int. J. Technol. Assess Health Care* 27 (1988).

116. Ogden, Mandatory Continuing Legal Education.

117. Rhode, Luban, & Cummings, *Legal Ethics*, at 301–302. Jenna Greene, A Muted Trumpet, *Nat'l L. J.*, Mar. 18, 2013, at A4; Eve Brensike Primus, Not Much to Celebrate, *Nat'l L. J.*, Mar. 18, 2013, at 26. ABA Standing Committee on Legal Aid and Indigent Defendants, *Gideon's* Broken Promise: America's Continuing Quest for Equal Justice 7–14 (2004).

118. Israel, On Mandatory CLE, at 3.

119. James C. Michell, Colossal Cave-In: Why Reform of MCLE Was DOA, *37 Ariz. Att'y* 36 (2001).

120. Thomas, Why Mandatory CLE Is a Mistake, at 14.

121. Thomas, Why Mandatory CLE Is a Mistake, at 15; Jack Joseph, Mandatory Continuing Legal Education—An Opponent's View, *Ill. B. J.*, Jan. 1997, at 256, 258 (noting that voluntary systems that fail to present effective programs will have empty classrooms).

122. Joseph, Mandatory Continuing Legal Education, at 258.

123. See New York City Bar Association Task Force on New Lawyers in a Changing Profession, Developing Legal Careers and Delivering Justice in the 21st Century 63 (2013), (noting programs of uneven quality with little interaction and no follow-up); Mitchell, Colossal Cave-In, at 36; James C. Mitchel, MCLE—The Joke's on Us, *Ariz. Att'y*, Aug./Sept. 1999; State Bar of California, MCLE Evaluation Commission Report, at 12 (noting that in telephone poll, 40 percent

of respondents rated the availability of programs in their field at the appropriate experience level as average or poor, and in a bar journal survey, half of respondents rated MCLE courses as unsatisfactory).

124. State Bar of California, MCLE Evaluation Commission Report, at 14.
125. New York City Bar Association Task Force, Developing Legal Careers, at 64–65.
126. Jeremy Perlin, Special Recognition, *ABA J.,* May 1998, at 76.
127. See N.Y. App. Div. Rules of Court Section 1500.222 (2000). See John Caher, State Board Adopts CLE Rules Allowing for Pro Bono Credit, *N.Y. L. J.,* Mar. 6, 2000, at 1.
128. This discussion of lawyer discipline draws on Deborah L. Rhode & Alice Woolley, Comparative Perspectives on Lawyer Regulation: An Agenda for Reform in the United States and Canada, *80 Fordham L. Rev.* 2761, 2764–2769 (2012).
129. Richard L. Abel, *Lawyers in the Dock: Learning from Lawyer Disciplinary Proceedings* 150 (2008). For the ABA's recommendations as to new model procedures for discipline at the state bar level, see ABA Commission on Evaluation of Disciplinary Enforcement, Report to the House of Delegates ix–xvii, 40–45 (1991).
130. See Rhode, *In the Interests of Justice,* at 158; see also Perceptions of the U.S. Justice System 63 (ABA ed.,1999).
131. ABA Commission on Evaluation of Disciplinary Enforcement, Report to the House of Delegates, at xxiv.
132. John C. Coffee, Jr., The Attorney as Gatekeeper: An Agenda for the SEC, *103 Colum. L. Rev.* 1293, 1316 (2003). For similar views, see Anthony E. Davis, Professional Liability Insurers as Regulators of Law Practice, *65 Fordham L. Rev.* 209, 231 (1996).
133. This argument draws on earlier work, including Deborah L. Rhode, Professional Regulation and Public Service: An Unfinished Agenda, in *The Paradox of Professionalism: Lawyers and the Possibility of Justice* 153, 161–168 (Scott L. Cummings ed., 2011); Rhode, *In the Interests of Justice,* at 158–165.
134. Barton, An Institutional Analysis, at 1207.
135. Richard Abel, *Lawyers on Trial: Understanding Ethical Misconduct* 476 (2011); Rhode, *In the Interests of Justice,* at 7–8, 208.
136. For discussion of efforts in California and Florida, see Abel, *Lawyers on Trial,* at 15–59, and Barton, *The Lawyer-Judge Bias,* at 139.
137. Judith L. Maute, Bar Associations, Self-Regulation, and Consumer Protection: Whither Thou Goest? *2008 J. Prof. Law.* 61–65.
138. Abel, *Lawyers in the Dock,* at 502.
139. Lance J. Rogers, Misconduct: Conference Panelists Call for Clarification of Obligation to Report Peer Misconduct, *23 Law. Man. Prof. Conduct* 297 (2007).

140. Michael S. Frisch, No Stone Left Unturned: The Failure of Attorney Self-Regulation in the District of Columbia, *18 Geo. J. Legal Ethics* 325 (2005); Maute, Bar Associations, at 62 n39, 64–65; Richard L. Abel, Comparative Studies of Lawyer Deviance and Discipline, *15 Legal Ethics* 187, 190 (2012).

141. Mark J. Fucile, Law Firm Risk Management by the Numbers, *20 Prof. Law.* 28 (2010).

142. Abel, *Lawyers in the Dock,* at 500; Judith A. McMorrow et al., Judicial Attitudes Toward Confronting Attorney Misconduct: A View from the Reported Decisions, *32 Hofstra L. Rev.* 1425, 1454 (2004). Disciplinary bodies have lacked authority to impose fines or order damages, though they can condition decisions on restitution. Where restitution is not ordered or the lawyer lacks sufficient assets, victims of intentional misconduct can seek compensation from client security funds, but they are insufficient to cover most claims. See Maute, Bar Associations, at 65 and n43, n44; ABA Center for Professional Responsibility, Standing Committee on Client Protection, Survey of Lawyers' Funds for Client Protection 2005–2007, 27 (2008) (reflecting that funds paid for about 10 percent of claims).

143. In re Caro, 945 N.Y.S. 2d 285, 287 (1ˢᵗ Dep't 2012); In re Johannes, 883 N.Y. S. 2d 471, 473 (App. Div. 1ˢᵗ Dep't 2009). For other cases of excessive leniency, see Stephen Gillers, Lowering the Bar: How Lawyer Discipline in New York Fails to Protect the Public, *17 N.Y. U. J. Legis. & Pub. Pol'y* 485, 510–534 (2014).

144. An estimated 20 to 50 percent of lawyers lack liability insurance. See Rhode, Luban, & Cummings, *Legal Ethics*, at 974.

145. See Maute, Bar Associations, at 62 n38. Only nine states have mandatory fee arbitration. See Lawyers.com, Fee Arbitration for Attorney Costs, available at http://alternative-dispute-resolution. lawyers.com/arbitration/Fee-Arbitration-for-Attorney-Costs.html. For discussion of disciplinary systems' lack of attention to performance issues and the rates of client dissatisfaction, see Rhode, *In the Interests of Justice*, at 159, 181; Deborah Rosenthal, Every Lawyer's Nightmare, *Cal. Law.*, Feb. 2002, at 23, 24. In Oregon's system, a majority of clients were not satisfied with the resolution of their complaints. See Oregon State Bar, Annual Report of the Oregon State Bar Client Assistance Office (2006).

146. Vivian Berger, Mediation: An Alternative Means of Processing Attorney Disciplinary Complaints, *16 Prof. Law.* 21, 24 (2005).

147. Leslie C. Levin, The Case for Less Secrecy in Lawyer Discipline, *20 Geo. J. Legal Ethics* 1, 2 n9, n10 (2007); see also Rhode, *In the Interests of Justice*, at 160–161.

148. Levin, The Case for Less Secrecy, at 20–21; Gillers, Lowering the
     Bar, at 489, 500, 501; Vesna Jaksic, Attorney Discipline Web Data
     Uneven, *Nat'l L. J.*, Sept. 10, 2007, at 1, 7.

149. Lynn Mather, How and Why Do Lawyers Misbehave? in *The Paradox
     of Professionalism*, at 130.

150. Mather, How and Why Do Lawyers Misbehave? at 111, 119. For
     example, almost half of Oregon lawyers believe that the disciplinary
     system is biased, and that the results are largely based on the size of
     the disciplined lawyer's firm. A majority of African American lawyers
     in Illinois believe that race plays a factor in disciplinary decisions.
     But only a small minority of white lawyers believe that race plays a
     role in the disciplinary process. See Levin, The Case for Less Secrecy,
     at 6–7.

151. Levin, The Case for Less Secrecy, at 7.

152. Levin, The Case for Less Secrecy, at 4–6.

153. None of the lawyers involved in Enron faced bar sanctions. Barton,
     The Lawyer-Judge Bias, at 253–254.

154. See Deborah L. Rhode & Paul D. Paton, Lawyers, Enron and Ethics,
     in *Enron: Corporate Fiascos and Their Implications* 625, 628 (Nancy
     Rappaport & Bala G. Dharan, eds., 2004); Fred C. Zacharias, The
     Myth of Self-Regulation, *93 Minn. L. Rev.* 1147, 1170 n109 (2009).

155. Paul F. Rothstein, "Anything You Say May Be Used Against You": A
     Proposed Seminar on the Lawyer's Duty to Warn of Confidentiality's
     Limits in Today's Post-Enron World, *76 Fordham L. Rev.* 1745, 1749
     n16 (2007) (noting the increased trend toward criminal prosecutions
     of lawyers in connection with clients' crimes); Laurel S. Terry, The
     Future Regulation of the Legal Profession: The Impact of Treating
     the Legal Profession as "Service Providers," *2008 J. Prof. Law.* 189
     (describing entities regulating lawyers); Zacharias, The Myth of
     Self-Regulation, at 1169–1170 (discussing agency rules and criminal
     prosecutions).

156. John Leubsdorf, Legal Ethics Falls Apart, *57 Buff. L. Rev.* 959, 961
     (2009).

157. For client agreements, see Christopher J. Whelan & Neta Ziv,
     Privatizing Professionalism: Client Control of Lawyers' Ethics, *80
     Fordham L. Rev.* 2577, 2582–2583 (2012). For insurance companies,
     see Davis, Professional Liability Insurers, at 209.

158. Wolfram, Lawyer Turf and Lawyer Regulation, at 1, 6–13.

159. Only one state, Oregon, requires insurance, and only five others
     require disclosure to the client if the lawyer does not have coverage.
     See Maute, Bar Associations, at 71.

160. Model Rules of Professional Conduct, Rule 8.4 (2011).

161. ABA Standards for Imposing Lawyer Sanctions 26–28 (2005), available at http://www.americanbar.org/content/dam/aba/migrated/cpr/regulation/standards_sanctions.authcheckdam.pdf. For inconsistency, see Gillers, Lowering the Bar, at 510–520.

162. See generally John M. Doris, *Lack of Character* (2002); Philip Zimbardo, *The Lucifer Effect: Understanding How Good People Turn Evil* (2007); Gilbert Harman, Moral Philosophy Meets Social Psychology: Virtue Ethics and the Fundamental Attribution Error, *99 Proc. Aristotelian Soc.* 315 (1999); Walter Mischel & Yuichi Shoda, A Cognitive-Affective System Theory of Personality: Reconceptualizing Situations, Dispositions, Dynamics, and Invariance in Personality Structure, *102 Psychol. Rev.* 246 (1995); Deborah L. Rhode, Moral Character as a Professional Credential, *94 Yale L. J.* 491, 557–559 (1985).

163. Rhode, Moral Character, at 558–559 (citing sources).

164. *In re Lamb*, 776 P.2d 765 (Cal. 1989).

165. *In re Lamb*, at 767–768.

166. *In re Lamb*, at 769.

167. Pan-Am Health Org., Domestic Violence During Pregnancy 1–2 (2000), available at http://www.planetwire.org/files.fcgi/2368_violencepregnancy.PDF; Loraine Bacchus et al., Domestic Violence: Prevalence in Pregnant Women and Associations with Physical and Psychological Health, *113 Eur. J. Obstet. Gynecol. & Reprod. Biol.* 6 (2004).

168. *In re Balliro*, 899 N.E.2d 794, 805 (Mass. 2009).

169. *In re Balliro*, at 796–798.

170. *In re Balliro*, at 804.

171. *In re Balliro*, at 804–805 (citing *In re Grella*, 777 N.E.2d 167 (Mass. 2002)).

172. *In re Boudreau*, 815 So. 2d 76, 76 (La. 2002).

173. *In re Boudreau*, at 78.

174. *In re Boudreau*, at 78–79.

175. *In re Boudreau*, at 79–80.

176. For drugs, see *Florida Bar v. Liberman*, 43 So. 3d 36, 37 (Fla. 2010) (disbarment for supplying friends with small amounts of methamphetamine and Ecstasy); *In re Lewis,* 651 S.E.2d 729, 730 (Ga. 2007) (two-year suspension for possession of cocaine); *In re Vegter,* 835 N.E.2d 494 (Ind. 2005) (public reprimand for marijuana possession); State *ex rel. Okla. Bar Ass'n v. Smith,* 246 P.3d 1090, 1095 (Okla. 2011) (public censure and one-year deferred suspension); Brian K. Pinaire et al., Barred from the Bar: The Process, Politics, and Policy Implications of Discipline for Attorney Felony Offenders, *13 Va. J. Soc. Pol'y & L.* 290, 319 (2006). For tax evasion, see

Pinaire et al., Barred from the Bar, at 319; Tax Evasion Aggravated by High Lifestyle Nets Year-Long Suspension for Two Lawyers, *26 Law. Man. Prof. Conduct* 14 (2010). For domestic violence, see Ignascio G. Camarena II, Comment, Domestically Violent Attorneys: Resuscitating and Transforming a Dusty, Old Punitive Approach to Attorney Discipline into a Viable Prescription for Rehabilitation, *31 Golden Gate L. Rev.* 155, 173 (2001). For an illustration of disagreements on the same facts, see *In re Lever*, 869 N.Y.S.2d 523, 524, 528 (App. Div. 2008), which involved an associate who used his office computer to solicit sex by pretending to be a 13-year-old girl. The referee recommended a six-month suspension; the court imposed a three-year suspension; and two judges voted to disbar him.

177. *Jordan v. DeGeorge*, 341 U.S. 223, 239 (1951) (Jackson, J. dissenting).

178. Abel, *Lawyers in the Dock*, at 512–514; Rhode, *In the Interests of Justice*, 163–164; Diane M. Ellis, A Decade of Diversion: Empirical Evidence That Alternative Discipline Is Working for Arizona Lawyers, *52 Emory L. J.* 1221 (2003).

179. Abel, *Lawyers in the Dock*, at 514; Rhode, *In the Interests of Justice*, at 162–163; Leslie L. C. Levin, Misbehaving Lawyers: Cross-Country Comparisons, *15 Legal Ethics* 357 (2012).

180. Steven K. Berenson, Is It Time for Lawyer Profiles? *70 Fordham L. Rev.* 645, 651–657, 680 (2001). For these and other reforms, see Rhode, *In the Interests of Justice*, at 162–165.

181. Levin, The Case for Less Secrecy, at 21–22.

182. ABA Commission on Evaluation of Disciplinary Enforcement, Lawyer Regulation for a New Century 33 (1992); Levin, The Case for Less Secrecy, at 22.

183. For an example, see *Attorney Disciplinary Board v. Keele*, 795 N.W.2d 507, 513–514 (Iowa 2009) (refusing to discipline a lawyer for illegal possession of a firearm where there was no nexus between that offense and his ability to function as a lawyer).

184. David Clementi, Review of the Regulatory Framework for Legal Services in England and Wales: Final Report 1 (2004).

185. Flood, Will There Be Fallout from Clementi? at 537, 540–542.

186. Office of Fair Trading, Competition in Professions: Progress Statement (2002).

187. Clementi, Review of the Regulatory Framework, at 15–17. The Legal Services Act lists "protecting and promoting the public interest" as its first objective. Legal Services Act, 2007, c. 29 Section 1 (U.K.). For discussion, see Laurel S. Terry, Steve Mark, & Tahlia Gordon, Adopting Regulatory Objectives for Legal Profession, *80 Fordham L. Rev.* 2685, 2699 (2012).

188. Department for Constitutional Affairs, The Future of Legal Services: Putting Consumers First 40 (2005).

189. Department for Constitutional Affairs, The Future of Legal Services, at 40.

190. Legal Services Act of 2007, Part 4. The approved regulator for solicitors is the Law Society of England and Wales, and disciplinary jurisdiction rests with the Solicitors Regulation Authority.

191. See Law Society General Regulations, s. 14(6), available at http://www.lawsociety.org.uk/documents/downloads/generalregulations.pdf.

192. Schneyer, Thoughts on the Compatibility, at 13, 27.

193. Legal Ombudsman Scheme Rules, Rule 5.37.

194. Legal Ombudsman Scheme Rules, Rule 5.38.

195. Legal Ombudsman Scheme Rules, Rule 5.40.

196. Bobette Wolski, Reform of the Civil Justice System 25 Years Past: Inadequate Responses from Law Schools and Professional Associations and How Best to Change the Behavior of Lawyers, *40 Common L. World Rev.* 40, 67 (2011).

197. Christine Parker & Adrian Evans, *Inside Lawyer's Ethics* 54–55 (2007).

198. Legal Profession Act of 2007; Parker & Evans, *Inside Lawyer's Ethics*, at 56; Leslie C. Levin, Building a Better Lawyer Discipline System: The Queensland Experience, *9 Legal Ethics* 187, 193–194 (2006).

199. Christine Parker, Tahlia Gordon, & Steven Mark, Regulating Law Firm Ethics Management: An Empirical Assessment of an Innovation in Regulation of the Legal Profession in New South Wales, *37 J. Law & Soc'y* 466, 472 (2010).

200. Parker, Gordon, & Mark, Regulating Law Firm Ethics Management, at 473.

201. Parker, Gordon, & Mark, Regulating Law Firm Ethics Management, at 473.

202. Parker, Gordon, & Mark, Regulating Law Firm Ethics Management, at 473.

203. Parker, Gordon, & Mark, Regulating Law Firm Ethics Management, at 488, 493.

204. Susan Forney & Tahlia Gordon, Adopting Law Firm Management Systems to Survive and Thrive: A Study of the Australian Approach to Management-Based Regulation, *10 U. St. Thomas L. J.* 152, 175 (2012).

205. John Briton & Scott McLean, Incorporated Legal Practices: Dragging the Regulation of the Legal Profession into the Modern Era, *11 Legal Ethics* 241, 250–251 (2010).

206. Briton & Mclean, Incorporated Legal Practices, at 253.

207. Model Rules of Professional Conduct, Rule 5.3 (a) (2002). See Ted Schneyer, The Case for Proactive Management-Based Regulation to Improve Professional Self-Regulation for U.S. Lawyers, *42 Hofstra L. Rev.* 233 (2013); Ted Schneyer, On Further Reflection: How "Professional Self Regulation" Should Promote Compliance with Broad Ethical Duties of Law Firm Management, *53 Ariz. L. Rev.* 577, 619–628 (2011).

208. Schneyer, Proactive Management-Based Regulation, at 254.

209. Roscoe Pound, *The Lawyer from Antiquity to Modern Times* 7 (1953).

Chapter 6

1. Legal Education Reform, *N.Y. Times,* Nov. 26, 2011, at A16. A prior version of this chapter appeared as Legal Education: Rethinking the Problem, Reimagining the Reform, *40 Pepp. L. Rev.* 437 (2013).

2. For an overview, see Brian Tamahana, *Failing Law Schools* (2012). For examples, see sources cited in Eli Wald & Russell G. Pearce, Making Good Lawyers, *9 St. Thomas L. Rev.* 403, 403–404 n1, n4, n5 (2011).

3. Wes Reber Porter, Law Schools' Untapped Resources: Using Advocacy Professors to Achieve Real Change in Legal Education, IAALS Online, Jul. 16, 2013, available at http://online.iaals.du.edu/2013/07/16/advocacy-professors-can-help-law-schools-achieve-real-change/.

4. For enrollments, see Karen Sloan, Enrollment Slump Continues, *Nat'l L. J.,* Jul. 21, 2014, at A1. The last time enrollment so low was in 1975, when there were almost 40 fewer schools. Mark Hansen, Law School Enrollment Down 11 Percent This Year Over Last Year, 24 Percent Over 3 Years, Data Shows, *ABA J.,* Dec. 17, 2013. For jobs and dissatisfaction, see the discussion infra.

5. William Henderson, Waking Up Law Professors, *Nat'l L. J. L. Sch. Rev.,* Nov. 3, 2011, available at http://legaltimes.typepad.com/lawschoolreview/2011/11/waking-up-law-professors.html; Mavlik Shah, The Legal Education Bubble: How Law Schools Should Respond to Changes in the Legal Market, *23 Geo. J. Legal Ethics* 843, 846–847 (2010).

6. Thomas Jefferson, *Selecting Writings* 966 (Merrill P. Peterson, ed., 1984).

7. ABA Standards and Rules of Procedure for Approval of Law Schools, http://www.americanbar.org/groups/legal_education/resources/standards.html.

8. David Segal, The Price to Play Its Way, *N.Y. Times,* Dec. 18, 2011, at B4.

9. David R. Barnhizer has made this point without linking it to accreditation. See David R. Barnhizer, The Purposes and Methods of American Legal Education, *36 J. Legal Prof.* 1, 40 (2011).

10. U.S. Government Accountability Office, Higher Education: Issues Related to Law School Cost and Access (2009). See also Martha Daugherty et al., American Bar Association Report of the Special Committee on the U.S. News and World Report Rankings 3–4(2010), available at http://ms-jd.org/files/f.usnewsfinal-report.pdf.

11. Steven J. Harper, *The Lawyer Bubble: A Profession in Crisis* 16 (2013).

12. Shah, The Legal Education Bubble, at 847; Debra Cassens Weiss, Study Partly Blames Higher Law School Tuition on 40 Percent Leap in Faculty Size, *ABA J.*, Mar. 2010. See also Gene R. Nichol, Rankings, Economic Challenge, and the Future of Legal Education, *61 J. Legal Educ.* 345, 349 (2012) (discussing ways schools maximize expenditures to improve rankings).

13. Richard A. Matasar, The Viability of the Law Degree: Cost, Value, and Intrinsic Worth, *96 Iowa L. Rev.* 1579, 1581 (2011); David Yellen, The Impact of Rankings and Rules on Legal Education Reform, *45 Conn. L. Rev.* 1389, 1397 (2013); American Bar Association Task Force on the Future of Legal Education, Report and Recommendations 2 (2014).

14. Yellen, The Impact of Rankings and Rules, 1895.

15. For the rankings methodology, see Robert Morse & Sam Flanagan, Law School Rankings Methodology, Mar. 14, 2011, available at http://www.usnews.com/education/best-graduate-schools/top-law-schools/articles/2014/03/10/methodology-2015-best-law-schools-rankings.

16. Stephen P. Klein & Laura Hamilton, Association of American Law Schools, The Validity of the U.S. News and World Report Rankings of ABA Law Schools (1998); Roger L. Geiger, *Knowledge and Money* 149 (2004); Terry Carter, Rankled by the Rankings, *ABA J.*, Mar. 1998, at 46, 48–49. Deborah L. Rhode, *In Pursuit of Knowledge* 7 (2006)

17. Klein & Hamilton, The Validity of the U.S. News Rankings.

18. Tamanaha, *Failing Law Schools*, at 78, 84 (quoting William Henderson).

19. Harper, *The Lawyer Bubble*, at 15; Karen Sloan, Prospective Law Students Still Have Stars in Their Eyes, *Nat'l L. J.*, Jun. 19, 2012.

20. Olufunmilauyo Arewa, Andrew P. Morriss, & William Henderson, Enduring Hierarchies in American Legal Education, Legal Studies Research Paper Series No. 2013–141, University of California at Irvine 76 (2013).

21. Tamanaha, *Failing Law Schools*, at 78.
22. Benjamin H. Barton, *Glass Half Full: America's Lawyer Crisis and Its Upside* (forthcoming, 2015).
23. William Henderson, Law School 4.0: Are Law Schools Relevant to the Future of Law? *Legal Prof. Blog*, Jul. 2, 2009, available at http://lawprofessors.typepad.com/legal_profession/2009/07/law-school-40-are-law-schools-relevant-to-the-future-of-law.html.
24. David Segal, Law School Economics: Ka-Ching, *N.Y. Times,* Jul. 17, 2011, at B6.
25. Brian Z. Tamahana, How to Make Law School Affordable, *N.Y. Times Op. Ed.,* Jun. 1, 2012, at A23; U.S. News and World Report, http://www.usnews.com./education/best-graduate-schools/the-short-list-grad-school/articles/2012/03/22/10-law-schools-that-lead-to-the-most-debt.
26. Karen Sloan, Bright Spots amid Glum Jobs Outlook, *Nat'l L. J.*, Apr. 21, 2014; NALP, Law School Grads Face Worst Job Market Yet—Less Than Half Find Jobs in Private Practice, NALP press release, Jun. 7, 2012, available at http://www.nalp.org/2011selectedfindingsrelease, http://www.nalp.org/classof2011; William D. Henderson & Rachel M. Zahorsky, The Law School Bubble: How Long Will It Last If Law Grads Can't Pay Bills? *ABA J.,* Jan. 2012, at 32, 36; Martha Neil, In "Perfect Storm" of Hard-to-Find Jobs and Stagnant Pay, Law Grads Can't Escape Hefty Student Loans, *ABA J.,* Feb. 6, 2012, available at http://www.abajournal.com/news/article/more_recent_law_grads_likely_are_filing_for_bankruptcy. Those reporting income may be on the higher end of the salary curve, so the actual median figure may be lower.
27. Political Calculations, Does It Pay to Go to Law School, Jul. 20, 2010, available at http://politicalcalculations.blogspot.com/2010/07/does-it-pay-to-go-to-law-school; Barton, *Glass Half Full*.
28. Bourne, The Coming Crash (noting higher debt burdens for African Americans and those from lower-income backgrounds): American Bar Foundation and National Association for Law Placement, *After the JD III: Third Results from a National Study of Legal Careers* 80–81 (debt disproportionately burdens Black and Hispanic lawyers).
29. Segal, The Price to Play, at B5 (quoting Keri-Ann Baker).
30. College Cost Reduction and Access Act of 2007, 21 Stat. 784, Public Law 110–184 (2007); Philip G. Schrag & Charles W. Pruett, Coordinating Loan Repayment Assistance Programs with New Federal Legislation, *60 J. Legal Educ.* 584 (2010). See ABA Commission on Loan Repayment and Forgiveness, Lifting the Burden: Law School Debt as a Barrier to Public Service (2003).

31. Joe Palazzolo, Law Grads Face Brutal Job Market, *Wall St. J.*, Jun. 26, 2012, at A1, A2; William Henderson, A Blueprint for Change, *40 Pepp. L. Rev. 461*, 476 (2013).

32. Steven J. Harper, Suffering in Silence, *Am. Law.*, Sept. 2011, at 83.

33. More than half of all student loans are delinquent or in deferral, see Bill Hardekopf, More Than Half of Student Loans Are Now in Deferral or Delinquent, *Forbes*, Feb. 1, 2013, available at http://www.forbes.com/sites/moneybuilder/2013/02/01/alarming-number-of-student-loans-are-delinquent/. For the unsustainability of the current system, see Henderson, A Blueprint for Change, at 462.

34. For further examples, see Lauren Carasik, Renaissance of Retrenchment: Legal Education at a Crossroads, *44 Ind. L. Rev. 735*, 745–746 (2011).

35. Marion Kirkwood, quoted in John W. Reed, On Being Watched: Modeling the Profession During Uncertain Times, *B. Exam.*, Jun. 2011, at 6, 8.

36. René Reich-Graefe, Keep Calm and Carry On, *27 Geo. J. Legal Ethics 55*, 63–66 (2014).

37. Bill Henderson, A Counterpoint to "the most robust legal market that ever existed in this country," *Legal Whiteboard*, Mar. 17, 2014, available at http://lawprofessors.typepad.com/legalwhiteboard/2014/03/a-counterpoint-to-the-most-robust-legal-market-the-ever-existed-in-this-country.html.; Bernard A. Burk, What's New about the New Normal: The Evolving Market for New Lawyers in the 21st Century, unpublished draft, Dec. 30, 2013; William Henderson & Rachel M. Zahorsky, Job Stagnation May Have Started before the Recession, and It May be a Sign of Lasting Change, *ABA J.*, Jul. 2011; Thomas S. Clay & Eric A Seeger, Law Firms in Transition: An Altman Weil Flash Survey (2010).

38. Henderson, A Blueprint for Change, at 478; Richard Susskind, *The End of Lawyers: Rethinking the Nature of Legal Services* (2009).

39. Ethan Bronner, Law School Applications Fall as Cost Rise and Jobs Are Cut, *N.Y. Times,* Jan. 30, 2013; Sloan, Enrollment Slump Continues, at A1.

40. Burk, What's New about the New Normal, at 59.

41. Barton, *Glass Half Empty*; Harper, *The Law School Bubble*, at 40.

42. The suits allege that the schools' reports of placement rates failed to disclose how many positions required a legal degree or were funded by the school, and that their reports of salary figures failed to disclose response rates. *Alaburda v. Thomas Jefferson School of Law* (California Superior Ct. May 26, 2011); *Gomez-Jinenez v. N.Y. Law School* (New York Superior Court, Aug. 10, 2011); *MacDonald v. Thomas M. Cooley Law School*, No. 11- CV-00831 (W.D. Mich. Aug. 10, 2011): Staci

Zaretski, Fifteen More Law Schools to Be Hit with Class Action Lawsuits over Post-Grad Employment Rates, *Above the Law,* Oct. 5, 2011. The first of these suits, brought against New York Law School, has been dismissed. Joe Palazzolo & Jennifer Smith, Law School Wins in Graduate Suit, *Wall St. J.,* Mar. 22, 2012, at B2. The ABA's new standards require such disclosures. Truth in Admitting, *Am. Law.,* Jul./ Aug. 2011; Mark Hansen, ABA Committee Approves New Law School Disclosure requirements, *ABA J.,* Jan. 17, 2012, available at http:// www.abajournal.com/news/article/aba_committee_recommends_ new_law_school_disclosure_requirements/.

43. David Segal, Is Law School a Losing Game? *N.Y. Times,* Jan. 8, 2011, at A1; Karen Sloan, What Are They Thinking, *Nat'l L. J.,* Jul. 12, 2010, at A1. For general accounts of the bias toward optimism, see Tali Sharot, *The Optimism Bias: A Tour of the Irrationally Positive Brain* (2011); Paul Brest & Linda Hamilton Krieger, *Problem Solving, Decision Making, and Professional Judgment* 405–408 (2010).

44. Kaplan Survey, Despite Challenging Job Market, Tomorrow's Lawyers Appear to Have a Healthy Outlook on Their Own Job Prospects, But Not Their Classmates', Apr. 12, 2010, available at http://press.kaptest. com/press-releases/kaplan-survey-despite-challenging-job-market-tomorrow%E2%80%99s-lawyers-appear-to-have-a-healthy-outlook-on-their-own-job-prospects-but-not-their-classmates%E2%80%99.

45. Tamahana, *Failing Law Schools,* at 143–145.

46. Henderson & Zahorsky, Job Stagnation.

47. See Deborah L. Rhode, Access to Justice: A Roadmap for Reform, 41 *Fordham Urb. L. J.* 1227, 1228 (2014); Deborah L. Rhode, Access to Justice: An Agenda for Legal Education and Research *12 J. Legal Educ.* 531, 531 n1 (2012).

48. The Higher Education Act of 1965, codified at 20 U.S.C. Section 1001 (2006), limited federal loans to students of higher educational institutions accredited by an organization that the Secretary of Education designated as the accrediting authority. In a subsequent ruling the Secretary required that the Council be able to act independently without final authority resting in the ABA. For a description of the process, see Judith Areen, Accreditation Reconsidered, *96 Iowa L. J.* 1471 (2011).

49. Areen, Accreditation Reconsidered, at 1492.

50. Areen, Accreditation Reconsidered, at 1490–1491.

51. Nancy B. Rapoport, Eating Our Cake and Having It, Too: Why Real Change Is So Difficult in Law Schools, *81 Ind. L. J.* 359, 366 (2006).

52. Rhode, Access to Justice, at 89, 198 n29; Herbert Kritzer, *Legal Advocacy* 193–203 (1998).

53. See Rhode, Access to Justice, at 15, 199 n29.

54. Edward Rubin, What's Wrong with Langdell's Method and What to Do About It, *60 Van. L. Rev.* 609, 610 (2007).

55. Lawrence Friedman, *A History of American Law* (2nd ed., 1985).

56. For adverse effects, see Roy Stuckey et al., *Best Practices for Legal Education: A Vision and a Road Map* 3 (2007), available at http://law. sc.duc/faculty/stuckey/best_practices-full.pdf. For women's lower participation rates, see sources cited in Katherine Bartlett, Deborah L. Rhode, & Joanna Grossman, *Gender and Law: Theory, Doctrine, Commentary* (6th ed., 2012) 544–551. For ineffective pedagogy, see Lawrence Krieger, What We're Not Telling Law Students—and Lawyers, *13 J. L. & Health* 1, 2–11 (1999); Gerald F. Hess, Seven Principles for Good Practice in Legal Education, *49 J. Legal Educ.* 367–369 (1999). For lack of feedback, see Erwin Chemerinsky, Rethinking Legal Education, *43 Harv. C. R. C. L. L. Rev.* 595, 597 (2008).

57. For the lack of empirical evidence, see Barnhizer, The Purposes and Methods of American Legal Education, at 7.

58. For the most prominent article making this claim, see Harry T. Edwards, The Growing Disjunction Between Legal Education and the Legal Profession, *91 U. Mich. L. Rev.* 34 (1992). For a more recent variation on the same theme, see David Segal, What They Don't Teach Law Students: Lawyering, *N.Y. Times,* Nov. 20, 2011, at A1.

59. LexisNexis, State of the Legal Profession Survey (2009), at 7.

60. Stuckey et al., *Best Practices for Legal Education*, at 18; sources cited in Charlotte S. Alexander, Learning to Be Lawyers: Professional Identity and the Law School Curriculum, *70 Md. L. Rev.* 465, 467 n.6 (2011). For client resistance to paying for training, see Segal, What They Don't Teach Law Students.

61. For new initiatives, see Patrick G. Lee, Law Schools Get Practical, *Wall St. J.*, Jul. 11, 2011, at B5. For their marginalization, see Segal, What They Don't Teach Law Students, at A1; Karen Sloan, Stuck in the Past, *Nat'l Law J.*, Jan. 16, 2012, at A1 (quoting Susan Hackett's dismissal of initiatives as "tweaking around the edges").

62. Segal, What They Don't Teach Law Students, at A1. See also Karen Tokarz et al., Legal Education at a Crossroads: Innovation, Integration, and Pluralism Required, *43 Wash. J. L. & Pol'y* 11 (2013) (finding only nineteen schools required clinic or internship).

63. Tokarz et al., Legal Education at a Crossroads.

64. Erwin Chemerinsky, Forward: The Benefits of Knowledge, Law School Survey of Student Engagement 5 (2012), available at http:// lssse.iub.edu/pdf/2012/LSSSE_2012_AnnualReport.pdf.

65. NALP Foundation for Law Career Research & Education & American Bar Foundation, *After the JD: First Results of a National Study of Legal Careers* (2004).

66. Jane Porter, Lawyers Often Lack the Skills Needed to Draw, Keep Clients, *Wall St. J.,* May 20, 2009, at B5; William Hornsby,

Challenging the Academy to a Dual (Perspective): The Need to Embrace Lawyering for Personal Legal Services, *70 Md. L. Rev.* 420, 437 (2011).

67. Lexis-Nexis, State of the Legal Industry Survey 7 (2009).

68. For lawyer leaders, see Deborah L. Rhode, *Lawyers as Leaders* (2013); Deborah L. Rhode, Lawyers and Leadership, *Prof. Law.*, Winter 2010, at 1. For expenditures on leadership development, see Doris Gomez, The Leader as Learner, *2 Int'l J. Leadership Stud.* 280, 281 (2007). For inadequate law school curricula, see Nitin Nohria & Rakesh Khurana, Advancing Leadership Theory and Practice, in *Handbook of Leadership Theory and Practice* 3 (Nitin Nohria & Rakesh Khurana, eds., 2010).

69. Neil W. Hamilton, Ethical Leadership in Professional Life, *6 St. Thomas L. J.* 358, 370 (2009).

70. For some examples, see Alexander, Learning to Be Lawyers, 477–482.

71. Richard Matasar, Does the Current Economic Model of Legal Education Work for Law Schools, Law Firms (or Anyone Else)? *N.Y. St. B. J.,* Oct. 2010, at 20, 24: Patrick G. Lee, Law Schools Get Practical, *Wall St. J.,* Jul. 11, 2011, at B5 (quoting Timothy Lloyd's observation that practical skills don't make "much of a difference").

72. Sloan, Stuck in the Past (quoting Wilkins).

73. Segal, What They Don't Teach, at A22; Rubin, What's Wrong with Langdell's Method, at 614. The problem is not unique to law schools. For inadequate recognition of teaching in academic reward structures, see Rhode, *In Pursuit of Knowledge*, at 63, 73.

74. William Sullivan et al., *Educating Lawyers: Preparation for the Profession of Law* (2007).

75. Sullivan et al., *Educating Lawyers*, at145, 187; Ann Colby & William Sullivan, Legal Education Gives Ethics Training Short Shrift, *S.F. Daily J.*, Jan 18, 2007, at 6.

76. This claim has been made before. See Deborah L. Rhode, The Professional Responsibilities of Professional Schools, *49 J. Legal Educ.* 24 (1999); and Deborah L. Rhode, Teaching Legal Ethics, *51 St. Louis L. J.* 1043, 1047–1049 (2007). For the focus of ethics classes, see Andrew M. Perlman, Margaret Raymond, & Laurel S. Terry, A Survey of Professional Responsibility Courses at American Law Schools in 2009, available at http://www.legalethicsforum.com/files/pr-survey-results-final.pdf. For the pressure that faculty feel to teach to the bar exam, see Steven Gillers, Eat Your Spinach, *52 St. Louis U. L. J.* 1215, 1219 (2007).

77. Perlman, Raymond, & Terry, A Survey of Professional Responsibility Courses.

78. For the assumption that values cannot be taught to adult law students, see Sullivan et al., *Educating Lawyers*, at 133; Neil Hamilton & Verna Munson, Addressing the Skeptics on Fostering Ethical Professional

Formation, *Prof. Law.* (2011). For the assumption that values should not be taught in a pluralist society, see W. Bradley Wendel, Teaching Ethics in an Atmosphere of Skepticism and Relativism, *36 U.S.F. L. Rev.* 711 (1992). For skepticism about the capacity of law schools, see Sullivan et al., *Educating Lawyers*, at 132–133; Carole Silver et al., Unpacking the Apprenticeship of Professional Identity and Purpose: Insights from the Law School Survey of Student Engagement, *17 J. Legal Writing Inst.* 373, 376–377 (2011).

79. Law School Survey of Student Engagement, Student Engagement in Law Schools: In Class and Beyond—2010 Annual Survey Results 4, 11, 12, 24, (2010). See Richard Acella, Street Smarts: Law Schools Explore Benefits of Teaching Ethics in a Clinical Setting, *ABA J.*, Jun. 2011, at 26.

80. See Wald & Pearce, Denial and Accountability; Sullivan et al., *Educating Lawyers*, at 139; Neil W. Hamilton, Assessing Professionalism: Measuring Progress in the Formation of an Ethical Professional Identity, *5 U. St. Thomas L. J.* 470, 475 (2008).

81. ABA Model Rules of Professional Conduct, Preamble (2011).

82. Rhode, If Integrity Is the Answer, What Is the Question? *72 Fordham L. Rev.* 333, 342 (2003); Sullivan et al., *Educating Lawyers*, at 135, 154; M. Neil Browne, Carrie L. Williamson, & Linda L. Barkacs, The Purported Rigidity of an Attorney's Personality: Can Legal Ethics be Acquired? *30 J. Legal Prof.* 55, 66 (2006); Steven Hartwell, Promoting Moral Development through Experiential Teaching, *1 Clin. L. Rev.* 505, 507–508 (1995); Neil Hamilton & Lisa M. Babbit, Fostering Professionalism through Mentoring, *37 J. Legal Educ.* 102, 116 (2007); National Research Council, Learning and Transfer, in *How People Learn* 51–78 (2000).

83. Linda F. Smith, Fostering Justice throughout the Curriculum, *18 Geo. J. Poverty L. & Policy* 427 430–431 (2011).

84. Law School Survey on Student Engagement, Student Engagement in Law Schools: A First Look 8 (2004). Only two schools reported faculty requirements. ABA Standing Committee on Professionalism, Report on Survey of Law School Professionalism Programs 46–47 (2006).

85. ABA Standing Committee on Professionalism, Report on Professionalism Programs.

86. Deborah L. Rhode, *Pro Bono in Principle and in Practice* 161–162 (2005). Only 62 percent of those responding to the ABA survey reported the availability of on-site supervision. ABA Standing Committee on Professionalism, Report, at 45.

87. Ronit Dinovitzer et al., *After the JD: First Results of a National Study of Legal Careers* 81 (2004).

88. AALS Commission on Pro Bono and Public Service Opportunities in Law Schools, Learning to Serve: A Summary of the Findings and Recommendations of the Commission on Pro Bono and Public Service Opportunities in Law Schools 2 (1999).

89. ABA Presidential Initiative Commission on Diversity, Diversity in the Legal Profession: Next Steps (2010); Robert S. Chang & Adrienne D. Davis, Making Up Is Hard to Do: Race/Gender/Sexual Orientation in the Law School Classroom, *33 Harv. J. L. & Gender* 1 (2010) (summarizing research); Angela Onwuachi-Willig, Emily Hough, & Mary Campbell, Cracking the Egg: Which Came First—Stigma or Affirmative Action?, *96 Cal. L. Rev.,* at 1299 n126; Celestial S. D. Cassman & Lisa R. Pruitt, Towards a Kinder, Gentler Law School? Race, Ethnicity, Gender, and Legal Education, *38 Davis L. Rev.* 1209, 1248 (2005); Richard Sander, Class in American Legal Education, *88 Denver U. L. Rev.* 631 (2011).

90. Karen Sloan, Legal Education's Diversity Deficit, *Nat'l L. J.,* May 12, 2014, at A1.

91. Kristin Holmquist, Marjorie Shultz, Sheldon Zedeck, & David Oppenheimer, Measuring Merit: The Shultz-Zedeck Research on Law School Admissions, *63 J. Legal Educ.* 565 (2014); Marjorie M. Shultz & Sheldon Zedeck, Predicting Lawyer Effectiveness: Broadening the Basis for Law School Admission Decisions, *36 Law & Soc. Inq.* 620 (2011).

92. See studies summarized in Mertz, Inside the Law School Classroom: Toward a New Legal Realist Pedagogy, *60 Vand. L. Rev.* 483, 509 (2007); and Adam Neufield, Costs of an Outdated Pedagogy? Study of Gender at Harvard Law School, *13 J. Gender, Soc. Pol'y, & L.* 511, 516–517, 530–539, 554–559 (2005); and findings of Sari Bashi & Mariana Iskander, Why Legal Education Is Failing Women, *18 Yale J. L. & Feminism* 389, 404–413, 423–437 (2006).

93. Jonathan Feingold & Doug Souza, Measuring the Racial Unevenness of Law School, *15 Berkeley J. Afr.-Am. L. & Pol'y* 71, 105, 108 (2013).

94. Ellen Nakashima, Harsh Words Die Hard on the Web: Law Students Feel Lasting Effects of Anonymous Attacks, *Wash. Post,* Mar. 7, 2007, at A1.

95. ABA Section of Legal Education and Admissions to the Bar, Statistics on Legal Education (2012–13), available at http://www.americanbar.org/content/dam/aba/administrative/legal_education_and_admissions_to_the_bar/statistics/ls_staff_gender_ethnicity.authcheckdam.pdf (minorities represent 16 percent of tenured professors and 21 percent of law school deans; women represent 30 percent of full professors and 20 percent of law school deans); Institute for Inclusion in the Legal Profession, IILP Review 2011 (2011);

Vikram David Amar & Kevin R. Johns, Why *U.S. News and World Report* Should Include a Faculty Diversity Index in Its Ranking of Law Schools, Apr. 9, 2010, available at http://writ.news.findlaw.com/amar/20100409html.

96. For bar commitments, see ABA Presidential Initiative on Diversity, Diversity in the Legal Profession; AALS Statement on Diversity.

97. Kennon M. Sheldon & Lawrence S. Krieger, Understanding the Negative Effects of Legal Education on Law Students: Longitudinal Test of Self-Determination Theory, *33 Personality & Soc. Psych.* 883, 884 (2007) (noting the shift from intrinsic to extrinsic motivations among law students due in part to controlling rather than supportive climate).

98. Sheldon & Krieger, Understanding the Negative Effects.

99. Todd David Peterson & Elizabeth Waters Peterson, Stemming the Tide of Law Student Depression: What Law Schools Need to Learn from the Science of Positive Psychology, *2 Yale J. Health Pol'y, Law & Ethics* 357, 359, 411–412 (2009); Lawyers and Depression, Dave Nee Foundation (2014), available at http://www.daveneefoundation.org/resources/lawyers-and-depression/. The problem is longstanding. Andrew Benjamin et al., The Role of Legal Education in Producing Psychological Distress among Law Students and Lawyers, *11 Law & Soc. Inq.* 225 (1986).

100. Lawyers and Depression.

101. Peterson & Peterson, Stemming the Tide, at 374–375; Sheldon & Krieger, Understanding the Negative Effects, at 884.

102. Karen Sloan, The View from 3L, *Nat'l L. J.,* Jan. 26, 2009, at A1 (quoting Eric Reed).

103. Fred Rodell, Goodbye to Law Reviews, *23 Va. L. Rev.* 38 (1936).

104. Adam Liptak, The Lackluster Reviews That Lawyers Love to Hate, *N.Y. Times,* Oct. 22, 2013.

105. Deborah Cassens Weiss, Law Prof Responds After Chief Justice Roberts Disses Legal Scholarship, *ABA J.,* Jul. 7, 2011.

106. Thomas A. Smith, The Web of Law, *44 San Diego L. Rev.* 309, 336 (2007). My own earlier study found that more than half of articles had never been cited. Deborah L. Rhode, Legal Scholarship, *115 Harv. L. Rev.* 1327, 1331 (2002).

107. Rhode, Legal Scholarship, at 1337; Max Stier et al., Law Review Usage and Suggestions for Improvement: A Survey of Attorneys, Professors, and Judges, *44 Stan. L. Rev.,* 1467, 1484, Table 4 (1992).

108. Robert Weisberg, Some Ways to Think about Law Reviews, *47 Stan. L. Rev.* 1147, 1148 (1995); Roger C. Cramton, The Most Remarkable Institution: The American Law Review, *36 J. Legal Educ.* 1, 708 (1986); Richard A. Wise et al., Do Law Reviews Need Reform?

A Survey of Law Professors, Student Editors, Attorneys, and Judges, *59 Loy. L. Rev.* 1 (2013).

109. Rhode, *In Pursuit of Knowledge*, 38; Arthur Austin, Footnote Skulduggery and Other Bad Habits, *44 U. Miami L. Rev.* 1009 (1990).

110. Arnold S. Jacobs, An Analysis of Section 16 of the Securities Exchange Act of 1934, *32 N.Y. L. Sch. L. Rev.* 209 (1987).

111. See Stier et al., Law Review Usage, at 1499; Submissions, *Harv. L. Rev.*, http://www.harvardlawreview.org/submisssions.php; Wise et al., Do Law Reviews Need Reform? at 6. In 2005, eleven law reviews issued a statement conveying their preference for "shorter articles" between 40 and 70 pages. Wise et al., Do Law Reviews Need Reform, at 6 n18.

112. Benjamin H. Barton, Is There a Correlation between Law Professor Publication Counts, Law Review Citation Counts, and Teaching Evaluations? An Empirical Study, *5 J. Emp. Legal Stud.* 619 (2008). In an overview of some thirty studies over three decades of teaching and scholarship outside law, two-thirds found no relationship. James Axtell, *The Pleasures of Academe* 241 (1998); Philip C. Wankat, *The Effective, Efficient Professor: Teaching, Scholarship and Service* 211 (2001).

113. Aldous Huxley, *Island* 163 (1962).

114. David Margolick, The Trouble with America's Law Schools, *N.Y. Times Mag.*, May 22, 1983.

115. Margolick, The Trouble with America's Law Schools (quoting William Cohen).

116. Tamahana, *Failing Law Schools*, at 47, 51 (citing data indicating that law professors earn the second highest salaries of academics, and that the majority's earnings are in the upper quartile of lawyer earnings).

117. Yale Law School Career Development Office, Job Satisfaction Survey 5 (2001–2005).

118. See Edward Rubin, The Future and Legal Education: Are Law Schools Failing and, If So, How? *39 Law & Soc. Inq.* 499, 500 (2014); Robert W. Gordon, The Geologic Strata of the Law School Curriculum, *60 Vand. L. Rev.* 339 (2007); Susan Sturm & Lani Guinier, The Law School Matrix: Reforming Legal Education in a Culture of Competition and Conformity, *60 Vand. L. Rev.*, 515, 519 (2007); Erwin Chemerinsky, Legal Education Must Change, But Will It?, *Nat'l L. J.'s L. Sch. Rev.*, Nov. 1, 2011. See also Richard A. Matasar, Defining Our Responsibilities: Being an Academic Fiduciary, *17 J. Contemp. Legal Issues* 67, 71 (2008) (noting that the curriculum remains focused not on what students want to learn but on what teachers want to teach).

119. Paul Campos, Stop Unlimited Loaning to Law School Students, *New Republic*, Jul. 23, 2013.

120. David Stern, The Avoidable Sticker Shock of Student Loan Repayment, *Nat'l L. J.*, Sept. 23, 2013, at 39.

121. Matasar, Does the Current Economic Model Work? at 26; Elizabeth Chambliss, Law School Training for Licensed "Legal Technicians"; Implications for the Consumer Movement, 65 *S. Car. L. Rev.* 579 (2014).

122. Tamahana, *Failing Law Schools*, at 173; Matasar, The Viability of the Law Degree, at 1579, 1618.

123. *In re Petition of Culver*, slip op. at 7 (Mont. 2002) (Trieweiler, J., dissenting).

124. Tamanaha, *Failing Law Schools*, at 177.

125. For example, in the July 2012 California bar examination, only 31 percent of first-time test takers and 10.5 percent repeat test takers from state-accredited law schools passed the exam. See General Statistics Report July 2012 California Bar Examination, available at http://admissions.calbar.ca.gov/Portals/4/documents/gbx/JULY2012STATS.122112_R.pdf. By contrast, 76.9 percent of first-time test takers and 24 percent of repeat test takers from ABA-approved law schools passed the bar exam. Among graduates of unaccredited schools, 22.2 percent of first-time test takers and 12.4 percent of repeat test takers passed. Id.

126. American Bar Association Task Force on the Future of Legal Education, Report and Recommendations, at 24.

127. For a similar proposal, see Tamahana, *Failing Law Schools*, at 173.

128. ABA Task Force on the Future of Legal Education, Report and Recommendations, at 24–25.

129. Laurel A. Rigertas, Stratification of the Legal Profession: A Debate in Need of a Public Forum, *J. Prof. Law.* 79, 100–110 (2012).

130. Michael Schudson, The Flexner Report and the Reed Report: Notes on the History of Professional Education in the United States, *55 Soc. Sci. Q.* 347 (1974).

131. The AALS report, Training for the Public Professions of the Law, appears as an appendix to the Carnegie report. Herbert L. Packer & Thomas Ehrlich, *New Directions in Legal Education* (1972).

132. Thomas Morgan, *The Vanishing American Lawyer* 196–197 (2010); Preble Stolz, The Two-Year Law School: The Day the Music Died, *25 J. Legal Educ.* 37 (1973).

133. Peter Lattman, Obama Says Law School Should Be 2, Not 3, Years, *N.Y. Times*, Aug. 24, 2013, at B3.

134. For the two-year proposal, see Samuel Estreicher, The Roosevelt-Cardozo Way: The Case for Bar Eligibility after Two Years of

Law School, *15 N.Y. U. Rev. Legis. & Public Pol'y* 599 (2012). For apprenticeships, see David Lat, Bring Back Apprenticeships, *N.Y. Times*, Feb. 2, 2012. For externships, see Alan Dershowitz, Make Law School Two Years-Plus, *New Republic*, Jul. 23, 2013; Paul M. Barrett, Do American Lawyers Need Less Law School? *Bloomberg Businessweek*, Sept. 3, 2013 (describing Lawyers for America externship program).

135. Barrett, Do American Lawyers Need Less Law School? (quoting Schrag).

136. Erwin Chemerinsky, ABA Report Lacking Solutions for Law Schools, *Nat'l L. J.*, Feb. 10, 2014, at 30.

137. Bruce Ackerman, Why Legal Education Should Last for Three Years, *Wash. Post*, Sept. 6, 2013; Bruce Ackerman, Three Years in Law School Are Barely Enough! *Balkinization*, Sept. 9, 2013, available at http://balkin.blogspot.com/2013/09/three-years-in-law-school-are-barely.html] and 146 [http://works.bepress.com/marjorie_shultz/14/.

138. Paul Lippe, Yale Law Prof Falls Short in Challenging Obama's 2 Year JD Idea, *ABA J.*, Sept. 11, 2013, available at http://www.abajournal.com/legalrebels/article?Profs_op-ed_opposing_a_two-year_jd/.

139. Rachel Van Cleave, Assessing the Value of Lawyers, *San Francisco Daily J.*, Sept. 24, 2013.

140. James E. Moliterno, The Future of Legal Education Reform, *40 Pepp. L. Rev.* 423, 433 (2013).

141. See discussion in Chapter 3.

142. See Richard Posner, Let Employers Insist if Three Years of Law School Is Necessary, *San Francisco Daily J.*, Dec. 15, 1999, at A4 (noting the lack of empirical or theoretical explanation for why three years of legal education is necessary); Mitu Gulati, Richard Sander, & Robert Sockloskie, The Happy Charade: An Empirical Examination of the Third Year of Law School, *51 J. Leg. Educ.* 235 (2001) (exploring challenges to the necessity of the third year of law school).

143. See Sullivan et al., *Educating Lawyers*, at 29–45.

144. Karen Sloan, ABA Pressed to Boost Law Students' Practical Training, *Nat'l L. J.*, Jul. 2, 2013.

145. A California State Bar Task Force has gone further and recommended that students be required to complete fifteen credits of practice-based experiential coursework. See State Bar Cal. Task Force on Admission Reg. Reform, Phase 1 Final Report, Jun. 24, 2013, available at http://www.calbar.ca.gov/portals/0/ documents/bog/bot_ExecDir/.

146. The ABA's MacCrate report identified critical skills: ABA Task Force on Law Schools and the Profession, Legal Education and Professional Development—An Educational Continuum (1992) (MacCrate Report). More recently Marjorie Shultz and Sheldon Zedeck conducted empirical research into practice skills that was designed

to improve admission criteria but that could also guide curricular reform: Marjorie M. Schultz & Sheldon Zedeck, Final Research Report: Identification, Development, and Validation of Predictors for Successful Lawyering (2008), available at http://www.law.berkeley. edu/finesLSACREPORTfinal-12.pdf.

147. The program requires five semesters and the same tuition as the three-year program, and admits only students with at least two years of post-undergraduate work experience. See Northwestern Law Accelerated JD Bulletin 3, available at http://www.law.northwestern. edu/academics/ajd/AJD.pdf.

148. Clark D. Cunningham, Should American Law Schools Continue to Graduate Lawyers Whom Clients Consider Worthless? *70 Md. L. Rev.* 499, 511–513 (2011).

149. Cunningham, Should American Law Schools Continue to Graduate Lawyers, at 509–510.

150. Gulati, Sander, & Sockloskie, The Happy Charade.

151. Lee, Law Schools Get Practical (describing Washington and Lee's case-based simulations run by practicing lawyers); New York City Bar Association Task Force on New Lawyers in a Changing Profession, Developing Legal Careers and Delivering Justice in the 21st Century 117–134 (2013).

152. One of the most ambitious examples is the Law Without Walls course pioneered by the University of Miami School of Law that involves students from over a dozen institutions here and abroad.

153. Sullivan et al., *Educating Lawyers*, at 135; Hartwell, Promoting Moral Development, at 505; Jane Harris Aiken, Striving to Teach Justice, Fairness, and Morality, *4 Clin. L. Rev.* 1, 23–25 (1998); James E. Moliterno, Legal Education, Experiential Education, and Professional Responsibility, *38 Wm. & Mary L. Rev.* 71, 81 (1997); Russell Pearce, Teaching Ethics Seriously: Legal Ethics as the Most Important Subject in Law School, *29 Loy. L. Rev.* 719, 734 (1998).

154. David Luban & Michael Millemann, Good Judgment: Ethics Teaching in Dark Times, *9 Geo J. Legal Ethics* 31, 39 (1995); Robert P. Burns, Legal Ethics in Preparation for Law Practice, *75 Neb. L. Rev.* 684, 692–696 (1998); Peter A. Joy, The Law School Clinic as a Model Ethical Law Office, *30 Wm. Mitchell L. Rev.* 35 (2004); Alan M. Lerner, Using Our Brains: What Cognitive Science and Social Psychology Teach Us about Teaching Law Students to Make Ethical, Professionally Responsible Choices, *23 Quinnipiac L. Rev.* 643, 694–695 (2004); Joan L. O'Sullivan et al., Ethical Decision Making and Ethics Instruction in Clinical Law Practice, *3 Clin. L. Rev.* 109, (1996). For examples, see Richard Acello, Street Smarts, *ABA J.* Jun. 2011, at 26.

155. Luban & Millemann, Good Judgment, at 39.

156. Aiken, Striving to Teach Justice, at 24–27.

157. AALS Commission on Pro Bono and Public Service Opportunities in Law School, Learning to Serve, at 2.

158. Cindy Adcock et al., Building on Best Practices in Legal Education— Pro Bono, in *Best Practices in Legal Education* (Roy Stucky et al., eds., 2d ed., 2011); Melissa H. Weresh, Service: A Prescription for the Lost Lawyer, *2014 J. Prof. Law.* 45, 75.

159. For the importance of role models, see Rhode, *Pro Bono in Principle*, at 63. For the importance of law faculty acting as models, see David Luban, Faculty Pro Bono and the Question of Identity, *49 J. Legal Educ.* 58 (1999).

160. Rules of the Court of Appeals for the Admission of Attorneys and Counselors at Law, Part 520.16 (2013); Don J. DeBenedictis, State Bar Announces Members of Skills Training Task Force, *San Francisco Daily J.*, Dec. 6, 2013.

161. Deborah L. Rhode, Midcourse Corrections: Women in Legal Education, *53 J. Legal Educ.* 475, 487 (2003). For discussion of other changes, see ABA Presidential Initiative Commission on Diversity, Diversity in the Legal Profession.

162. For effective teaching strategies, see Michael Hunter Schwartz, Gerald F. Hess, & Sophie M. Sparrow, *What the Best Law Teachers Do* (2013).

163. Peterson & Peterson, Stemming the Tide, at 384, 408–415.

164. See sources cited in Deborah L. Rhode, David Luban, & Scott Cummings, *Legal Ethics* 961(6th ed., 2013).

165. Wise et al., Do Law Reviews Need Reforms?, at 62.

166. Huxley, *Island*, at 163.

Chapter 7

1. Ralph C. Cavanagh & Deborah L. Rhode, Project: The Unauthorized Practice of Law and Pro Se Divorce: An Empirical Analysis, *86 Yale L.* 104, 123–129 (1976).

2. My most recent effort is Deborah L. Rhode & Lucy Ricca, Protecting the Public or the Profession? Rethinking Unauthorized Practice Enforcement, *82 Fordham L. Rev.* 2587 (2014).

3. For a leading case, see *Florida Bar v. Brumbaugh*, 355 So.2d 1186 (Fla. 1978).

INDEX

———◦◦◦———